Securing Life

Securing Life

The Enduring Message of the Bible

Robert P. Vande Kappelle

WIPF & STOCK · Eugene, Oregon

SECURING LIFE
The Enduring Message of the Bible

Copyright © 2016 Robert P. Vande Kappelle. All rights reserved. Except for brief quotations in critical publications or reviews, no part of this book may be reproduced in any manner without prior written permission from the publisher. Write: Permissions, Wipf and Stock Publishers, 199 W. 8th Ave., Suite 3, Eugene, OR 97401.

New Revised Standard Version Bible, copyright 1989, Division of Christian Education of the National Council of the Churches of Christ in the United States of America. Used by permission. All rights reserved.

Wipf & Stock
An Imprint of Wipf and Stock Publishers
199 W. 8th Ave., Suite 3
Eugene, OR 97401

www.wipfandstock.com

PAPERBACK ISBN: 978-1-5326-0033-3
HARDCOVER ISBN: 978-1-5326-0035-7
EBOOK ISBN: 978-1-5326-0034-0

Manufactured in the U.S.A.   MAY 26, 2016

To valued mentors who have taught me
the enduring message of the Bible:
Bernhard W. Anderson
Karen Armstrong
Marcus Borg
Walter Brueggemann
Bruce M. Metzger
John Shelby Spong

"You will know them by their fruits"

—Matt. 6:16

Contents

Preface | ix
Introduction | 1

Part I: Introductory Topics

1. Biblical Information: Books, Genres, and Central Themes of the Bible | 21
2. Biblical Inspiration: How the Bible Became Scripture | 33
3. Biblical Interpretation: The Science and Art of Reading the Bible | 51

Part II: Theological Topics

4. Biblical Theology: Humans as Related to God | 67
5. Biblical Anthropology: Humans as Related to Self, Nature, and Culture | 80

Part III: Literary Topics—The Hebrew Bible

6. Covenant | 95
7. Community | 110
8. Creation | 132

Part IV: Literary Topics—The New Testament

9. New Covenant | 155
10. New Community | 174
11. New Creation | 192

Epilogue: Reading the Bible (Or How the Bible Reads Us) | 216
Bibliography | 221
Subject/Name Index | 225

Preface

Christianity, the predominant, most accessible, and most diffuse of the world's religions, has arguably inspired the world's greatest art, music, and architecture. It has also inspired its most memorable speeches, sermons, and lectures; its most elevated theology and philosophy; and its most elegant rhetoric and prose. At the heart of this movement that has captured the imagination of people around the globe is its scripture, known as the Holy Bible, a library of books divided into testaments, one Jewish and the other Christian.

The Bible, the all-time best-selling book, is the most read, best known, most published, and most widely disseminated book in the world. Its value is inestimable, for it has single-handedly changed the course of world history, guiding empires, influencing legal systems, and impacting the lives of untold millions around the globe. Columbus took a copy to the New World, Charles Lindbergh stowed a copy in the cramped quarters of the Spirit of St. Louis on his epic trans-Atlantic flight, and astronaut James Irwin, who carried a copy on his moon walk, became the first person to quote from the Bible while on the moon: "I will lift up my eyes unto the hills, from whence cometh my help" (Ps. 121:1, KJV).

For two thousand years this book, in part or in whole, has been viewed as sacred by generations of believers, its sacredness related not to the origin of the Bible but rather to its status within the Christian community. At the time of their composition, the books of the Bible were not considered to be part of scripture, Rather, the various parts of the Bible became sacred through canonization, a process that took several centuries. For Christians, the status of the Bible as sacred scripture means it is the primary collection of writings they know, definitive for faith and practice. The sacredness of scripture is validated by its ability to inspire believers in every age, thereby authenticating its enduring message.

PREFACE

My love affair with scripture began at the age of four, lasted through a forty-year teaching career in the field of biblical studies, and has not wavered since. This book is the twelfth of my scholarly career, a number in the Bible that represents faithful witness to God, whether through Israelite tribes in covenant with God or through apostles in new covenant with God through Christ. The number forty is biblically symbolic, representing a spiritual time of testing, growth, and transformation. Whenever God prepared someone for a spiritual purpose, it took forty days. We are told that the Deluge lasted forty days upon the earth (Gen. 7:4); Moses spent forty days on the Mount awaiting Torah (Exodus 24:18); the twelve spies, each representing one tribe of Israel, spent forty days investigating the Promised Land (Numbers 13:25); Elijah took a forty-day sojourn to Horeb (Sinai), where he stood "before the Lord" (I Kings 19:8, 11); Jonah called on Nineveh to repent within forty days (Jonah 3:4); Jesus fasted forty days and nights in the wilderness (Matt. 4:2), one day for every year the Israelites wandered in the wilderness, and he remained on earth forty days after his resurrection (Acts 1:3).

Forty years, the biblical length of life and hence a generation of time, represents not only the interim the Israelites spent wandering through the wilderness, a transitional period between their liberation from Egypt and the conquest of the Promised Land characterized by testing and transformation, but all indeterminate periods of spiritual growth and transformation. Having reached my own promised land—retirement—I am pleased and honored to share insights on scripture attained during my "wilderness sojourn."

My journey of faith has been nurtured by Bernhard W. Anderson, Karen Armstrong, Marcus Borg, Walter Brueggemann, Bruce M. Metzger, and John Shelby Spong, master teachers and pioneers in the field of biblical and theological spirituality.[1] I have been fortunate to have known these individuals personally, having studied under their tutelage at Princeton Theological Seminary, Boston College, and Chautauqua Institution. I dedicate this book to these mentors and to all whose scholarship has advanced my thinking and living.

My gratitude extends to David Novitsky, Olga Solovieva, Dan Stinson, and Walt Weaver, friends and colleagues at Washington & Jefferson College. This book, indeed my academic career, would not have been possible without joyous companionship and judicious advice provided by my wife Susan, and I am grateful for her ongoing support.

1. A partial list of their works appears in the bibliography.

Introduction

Whatever its original setting and intent, in whole or in part, the canonical scripture is intended for all people alike—irrespective of gender, race, social class, occupational state, educational status, geographical location, and personality type—and for every season of life.

While the Bible is read by Africans, Americans, Asians, and Europeans alike, its interpretation and application are diverse. Despite being read by conservatives, liberals, and moderates alike, the Bible seems to have a conserving effect on conservative readers, a moderating effect on moderate readers, and a liberating effect on liberal readers. Why is this so? The answer, I believe, is attributable to four factors, including (1) the extent to which one reads out of the text its intended meaning (what scholars call "exegesis") or into the text *one's interests, bias, or meaning* (what scholars call "eisegesis"); (2) *selective reading*, namely, the practice of picking and choosing passages that support one's point of view while avoiding perplexing passages or passages that contradict cherished beliefs; (3) *the polyvalence of scripture*, namely, that each biblical text bears multiple layers of meaning (these are identified, examined, and interpreted through what scholars call the hermeneutical process); and finally (4) the nature and depth of one's faith journey and perspective, including *whether one views scripture with first- or second-half-of-life lenses.*

The Further Journey (Second Half of Life)[1]

While many models—biological, social, psychological, cognitive, moral, ecological, religious, existential, mystical—exist to help conceptualize life's

---

1. This topic is discussed in Richard Rohr's *Falling Upward* and also in my book *Dark Splendor*.

journey,[2] one I find compelling is known as the "second half of life." This "further journey" is not chronological, nor does one magically stumble upon it at midlife or in times of crisis, though these often serve as catalysts. While the second journey represents the culmination of one's faith journey, it is largely unknown today, even by people we consider deeply religious, since most individuals and institutions remain stymied in the preoccupations of the first half of life, establishing identity, creating boundary markers, and seeking security. The first-half-of-life task, while essential, is not the full journey. Furthermore, one cannot walk the second journey with first-journey tools. One needs a new toolkit.

As a child I was an achiever, fully embracing first-half-of-life tasks. Given a job, I did it to the best of my ability, quickly and efficiently. The sky was the limit, no task insurmountable. Having grown up in Latin America, the son of missionary parents, I attended a preparatory school near New York City to complete my high school education. The school adhered to Christian standards, requiring a class in religion annually. In our senior year, that course was taught by the headmaster, a distinguished Christian scholar. At the start of the course he issued a challenge to the senior class, that whoever memorized a book of the New Testament, such as Paul's letter to the Philippians, would receive a leather-bound version of the Bible—chosen by the student—inscribed with the pupil's name on the front cover. Many students raised their hand, indicating they would commit to the project, but in the end only two completed the task. When the headmaster asked me which version of the Bible I desired, I had no answer, for my only goal was to complete the task. At graduation the headmaster presented me a genuine morocco red-leather Bible with my name inscribed on the front—correctly spelled! Completing that task required commitment and discipline, essential virtues for the first half of life. But first-half-of-life virtues can only take you partway home.

Evidence suggests that there is another great undertaking to human life. The first task is to build a strong "container" or identity; the second is to find the contents that the container is meant to hold.[3] The first task—surviving successfully—is obvious, one we take for granted as the purpose of life. We all want to complete successfully the task that life first hands us: establishing an identity, a home, a career, relationships, friends, community, and security, all foundational for getting started in life. Many cul-

2. Such models are defined and explained in chapter 1 of *Dark Splendor*, 3–22.
3. Rohr, *Falling Upward*, xiii.

tures throughout history, most empires in antiquity, and the majority of individuals in the modern period have focused on first-half-of-life tasks, primarily because it is all they have time for, but also for lack of vision.

Most of us are never told that we can set out from the known and the familiar to take on a further journey. Our institutions, including our churches, are almost entirely configured to encourage, support, reward, and validate the tasks of the first half of life. Shocking and disappointing as it may be, we struggle more to survive than to thrive, focusing on "getting through" or on getting ahead rather than on finding out what is at the top or was already at the bottom. As wilderness guide Bill Plotkin puts it, many of us learn to do our "survival dance," but we never get to our actual "sacred dance."

According to Plotkin, the stage of adolescence—beyond which most adults never move—holds the key to both individual development and human evolution. In this stage individuals develop their distinctive ego-based consciousness, which represents both their greatest liability as well as their greatest potential. If they are to become fully human and move to the stages of genuine adulthood, people in the adolescent stage must let go of the familiar and comfortable while submitting to a journey of descent into "the mysteries of nature and the human soul." Individuals who remain within the constraints of a largely adolescent world regress into "pathological adolescence," characterized by materialism, sexism, competitive violence, racism, egoism, and self-destructive patterns. Patho-adolescent societies are perpetuated by leaders and celebrities described as self-serving politicians, moralizing religious leaders, drug-induced entertainment icons, and greedy captains of industry. If society is going to develop soulcentrically, it must be overseen by wise elders, not by adolescent politicians and corporate officers.

How can you know you are entering the second half of life? The following road markers are quite reliable: when you

- experience new urges
- sense a new vision
- are ready to let go of old securities
- are ready to risk giving up the patterns of the past for the promise of the future
- are as focused on the "inner" life as on the outer dimension of life.

While individuals can describe their experience of the second journey and even serve as mentors, they cannot define or outline the journey for others. This is due both to the uniqueness of the journey and to a subtle factor, known by generations of mystics and spiritual masters but elusive to many of our contemporaries: One does not choose this second journey; rather it chooses you. It finds you by means of your soul, your personal center and true home, the source of your true belonging. The soul comes to our aid through dreams, deep emotion, love, the quiet voice of guidance, synchronicities, revelations, hunches, and visions, and at times through illness, nightmares, and terrors. This is the identity that defines you, aligning you with your powers of nurturing, transforming, and creating, with your powers of presence and wonder. It is the soul that guides you, preparing the way and declaring you ready for this further journey.

Biblical Interpretation for Both Halves of Life: A Personal Example

One of the greatest rewards of teaching comes when teachers learn from their students. That occurred recently during my seminar on the book of Revelation. The class was examining the topic of heaven in Revelation, asking whether heaven should be viewed primarily as a place of destiny or as a literary device to help readers gain perspective. Important questions arose about the nature of worship, the focus of Christian life, and the role of scripture: Should the focus of the Christian life be on the challenges and possibilities of the present or on conjecture about the afterlife? Should the motivation for worship come from gratitude for the gift of life or from desire for heaven? Is the book of Revelation's intent to energize believers to greater faithfulness in their daily lives or to predict the future? Does reading Revelation as a code book about end-time events prepare us for the future or distract us from the tasks at hand? While the argument could be made that perhaps both sets of options might be correct, I was attempting to stretch their imagination and their critical thinking skills.

At one point in the discussion I introduced the famous declaration by Rabia (717–801), the medieval Sufi saint:

> O God, if I worship you from fear of hell, burn me in hell;
> And if I worship you in hope of paradise, bar me from paradise.
> But if I worship you for your own sake, grant me then your everlasting beauty.

INTRODUCTION

A freshman disagreed with Rabia's premise that love should be the motivating factor in religious worship, noting that the Bible commends the "fear" of the Lord, which he took literally to mean that people should worship and obey God out of fear of punishment. "Doesn't religion begin at home," he questioned, "with fearing our parents"? The student's insistence on literalism prompted further discussion.

"In the near future," I noted, "some of you will get married and have children. Do you want your children to fear you or to love and respect you?"

"Yes, of course, we would want them to love and respect us."

"If that's how you would want your children to relate to you," I replied, "isn't God's parenting better than ours?"

An older student, whether supporting the first student's understanding or simply playing the devil's advocate, questioned the meaning of Matthew 10:28, where Jesus is quoted as saying: "Do not fear those who kill the body but cannot kill the soul; rather, fear him who can destroy both soul and body in hell."

I encouraged the students to examine the context to determine whether the author's intention was to increase or decrease fear. Noting that verses 28 and 31 exhort believers not to be afraid, I explained that when the Bible speaks of fearing God, the stress is normally upon honoring, respecting, and obeying God, rather than cowering or trembling out of fear of divine punishment. One of the principles of biblical interpretation, which we had studied earlier in the term, affirms that "the symbolic is to be interpreted in the light of the didactic," meaning that secondary or obscure things in scripture should be subject to primary and plain teaching. Using this principle, I encouraged the students to focus on the supreme depiction of God in the Bible. If God is love, as the Bible proclaims, one we can call "Daddy,"[4] as Jesus did, shouldn't we relate to God as friend rather than as foe, as someone to love rather than someone to fear?

At that point a nineteen-year-old sophomore, wise beyond his years, asked perceptively: "Isn't it possible that this text contains two separate messages, one intended to strike fear into the heart of nominal or unrepentant Christians, and another to exhort devout believers to greater trust and faithfulness? Is it possible that biblical passages contain two messages, one for 'first-half-of life' Christians and the other for 'second-half-of life' Christians?'" The discussion ended on that high note.

---

4. The term Abba, an intimate reference to God in the New Testament, is commonly translated "Daddy"; see Mark 14:36, Romans 8:15, and Galatians 4:6.

After class a student approached me, the one who had asked us to read Matthew 10:28. We spoke about red-letter versions of the Bible, the ones that highlight the words of Jesus in red, and I indicated that in my estimation this device was one of the worst things we could do to the Bible, because highlighting the words of Jesus in this way gives the impression that such passages are verbatim words of Jesus. I explained that each Gospel, as each book of the Bible, is written from a specific point of view, which the original author or authors conveyed to a specific audience in a particular setting. The setting of Matthew's Gospel was quite possible a religious academy in Antioch, Syria, where Jewish Christians were preparing to evangelize fellow Jews. That Gospel likely served as a primer for early converts, presenting the teachings of Jesus selectively and in a manner that could be easily memorized and remembered. Written by a Jewish Christian for Jewish Christians, Matthew's Gospel appealed to Jewish legalism, with its love of rules and regulations. In most cases, the stories in the Gospels should not be taken literally, or the words verbatim.

As a religious scholar with over forty years of teaching experience, my knowledge and ability to interpret scripture is more advanced than that of my students. While some of that can be attributed to chronological age, since the majority of my students are fifty years younger than I, another factor, the "second half of life," is also at stake. The awareness I reached that day, while obvious now, continues to be transformative: Our religious perspective (including biblical and theological understanding) is greatly affected by whether we are in the first or second phase of our faith journey.

Biblical Interpretation for Both Halves of Life: A Pauline Example

Paul's argument in his letter to the Galatians about the relation of the law principle (Hebrew Torah) and the faith principle (Christian Gospel) seems to anticipate our model of the two halves of life. Paul begins his argument in chapter 3 by calling his listeners "foolish Galatians," for they had seemingly regressed from the second journey (living by faith: "the only thing that counts is faith working through love"; 5:6) to the first journey (living by "works of the law"). Having begun their Christian experience with freedom, trust, and the Holy Spirit (with the "second half of life" task), that is, with the presence of the living Christ (see Rom. 8:9–11), the Galatians had regressed to life in the flesh, that is, to legalistic efforts (to "first half of life" tasks). Their regression forced Paul to clarify the role of the Old Testament law (Torah) and its relation to the "law of Christ," by which he means the law of love: "The whole law is summed up in a single commandment, 'You shall love your neighbor as yourself'" (5:14).

In chapter 4:21—5:1 Paul speaks of two covenants or ways of life—the way of slavery and the way of freedom—concluding that we should choose the latter: "For freedom Christ has set us free. Stand firm, therefore, and do not submit again to a yoke of slavery." What is this yoke of slavery? I submit it can be seen as the first phase of the journey, characterized by adhering closely to life-shaping laws.

The rule of moral and religious laws is important, Paul argues in Galatians 3:19-24, for the Old Testament laws came from God and were given to provide moral, civil, and practical guidance. Those laws, however, have a temporary and intermediary role, to bring us to maturity and faith in Christ. Before Christ came (Gal. 4:4), the law had a custodial role, functioning as a "disciplinarian" or tutor (Gal. 3:24), much as a household slave who supervises the discipline of the child. But now that faith has come, we are no longer under this slave, but have become adults, full members in the household of God. Spiritual maturity sets us free to embark on the "further journey."

While conservatives find harmony in biblical thought and teaching, attributing unity of meaning and intention to divine authorship, liberals find tension, disagreement, and even contradiction within the texts, attributing these to human authorship and to historical, cultural, theological, and social differences reflected in the texts. Does the Bible contain a consistent message, to be accepted by all readers alike? Should biblical texts be limited to specific meaning and perspective, acceptable by all, or should they be considered polyvalent, containing multiple levels of meaning? Does polyvalence imply that some texts have no certain or final meaning? Is it possible that biblical texts contain conserving and liberating messages simultaneously?

While this book addresses these questions, it does not approach the Bible as an answer book, human or divine, but rather as a collection of books, multifaceted in nature, its enduring purpose being to provide us with perspective for living faithfully and fully through the stages and seasons of our lives.

Ways of Being Christian: Two Paradigms

It is no secret that we are living in a time of major change, resulting in monumental religious conflict, chiefly in North American mainline denominations. While there are many ways of being Christian in our day, two paradigms—two overarching interpretive frameworks—may be helpful to describe the current conflict in Christianity. The first, the Precritical Paradigm, has been a common form of Christianity for the past several hundred years. This approach should not be associated with Christianity as a whole, though it remains a major voice, perhaps the majority voice in global Christianity. Its adherents

a. view the Bible as a divine product, as the unique revelation of God;

b. interpret the Bible literally;

c. equate faith with belief; the Christian life centered in believing now for the sake of salvation;

d. view the afterlife as central; the Christian life being about requirements and rewards, with the main reward a blessed afterlife;

e. view Christianity as the only true religion, and belief in God, the Bible, and Jesus as the way to heaven.

This paradigm should not be equated with "the Christian tradition," as though it were the dominant or only way of being Christian throughout history. In actuality it is the product of modernity, shaped by the birth of modern science and scientific ways of knowing. Since the Enlightenment of the seventeenth century, modernity has questioned both the divine origin and the literal-factual truth of many parts of the Bible, and the Precritical Paradigm is a response to that modern critique.

A second way of seeing Christianity, the Postcritical Paradigm, has been in existence for over a hundred years and has become an increasingly attractive movement within mainline Protestant denominations and in the Catholic Church. Like the earlier paradigm, its central features are a response to the Enlightenment, only in this case it embraces many Enlightenment ideals, including an appreciation of science, historical scholarship, religious pluralism, and cultural diversity. It also arose out of awareness of how Christianity had contributed to racism, sexism, nationalism, exclusivism, and other harmful ideologies. Its adherents

a. view the Bible as a human response to God;

b. interpret the Bible historically and metaphorically;

c. view faith relationally rather than dogmatically—faith being the way of the heart, not the way of the head;

d. view the Christian life as one of relationship and transformation. Being Christian is not about meeting requirements for a future reward in an afterlife, and not very much about believing. Rather, the Christian life is about a relationship with God that transforms life in the present;

e. affirm religious pluralism. This paradigm considers Christianity as one of the world's great enduring religions, as a particular response to the experience of God in our Western cultural stream.

From the perspective of the Postcritical Paradigm, the Precritical Paradigm seems anti-intellectual and rigidly (but selectively) moralistic. Its insistence on biblical literalism seems inadequate, as does its rejection of science whenever it conflicts with literalism. It seems to emphasize individual purity more than compassion and justice. And its exclusivism, its rejection of other religions as inadequate or worse, is objectionable. Can it be that God is known in only one religion—and perhaps only in the "right" form of that religion?

Second-Half-of-Life Spirituality

Like individuality, each person has a spirituality native to his or her own personality. Like personality, spirituality also yearns for growth and expression. One's spirituality, like one's personality, can never be determined by someone else. It can be influenced by others, as in the case of parents and other authority figures, but ultimately the choice of spirituality must be one's own. The goal of spirituality is maturity: in wisdom, lifestyle, and understanding. Such wisdom includes our knowledge, understanding, and application of scripture.

While disagreements over matters such as the role of religion, the Christian life, the interpretation of scripture, the meaning of God, and doctrines such as belief in heaven and hell are attributable to upbringing, chronological age, social standing, and academic training, many disagreements are affected by our spiritual journeys, particularly by our place on that journey. This explains why some people more open to growth, change, and transformation than others. While intellect and background are factors, spiritual growth, curiosity, and development are often indicative of second-half-of-life spirituality.

The second-half-of-life journey has been likened to a second simplicity or a second naiveté. Whatever we call it, this condition is the very goal of mature adulthood and mature religion. First naiveté is the earnest and dangerous innocence we sometimes admire in young zealots, but it is also the reason we should not elect them or follow them as leaders. It is probably necessary to be impetuous when we are young, taking risks and eliminating most doubt. In the long run such approaches to life are not wise. Mature wisdom is content to live with mystery, doubt, and "unknowing," and in such living ironically resolves that very mystery to some degree. It takes a great deal of learning to finally "learn ignorance," as so many religious sages discovered. As T. S. Eliot puts it in the *Four Quartets*: "We had the experience but missed the meaning." Eliot's verse suggests that people in the second half of life need not expect to have the same experience as others; rather, simple meaning now suffices.

This new coherence, a unified field that embraces paradox, is precisely what characterizes second-half-of-life people. It feels like a return to simplicity after having learned from all the complexity. Finally, one understands that "everything belongs," even the sad, absurd, and futile parts. In the second half of life we can devote ourselves to integrating even the painful parts of our life into the now unified field, including people who are different or marginalized. If we can forgive yourselves for being imperfect and falling, we can now do it for others.

As noted above, the transformation that brings us to the second half of life is often more about unlearning than learning. Perhaps it is simply a more profound learning. Life is more spacious now, the boundaries of the container having been enlarged by transformative experiences and relationships. For many people, the second half of life is characterized by seven transformational qualities:

1. Less fear and therefore less hostility. Because one has less need to eliminate the negative or fearful from one's life, there is less need to punish other people. Superiority complexes have been shown to be useless, ego based, counterproductive, and often entirely wrong.
2. Less combative. By the second half of life one has learned that most frontal attacks simply add to the amount of evil within. Along with an inflated self-image, they incite retaliation from those one has attacked.

INTRODUCTION

3. Less need of attention. When "elders" speak, they need few words to make their point. Second simplicity has its own kind of brightness and clarity, but much of it is expressed nonverbally, and only when really needed. In the first half of life, one is defined through differentiation; now one looks for commonality. One does not need to dwell on the differences between people or exaggerate the problems. Creating dramas has become boring.

4. Less assertive. In the second half of life it is good just to be a part of the general dance. We do not have to stand out or be better than others; life is more participatory than assertive, and there is no need for strong or further self-definition.

5. Less self-concerned. At this stage we no longer have to prove that we are the best, that our ethnicity is superior, our religion the only one accepted by God, or that our role and place in society deserve special treatment.

6. Less dogmatic. People in the second half of life are less condemning. They no longer see God as small, punitive, or tribal. They once defended signposts; now they have arrived where the signs pointed. One's growing sense of spaciousness is no longer found mostly "out there" but especially "in here." The inner and the outer have become one. In the second journey, we have less final opinions about things and people as we allow them to delight or sadden us. We no longer need to change or adjust other people in order to be happy ourselves. Ironically, we are more than ever before in a position to change others—but we do not need to—and that makes all the difference. Now we aid and influence others simply by being who we are.

7. Less possessive. At this stage we are no longer preoccupied with accumulating additional goods and services; rather, our desire and effort should be to pay back to the world some of what we have received. Our concern is not so much to have what you love but to love what you have—here and now. This is such a monumental change from the first half of life that it is almost the litmus test of whether one is in the second half of life at all.

Such transformation involves risk-taking in the following areas: (1) forgiveness (repudiating retaliation or "getting even"); (2) prayer (learning to listen in silence); (3) changing one's attitude ("unlearning"); (4)

quiet persuasion (becoming an elder statesman); (5) becoming an agent of change (which starts with actively working for peace); and (6) influencing events (indirectly rather than directly, by modeling the transformative qualities of the second simplicity).

If unlearning is a way to deeper spirituality, the following pathways represent "paradigm shifts," attitudinal transformations, in the journey from the first to the second half of life:

- Impatience to greater patience;
- Critical to more accepting;
- Pessimism to optimism;
- Stoical to joyful;
- Independent to dependent;
- Aloof to affectionate;
- Self-centered to other-oriented
- Frugal to generous.

These observations do not represent precepts to be followed or new commandments to be obeyed. The second half of life is not about precepts or commandments, for there is only one guideline for the second half of life: to love the Lord your God with your entire mind, heart, soul, and strength, and your neighbor as yourself. The rest is commentary.[5]

When we grow spiritually, journeying into the second phase of life, our faith grows exponentially. With this freedom comes a new understanding of scripture, the creeds, God, and of the Christian life. As a Christian—a "little Christ," a bearer of the image of God—we were born to co-create the future with God. That task will be nourished by the study of scripture presented in this book.

A strong correlation can be found between the biblical tradition and the second half of life, particularly if this form of spirituality represents the ability to live life authentically in the real world. Such spirituality represents the arena where humans struggle to cope with the chaos of daily life, where good and evil compete for human loyalty, and where the divine and the human meet. Popular thinking often limits divine-human exchange to specifically religious activities and places, claiming that God is to be found

---

5. The discussion regarding second-half-of-life qualities is adapted from my book *Dark Splendor*, 96–98; see also Rohr, *Falling Upward*, 118–25.

INTRODUCTION

primarily in the privacy of the individual soul. Biblical literature provides a resource for a more holistic spirituality, one that perceives outer and inner life, individual and community life, and God and the world as inextricably intertwined. Understanding the realm of divine-human encounter to be ordinary human life, second-half-of-life spirituality promotes the pathway of relationship.

The implications for such an understanding of spirituality are enormous. Second-half-of-life spirituality leaves little room for dualistic thinking or living. Ordinary life and the life of faith are not separate or antithetical spheres, for all life exists in the presence of its Creator. From this perspective, the struggles and conflicts of daily life should not to be shunned or avoided as though they are evil, but rather embraced in full consciousness of their revelatory and healing potential.

Second-half-of-life spirituality appreciates the ambiguity of human experience. It finds in ambiguity and confusion the opportunity for breakthrough into mystery. It struggles against rote religious answers to human problems. Second phasers know that life is not a simple set of truths to be followed indiscriminately, but a continual encounter with conflicting truths, each making competing claims upon the seeker. But the point of ambiguity or paradox is not to bring the individual to an intellectual impasse or a spiritual angst, but to lead one beyond the obvious into deeper understanding. Offering a spirituality of discovery, second-half-of-life spirituality requires openness, discernment, and choice. Because such an approach views life as paradoxical, it also calls for patience, trust, and a glad heart.

Jefferson Bethke's video "Why I Hate Religion, But Love Jesus" became an overnight sensation when it first appeared on YouTube in 2012, with seven million views in the first forty-eight hours. Recited in rap, Bethke's verse contrasts self-righteous attitudes with the teachings of Jesus. using hyperbole to distinguish between first- and second-half-of-life religious attitudes and perspectives:

> See, the problem with religion is it never gets to the core;
> It's just behavior modification, like a long list of chores. . . .
> Now I ain't judging; I'm just saying, quit putting on a fake look
> 'Cause there's a problem if people only know you're a Christian by your Facebook. . . .

Written to highlight the difference between Jesus and "false" religion, additional lines intensify the distinction further: "Religion says 'do,' Jesus says 'done'"; "Religion says 'slave,' Jesus says 'son'"; "Religion makes you blind, but Jesus makes you see."

This four-minute video shows a young adult transitioning from a first-half-of-life to a second-half-of life perspective. While I disagree with Bethke's strident dismissal of traditional religion, his words clearly validate the gap between his perspective and that of many adult parishioners in American churches. This video demonstrates that one need not be fully adult to embark on the second-half journey.

Securing Life

According to the Bible, humans live in a moral universe. Discovering this "rational rule" enabled biblical authors to secure existence by acting in harmony with the fundamental order that sustained the cosmos. One's conduct either strengthens the existing order or contributes to the forces of chaos that threaten survival itself. Once biblical authors discovered this moral or rational principle, it became their task to transfer it from the realm of nature to the human sphere. They accomplished this goal through analogy. The search for proper analogies had as its goal *securing life*. Such life, called salvation or abundant life in John's Gospel (10:10), comes from a relationship with God. In the Bible, a person who is "saved" (10:9) has secured life. Such life is not different in degree from ordinary life, but different in kind: abundant life, an extension of God's love, is measureless and unlimited. Second-half-of-life people today are turning to the Bible for wisdom in daily living, recognizing that God is encountered *through* human experience, not despite it.

Basic Principles and Perspectives

Securing Life is grounded in the conviction that humans have the capacity to transcend conventional understanding of scripture, exhibiting a genuine and wholesome faith that is dynamic rather than static, future-oriented rather than past-oriented, and affirmed rather than passively acquired. This capacity is fueled by two principles: (1) that whatever does not grow dies (this principle encourages us to remain open to change and newness); and

(2) that all truth is God's truth (this principle encourages us to remain open to truth wherever it may be found and wherever it leads).

From a neuroscientific perspective, it seems that the brain has two basic functions or goals: self-maintenance and self-transcendence. The self-maintenance function of the brain incorporates all of the things we associate with first-half-of-life concerns, everything that helps us survive. However, self-maintenance is only part of the story because an organism doesn't merely maintain one steady state throughout life. People change, and as a result, the brain must have the ability to change and adapt as well. To some extent, self-transcendence is part of self-maintenance because, presumably, an adaptable brain enables us to handle the vagaries of life more effectively. Thus there is a certain degree of stability within the brain and its connections. This allows us to be who we are throughout our lives. However, the brain also has flexibility, variability, and changeability. It has the ability to change by rewiring the connections between neurons, and possibly even changing the function of the neurons in a process referred to as neuroplasticity. Neuroscientists are now appreciating the role of religion in providing powerful mechanisms to accomplish these goals.[6]

A basic premise of this book is that the Bible, like religion in general, has both a conserving and liberating effect, providing perspective for both halves of life:

- perspective for *formation* (such first-half-of-life perspectives, while characterized as traditional, conventional, or conservative, are essential but not definitive or ultimate ways of reading and applying scripture);

- perspective for *transformation* (such second-half-of-life perspectives, characterized as progressive, radical, or liberal, are essential, definitive, and ultimate ways of reading and applying scripture).

Securing Life examines both ways to read and understand scripture. If you are a first-phase Christian, this book will expand your thinking and enlarge your boundaries. If you are a second-phase Christian, this book provides a toolkit for ongoing growth and transformation, engaging you in new ways to think about religion, theology, and scripture.

---

6. Newberg, *The Spiritual Brain*, 153–55.

Overview

Those who read the Bible canonically, beginning with Genesis (Creation) and ending with Revelation (Consummation), do so to gain literary and theological perspective. They are not, however, reading the Bible chronologically, for the sources and books that comprise the Bible were not written in that order.

Biblical scholars customarily date Israel's first national epic as the product of a literary awakening that occurred during the reigns of David and Solomon, a period known as the United Kingdom. In this view, an unknown author in Judea known as "the Yahwist" (or Jahwist) composed a masterful prose epic using preliterary units of tradition to create Israel's first written source. This source, called J, was written about 950–900. He (or she) was interested in personal biography and in ethical and theological reflection. E, the second source, was composed between 850–750 BC in the Northern Kingdom of Israel by an unknown author identified as the Elohist. This source is more objective than J, being less interested in theological reflection. About 715 BC an unknown editor combined J and E into what is known as the Old Epic or JE.

While the period from Abraham to Moses to David was one of oral tradition, this does not mean that beginning with David (1000 BC) oral tradition was superseded by literary records or that before David there were no written records. What it means is that the Yahwist was the first to record the all-Israelite epic, a core story which up to that time had survived orally through stories, poems, songs, and other "memory units." Some units of oral tradition were non-Israelite in origin and were later taken over by the Israelites. For example, the stories of Abraham's sacrifice of Isaac (Gen. 22) and Jacob's dream at Bethel (Gen. 28) could have been Canaanite cult legends whose original cultural meaning is now lost to us. These independent units of tradition were not simply borrowed but rather were appropriated by Israel and given new meaning.

The compositional approach used by the Yahwist is fascinating. Rather than starting chronologically with creation, adding accounts of the patriarchs, the Exodus, the conquest, the tribal confederacy, and finally, the monarchy, the J writer worked backward, "viewing earlier stories through the prism of the crucial historical experiences that created the community of Israel."[7] Starting with the Mosaic tradition (the material that extends

---

7. Anderson, *Understanding the Old Testament*, 145.

from the oppression in Egypt to the entrance into Canaan), the Yahwist linked it with the Patriarchal tradition (the pre-Mosaic material found in Genesis 12–50), and finally with the Primeval tradition (the early material in Genesis that extends from the Creation, through the Flood, to the new beginning after the Flood).

The all-Israelite epic, read chronologically through its three movements or "acts," begins ecumenically (with fundamental human experiences), continues with Israel's ancestors, and culminates in the Mosaic tradition. The Yahwist, it appears, was the first author to link the Mosaic tradition to a universal and cosmic context.

Like the Yahwist, *Securing Life* examines the biblical experience as the unfolding drama of God's historical purpose, moving backward from Covenant (Mosaic period) through Community (Patriarchal tradition) to Creation (Primeval tradition) and then forward from New Covenant (Pauline tradition) through New Community (Gospel tradition) to New Creation (Apocalyptic tradition) into an open-ended future. Those motifs are preceded by five preparatory chapters, three dealing with introductory matters (chapter 1 provides an overview of the Bible, including its books, genres, and themes; chapter 2 examines biblical inspiration, including how the Bible was composed and became scripture; and chapter 3 provides hermeneutical guidelines for biblical reading and interpretation), one (chapter 4) with biblical theology (the doctrine of God), and one (chapter 5) with biblical anthropology (the doctrines of sin and salvation).

Part I

Introductory Topics

Chapter 1

Biblical Information
Books, Genres, and Central Themes of the Bible

Do you know the books of the Bible in order? Can you find a particular verse or locate specific topics and doctrines in the Bible quickly and efficiently? Have you read the Bible from cover to cover, once, twice, many times? Have you memorized verses, passages, even books of the Bible? To each question, I can answer in the affirmative, having accomplished these tasks before I reached puberty. By the time I enrolled at Princeton Theological Seminary to prepare for ministry I had read through the Bible several times, taken numerous college courses in biblical and theological studies, and memorized entire books of the Bible.

As a child I recall participating in sword drills. A sword drill has nothing to do with fencing. It is a competition designed to improve one's knowledge and use of the Bible, a fun way for children to learn the books of the Bible and their location by turning quickly to a specific verse. The first person to find the reference reads the passage and gains a point. Some competitions allow contestants to quote a verse without looking it up, rewarding memorization. At higher levels, participants are given unfinished quotations to complete; they also compete in topical and doctrinal drills, where they are asked to locate verses on topics such as creation, prayer, heaven, and the end of the world.

If you grew up in a fundamentalist or evangelical church, as I did, the Bible was the "sword of the Lord," and you were encouraged to get "into the Word," studying it in depth to become proficient in biblical knowledge. As the "Word of God," the Bible is considered holy and sacred above all books and reliable in every detail. Details were important, and I quickly mastered biblical trivia, knowing the answers to questions such as how long Moses lived (120 years), who lived the longest life (Methuselah, 969 years), or the identity of such biblical characters as Enoch, Melchizedek, and Elihu.

Most children nowadays do not know the Bible in this way. In fact, they may not even own a Bible, and if they do, they are likely biblically illiterate. According to a survey in 2006, about 47 percent of Americans polled claimed to read the Bible at some point in a week (up from a low of 31 percent in 1995). That's encouraging! But an earlier survey found that while 82 percent of Americans claimed to believe that the Bible is either the literal or "inspired" Word of God, with more than half saying they read the Bible at least monthly, many could not distinguish an apostle from an epistle, half couldn't name one of the four Gospels, and fewer than half knew who delivered the Sermon on the Mount. That's discouraging!

The Jewish Bible (known to Christians as the Old Testament) and the Christian New Testament are ancient. Some portions of the Old Testament may have been written around three thousand years ago, while the books of the New Testament are about two thousand years old. In the twenty-first century, why should we study such archaic writings?

Many people, of course, read the Bible as scripture, meaning it is fundamental to their identity. They consider the Bible the Word of God and are committed to living their lives on the basis of the values they find therein. They read the Bible weekly in worship and live liturgically, their lives impacted deeply by ritual observances based on stories found in these texts, such as the Jewish Passover and Yom Kippur or the Christian Easter and Christmas.

There are other less religious reasons the Bible should be studied today. These are particularly relevant for readers who have little or no connection with the Bible as sacred text, but are important for those who are guided by its spiritual values and moral teachings. In addition to its spiritual and religious significance, the Bible continues to have a profound cultural influence on the Western world, including artistic, literary, political, and legal influence. The Bible, after all, is great literature, and those who ignore it cannot be considered educated.

The word "Bible" derives from the Greek *biblia*, which means "books." The Bible is not a single book but rather a collection of writings. It is a library of diverse pieces of literature that were collected together as scripture by Jewish and Christian communities. In the ancient world "book" really meant "scroll." With the development of the codex (a book with leaves or pages), a collection of books could be bound together in a single volume, and the Bible represents such a format.

Why Genre Matters

Whenever we read a book, whether we are aware of it or not, we make certain judgments even before we start reading. If we pick up a romance novel, we expect to read about broken hearts or extramarital affairs, but we certainly do not expect to read an enduring literary work. If you read a book on the Vietnam war or the Iraq war, we expect to read about historical events that led to the conflict or the political maneuverings that brought it to conclusion. You would not expect a tourist guide of places to visit in Saigon or Baghdad.

When you make judgments about different types of literature, you are making decisions about the genre of the work. The same holds true in other artistic endeavors, such as art or music. For example, most people can distinguish between impressionism or realism in art, or jazz from folk music. Painters, composers, and performers know that there are certain rules that govern their work. Sometimes they deviate from these rules in order to create interest or excitement, but when they go too far, they find themselves working in a different genre or possibly even creating a new genre. The same holds true for literature. Knowing whether the genre of a work is a novel, a biography, or science fiction is an important step in understanding how to interpret it.

The same holds true for the New Testament books; knowing their genre can dramatically impact interpretation. Some people look at the Gospels, for example, and think of them as histories (in the modern sense of the word) or eyewitness accounts of the life of Jesus. However, scholarly research into the gospel writers and their intended audiences shows that they were intended as faith proclamations for communities committed to belief in Jesus as the Christ. Similarly, some people read the book of Revelation and think it will give them a timetable of the events that must take place before the end of the world. However, without a proper understanding of the apocalyptic genre, they will miss the intended message of Revelation. The book is highly symbolic, and while it appears to be about the end time, its real message is pastoral, hopeful, and timely.

Basic Information on the Old Testament

The Jewish Bible (known as the Hebrew scriptures or to Jews simply as Tanakh) and the Christian Old Testament are similar but not identical. For the Jewish community, the Bible is composed of twenty-four books divided into three sections: Torah (Law), Nebiim (Prophets), and Kethubim (Writings). While these books, written almost entirely in Hebrew, are fundamentally the same as the Christian Old Testament, the arrangement differs. To understand the Hebrew Bible, imagine three concentric circles. The inner circle, the Torah, presents the basic story of the people and includes laws for everyday life. The next circle, the Prophets, is a commentary on the life of the people to whom the Torah is given. The outer circle, the Writings, is a diverse collection that extends outward from Israel's worship and festivals to wisdom reflection.

The Christian Bible, after the first five books (known as the Books of Moses or the Pentateuch), displays a different order and add up differently, making thirty-nine distinct books, in contrast to the twenty-four of the Tanakh. The differences are partly accounted for by the fact that the early Christians were a Greek-speaking community who read the Hebrew Bible in Greek, particularly in a translation begun in the third century BC called the Septuagint. The Septuagint placed the prophetic writings last, while the Hebrew Bible concludes with the Writings (ending with 1–2 Chronicles). Traditionally, Christians prefer the Greek order because the prophetic books look ahead to a new beginning for Israel, creating a more effective transition to the New Testament. In addition, these books provide a prophetic bridge between the testaments, directly connecting Old Testament prophecy with New Testament fulfillment. For example, Matthew's opening narrative regularly references how the birth of Jesus fulfills Old Testament prophecy: "All this took place to fulfill what had been spoken by the Lord through the prophet" (Matt. 1:22; see also 2:5; 15, 17, 23). The Septuagint also includes a number of works that are not part of the Hebrew Bible, though these works once enjoyed considerable favor in Jewish circles.

Among Christian groups there is also disagreement concerning the contents of the Old Testament. Some Christian churches, including Roman Catholic, Eastern Orthodox, and a few Protestant groups, add six or seven additional books (plus additions to existing books) to the twenty-four books of the Tanakh. These additional works are called "deuterocanonical" (lit. "second canon," meaning that they came into the biblical canon at a later time than the books of the Hebrew Bible) by these groups and the "Apocrypha" by most Protestant groups, whose Old Testament has the same books as the Tanakh, although arranged somewhat differently. The following table illustrates these differences.

The Hebrew Bible (Tanakh)

The Torah (five books): Genesis, Exodus, Leviticus, Numbers, Deuteronomy

The Prophets (eight books):

- Former Prophets: Joshua, Judges, Samuel (counts as one book), Kings (counts as one book)
- Latter Prophets: Isaiah, Jeremiah, Ezekiel, the Twelve (counts as one book: Hosea, Joel, Amos, Obadiah, Jonah, Micah, Nahum, Habakkuk, Zephaniah, Haggai, Zechariah, Malachi)

The Writings (eleven books): Job, Psalms, Proverbs, Ruth, Song of Songs (also known as Song of Solomon), Ecclesiastes, Lamentations, Esther, Daniel, Ezra-Nehemiah (counts as one book), Chronicles (counts as one book)

The Christian Old Testament

The Pentateuch: (five books): Genesis, Exodus, Leviticus, Numbers, Deuteronomy

Historical Books (twelve books): Joshua, Judges, Ruth, 1 and 2 Samuel, 1 and 2 Kings, 1 and 2 Chronicles, Ezra, Nehemiah, Esther

Poetry and Wisdom Books (five books): Job, Psalms, Proverbs, Ecclesiastes, Song of Solomon

Prophetic Books (seventeen books)

- Major Prophets: Isaiah, Jeremiah, Lamentations, Ezekiel, Daniel
- Minor Prophets: Hosea, Joel, Amos, Obadiah, Jonah, Micah, Nahum, Habakkuk, Zephaniah, Haggai, Zechariah, Malachi

The Deuterocanonical (or Apocryphal) Books

Historical Books: Tobit, Judith, Additions to Esther; 1 and 2 Maccabees

Poetry and Wisdom: Wisdom of Solomon, Ecclesiasticus

Prophets: Additions to Daniel

The first fourteen books of the Old Testament (the first ten books of the Tanakh) have a narrative framework, recounting a story that begins with the creation of the heavens and the earth by God in Genesis and continues with the formation and flourishing of the nation Israel, and concludes with the chaos of the destruction of ancient Israel. The Pentateuch begins with prehistory (Genesis 1–11), including accounts of cosmic origins, the first humans, a disastrous flood, restoration after the flood, and the spread of humanity. The central historical narrative features ancestral stories (Genesis 12–50), beginning with the journey of Abraham and Sarah to the land of Canaan and eventually into Egypt, where they become slaves to Pharaoh. Eventually Moses leads the Israelites out of Egypt (Exodus 1–18), climaxing in a dramatic encounter with God at Mount Sinai, where they enter into a covenant with Yahweh (Exodus 19:1—Numbers 10:10). At the end of a forty-year sojourn through the wilderness, the tribes of Israel stand on the east bank of the Jordan River, ready to enter the land of promise. The account of wandering is accompanied by extensive ritual and legal legislation (such as the Book of the Covenant in Exodus 20:22—23:33 and the Holiness Code in Leviticus 17–26).

The final book of the Torah (Deuteronomy) marks a transition to the next section of the Bible (known as the Historical Books or to Jews as the Former Prophets), as Moses recounts to the people the journey on which God has led them, exhorts them to keep the law given by God, and prepares them for life in the land they are about to enter.

The Historical Books recount the dramatic story of the conquest and settling of the land of Canaan by the tribes of Israel under the leadership of Joshua (Joshua 1—Judges 2); the exploits of leaders known as judges who emerge to defend the tribes when they are threatened (Judges 3–21); the capture of Jerusalem and the creation of the nation of Israel under King David and his son Solomon, the building of the temple in Jerusalem, the division of the nation into the kingdoms of Israel (in the North) and Judah (in the South), and finally the conquest of the two kingdoms by the Assyrian and Babylonian empires, culminating in the destruction of the temple and the beginning of the exile in Babylon (1 and 2 Samuel, 1 and 2 Kings). The story throughout the Historical Books is told from the perspective introduced in the book of Deuteronomy, that the nation prospers when leaders and people are faithful to the law God revealed to them at Sinai. Hence, scholars often call this section the Deuteronomistic History.

BIBLICAL INFORMATION

In the Jewish canon narrative books are treated as prophecy because they are said to contain accurate and reliable lessons about history. A prophet, in Israel's religious tradition, was not a predictor of the future, but a reader of the present. That is to say, a prophet was one who could look at society critically and discern the will of God for the present time, then speak that will to the people. The authors of these Historical Books were prophets in this sense. They looked at Hebrew society of their time and judged that a particular lesson from Israel's history was needed to insure God's blessing.

The books of the Latter Prophets include collections of oracles and writings of the prophets, usually in poetic form, as well as stories about the prophets. The first three are called the major prophets because they are longer in length, while the shortest are called minor prophets.

The remaining books, a diverse collection of literature known as the Writings in the Tanakh, include religious poetry (Psalms and Lamentations), love poetry (Song of Solomon), conventional wisdom sayings (Proverbs), and skeptical wisdom (Ecclesiastes and Job). In addition, the Writings include a group of historical writings (Ezra, Nehemiah, and 1 and 2 Chronicles), called by scholars the Chronicler's History. These books revisit the story of the formation and collapse of the nation Israel, already introduced in the Former Prophets, and extends it to the return following the Babylonian exile, focusing on the rebuilding of the Jerusalem temple, the walls of the city, and the renewal of the covenant with God. The Writings also include Ruth and Esther, short stories about heroic women who play crucial roles in the life of Israel. In Jewish tradition, five of the books in the Writings (Ruth, Esther, Song of Songs, Ecclesiastes, and Lamentations) are grouped together as the Megilloth or festival scrolls and assigned to be read at specific religious holidays.

Daniel, the remaining book in the Writings, is the only fully apocalyptic book in the Tanakh. It includes visions of a dramatic time in history known as the Maccabean period and hopes for a new age, the kingdom of God. In the Christian Old Testament this book is included with the prophetic books.

The deuterocanonical (or apocryphal) books reflect the same literary variety as the Old Testament. Tobit and Judith are short stories, recounting the exploits of heroic figures. Maccabees extends the historical narrative begun in the Historical Books. Edifying tales (Susanna and Bel and the

Dragon) and poems (The Prayer of Azariah and the Song of the Three Men) are added to Daniel in the Deuterocanon.

Basic Information on the New Testament

An offshoot of Judaism, the early Christian community added twenty-seven early Christian writings to the Jewish Bible, which they formerly called simply "scripture." The addition became known as the New Testament. Considerably shorter than the Old Testament and written entirely in Greek, the New Testament can be grouped into five divisions, as the following chart shows.

The New Testament

Gospels (four books): Matthew, Mark, Luke, John

Historical (one book): Acts

Epistles (Letters) of Paul (thirteen books): Romans, 1 and 2 Corinthians, Galatians, Ephesians, Philippians, Colossians, 1 and 2 Thessalonians, 1 and 2 Timothy, Titus, Philemon

General (Catholic) Epistles (eight books): Hebrews, James, 1 and 2 Peter, 1, 2, and 3 John, Jude

Prophetic (1 book): Revelation

The books of the New Testament are not arranged according to chronology, that is, according to the order in which they were written, but rather according to the order in which the material they report happened.

- Gospels—deal with the life of Jesus
- Acts—deals with the birth of the church
- Epistles of Paul—deal with the growth of the church
- General Epistles—deal with the general nature of the church
- Revelation—deals with the immediate and distant future of the church

The New Testament begins with four works known as Gospels. Each is a narrative of the life and teachings of Jesus of Nazareth, proclaiming him to be the Christ, which means the Messiah, the one anointed by God to fulfill the promises made to Israel. What began as a largely oral tradition, handed down in no particular order, gradually became a set of texts. The first three Gospels, similar in structure and content, are known collectively as the Synoptics, whereas John, the last to be written and distinct in structure and point of view, is known as the Fourth Gospel.

The Gospels are followed in the New Testament by Acts of the Apostles, an historical narrative that recounts a geographic shift—the spread of the Christian message from Jerusalem to Rome—and an ethnic shift—from a church predominantly Jewish to one predominantly Gentile in nature. Acts focuses on the role of two prominent individuals: Peter, an apostle of Jesus, and Paul, commissioned apostle by the risen Christ. Modern scholarship supports the view that the Gospel of Luke and the Acts of the Apostles share authorship and purpose, joint volumes in a connected historical narrative of the birth of Christianity.

Thirteen of the twenty-seven books of the New Testament are letters attributed to Paul, who helped shape Christian belief, practice, and ethics and was instrumental in the spread of Christianity across the Mediterranean world. Scholars disagree over which letters were actually written by Paul, suggesting at least three categories: authentic, disputed, and pseudepigraphic. As a way of dealing with this classification, the following views of Pauline authorship have been proposed:

- *Radical Paul* (seven authentic letters): 1 Thessalonians, 1 and 2 Corinthians, Philippians, Galatians, Romans, Philemon

- *Conservative Paul* (three disputed letters; if not Pauline, they are Deutero-Pauline, that is, written by an admirer of Paul): 2 Thessalonians, Colossians, Ephesians

- *Reactionary Paul* (three letters, written by an anti-Paulinist, in order to make Christianity appear compatible with Roman values): 1 and 2 Timothy, Titus.

Paul's authentic letters typically follow epistolary correspondence common in the Greek-speaking world of the first century. Most of these letters are addressed to Christian communities in the northern Mediterranean world, churches Paul visited during his three missionary journeys. The author gives thanks for the people's faithfulness, chastises them for their failings, exhorts them to live as disciples of Jesus Christ, and clarifies his understanding of the meaning of the Christian gospel. Philemon is addressed to a friend of Paul. Three of the letters attributed to Paul but actually written to deradicalize Paul are 1 and 2 Timothy and Titus. Called the

Pastoral Letters because of their concern with leadership in the Christian churches, their target audience is other Christian missionaries.

Like other New Testament documents, the Pauline letters are not arranged chronologically, that is, in the order in which they were written, but rather according to two criteria: length and audience. The first nine letters, written to churches, precede the last four, written to individuals; Romans, the longest letter written to a community, appears first, and Philemon, the shortest letter written to an individual, appears last.

The Pauline letters, while varied and complex in content, have been classified thematically as follows:

- *Eschatology* (addressing the meaning and expected return of Christ): 1 and 2 Thessalonians
- *Soteriology* (addressing the way of salvation): Romans, Galatians, 1 and 2 Corinthians (all letters in this group are said to be authentically Pauline)
- *Christology* (addressing the doctrine of Christ): Ephesians, Colossians, Philippians, and Philemon
- *Ecclesiology* (addressing leadership for the local church): 1 and 2 Timothy, Titus

The other New Testament letters, called General or Catholic Epistles because their message is universal and intended for the church at large, are general tracts on Christian themes. The book of Hebrews appears not to be a letter but an early Christian sermon. These epistles are named either for the type of audience (Hebrews) or the claimed author (James; 1 and 2 Peter; 1, 2 and 3 John; Jude). The authors of the letters of James and Jude have been traditionally identified as brothers of Jesus and early Christian leaders. Peter is an apostle of Jesus prominent in the Gospels and Acts. It is generally assumed that the "John" of the first epistle is not "the elder" identified in the other two letters of John.

The final book of the New Testament, written by a prophet named John and aptly named the book of Revelation, is, like the Old Testament book of Daniel, an apocalyptic work. It features visions of the end, describing the course of future events leading up to the defeat of evil and, with the triumphant return of Jesus Christ, the beginning of a new age. It is principally concerned with faithfulness, both of Christians and of God.

BIBLICAL INFORMATION

The Bible: A Narrative Drama in Five Acts

Since the Jewish and Christian Bibles are not single books but collections of works, they have a variety of themes and conflicting points of view. However, read canonically, the Bible contains a unified story. Biblical theologians see the Bible as a narrative drama, with God as the main character. While scholars disagree on the number of episodes in the biblical drama or on what to call them, the following headings adequately describe the plot: Creation, Covenant, Christ, Church, and Consummation.

The Bible focuses on the involvement of the Creator of the universe in the unfolding story of life. The book of Genesis begins with the origins of the cosmos and quickly moves to a story revolving around God's special relationship with human beings, particularly with the nation of Israel. It is the story of God's faithfulness and of the fulfillment humans enjoy when they respond with obedience to the way of life to which God calls them. A central theme in the Old Testament is God's special relationship with the people of Israel, founded on God's promise made to a couple named Abraham and Sarah that their descendants would become a great nation with a land of their own and that through this nation (which became known as Israel) all the peoples of the earth would be blessed. Because of this special relationship, the people of Israel are expected to follow the path God reveals to them through Torah, God's law given through Moses and reaffirmed by prophets, priests, and kings at various points in the story of the nation. However, Israel's leaders and people fail to keep these expectations and the Old Testament recounts the tragic story of God's judgment as Israel breaks up. Nevertheless, the underlying theme of God's faithfulness reappears in a variety of contexts, such as in Isaiah's Suffering Servant poems (Isa. 42:1–4, 49:1–6, 50:4–11, and 52:13—53:12), Jeremiah's promise of a new covenant (Jer. 31:31–34), and Daniel's Son of Man vision (Dan. 7:13–14). These references would become vital to the fledgling Christian community's self-understanding, creating a sense of hope that all God's promises were being fulfilled in Jesus Christ (see 2 Cor. 1:20).

The Christian Bible reorganizes the books of the Tanakh so that the focus is on the hope that God is acting in a new and decisive way to redeem Israel. From that perspective, the New Testament is the story of the church, a "new Israel" that includes not only physical descendants of Abraham but all people who respond faithfully to God's new revelation (Gal. 3:6–9, Rom. 4:16–25) in Jesus Christ. Therefore, the New Testament begins with the story of the life, death, and resurrection of Jesus in the Gospels and follows with the account of the formation of a new community of faith founded on faith in Jesus, through whom all humans are brought back to a right relationship with the Creator. The New Testament ends by looking to the return of Jesus and the creation of a "new heaven and new earth" (Rev. 21:1, 5), a consummation in which the harmony God intended at the beginning will finally be realized.

The books of the Old and New Testament constitute the Christian canon, for Christians the authoritative Word of God. The reasons for its authoritative nature and the process of its canonization will be explored in chapter 2.

Chapter 2

Biblical Inspiration

How the Bible Became Scripture

Foundational to reading the Bible is a decision about how to view its nature: is it a divine product, a human product, or somehow both? When traditional Christians call the Bible the Word of God,[1] they generally assume its inspiration. The point of inspiration is that it gives the biblical text the same authority as if the words came from the mouth of God. If scripture were no longer considered inspired, it would cease being God's Word for them. If the Bible were not God's Word, students, scholars, and progressive thinkers might study it as inspiring literature but, having lost its mystique, it would be abandoned by "Bible-reading" Christians.

As important as biblical inspiration is to most Christians, when pressed to define the concept, some might reply with a shrug of the shoulders, others with a vague reference to the divine origin of the Bible, and still others might allude to 2 Timothy 3:16–17: "All scripture is inspired by God and is useful for teaching, for reproof, for correction, and for training in righteousness, so that everyone who belongs to God may be proficient, equipped for every good work." Conservative scholars note that the Greek

---

1. Keep in mind that none of the authors of the books in the Bible wrote thinking they were writing the "Word of God." That was something decided much later. Furthermore, there is only one reference to "Word of God" in the Bible as a whole, and that reference does not concern written scripture but rather Jesus of Nazareth, as we find in the opening verses of the Gospel of John (John 1:1, 14; see Rev. 19:13). For Christians traditionally, the canonical Bible is a witness that points to the Word. In so doing, it points away from itself. In proclaiming Jesus as the Word, scripture becomes again for us the Word of God, Achtemeier, *Inspiration of Scripture*, 163–64.

word translated as "inspired" here literally means "God-breathed," a reference traditionally taken to mean that the authors were directed by God to produce documents that accurately reflected God's message to humanity. While many understand the term inspiration to describe something that happened to the authors, literalists note that this verse bypasses the authors and their humanity, speaking only of the written product as inspired.

Another passage often cited by conservative Christians is 2 Peter 1:20–21: "First of all you must understand this, that no prophecy of scripture is a matter of one's own interpretation, because no prophecy ever came by human will, but men and women moved by the Holy Spirit spoke from God." Verse 21 describes the inspiration process as one in which the human authors were "moved" by the Holy Spirit. In biblical times, the Greek verb used here referred to the moving of a ship's sails by the wind, an apt biblical metaphor for the role of the Holy Spirit.

While such a view of biblical authorship may be inaccurate, having a Bible inspired in this manner is foundational for first-half-of-life living and thinking. The implications of such an inspired Bible for theology are enormous: God exists, God is benevolent, and God communicates directly with us, endowing us with providential resources and values to safeguard our dignity and identity. Those who view scripture this way refer to the Bible as anchor, compass, and shelter in the time of storm. Such inspiration implies biblical reliability, down to tiniest details. Of course, when conservative Christians quote scripture to authenticate its own inspiration, they practice circular reasoning, always questionable.

Theories of Inspiration

Christians who look to the Bible as a source of religious teaching or for guidance concerning how to live bring to their reading presuppositions that affect interpretation. These presuppositions influence their understanding of inspiration and the authority of the Bible. Some church traditions say that God is the author of the Bible in the sense that God actually dictated the words of the Bible to human writers who recorded the words verbatim. This approach is called a *literalist view* of inspiration. Other church traditions hold that the human authors of the Bible are real authors in every sense, but that the words of scripture are still somehow what God wanted to communicate to humanity. This approach, called a *contextualist view* of inspiration, allows that God is the author of the Bible without specifying how the Bible is inspired, except to emphasize that the freedom, individuality, and creativity of the human authors are preserved. Of course, actual understandings of inspiration are often subtler and more complex than these approaches might suggest.

This book takes as its starting point an understanding of inspiration that accepts the full and free involvement of the Bible's human authors. This approach is called contextualist because it emphasizes that to understand scripture readers need to take into account the historical, political, cultural, literary, and religious contexts in which the documents were written. This approach is compatible with contemporary historical and literary methods of studying the Bible.

Concerning the authority of the Bible, communities and individuals that hold a contextualist approach to inspiration might say that the Bible is best described as compelling and persuasive. This means that the Bible has authority insofar as it compels us to respond with faith, hope, and love. Further, it does not legislate a particular moral action in response to specific situations, but it provides a series of guidelines upon which Christians can reflect on modern issues and concerns. William Countryman, a theologian and professor of the New Testament, explains the authority of scripture in this way: While the church participated in creating the Bible and acts as its interpreter, the Bible functions as the church's judge, constantly calling it to conversion.[2] Therefore, the authority of the Bible is closely connected to its power to transform.

Biblical Inspiration for Both Halves of Life

Biblical scholars suggest three broad possibilities regarding the inspiration of the Bible, to which we add a fourth as corollary:

- *verbal inspiration*—the view that every word of the Bible is divinely inspired and therefore inerrant;

- *human response to inspiration*—the view that biblical writers were witnesses to divine revelation; their words and experiences may be human but they serve as vehicles to a higher voice and a deeper reality;

- *inspired imagination*—the view that the Bible is great literature, designed to capture the imagination; though the books of the Bible contain heightened insight, their message is conditioned by historical,

2. Countryman, *Biblical Authority or Biblical Tyranny?*, 52–57.

sociological, and cultural factors. When the Bible is studied academically, it is this view that scholars espouse.

The first view, simple, clear, and unambiguous, lends itself well to the perspectives and tasks of the first journey; the second and third views to the perspectives and tasks of the second journey. To these options we add as corollary *inspired process*, the view that scripture requires ongoing interpretation. This assertion, flowing naturally from the preceding options, recognizes that the sacredness of scripture is validated by its ability to inspire Christians in every age. Scripture, defined and finalized by the canonical process, has an open-ended quality in that it is dynamic and alive, thereby extending the revelatory process to the present. Viewing scripture as "inspired process" safeguards the original revelation while authenticating its ongoing meaning.

To Think or Not to Think: A Personal Example

To expand our understanding of biblical inspiration, we must contextualize the Bible, and this includes examining how it was written and transmitted, including the canonical process. I begin with a personal reflection from my college experience. Having attended a Christian college preparatory school near New York City, it was natural to continue my college education at a nearby Christian institution. Adequate grades and strong references qualified me for a full scholarship at a private evangelical college. While I thrived socially in this protected environment, I felt intellectually constrained.

The core curriculum, required of all students, included courses in Bible and theology. For one such class I proposed writing a term paper on the canonical process, wishing to investigate how the various books of the Bible had been selected as normative for Christians. The professor's response was unexpected: "Select another topic," he declared. "The topic you have chosen is unacceptable." That ended the discussion and I was forced to find another topic. In my professor's estimation, I had chosen to examine the human side of the Bible, a risky approach that might diminish my zeal, divert me from my spiritual goals, and compromise my faith. Rather than deter my progress, that "no" opened the door to graduate studies at Princeton Theological Seminary, an experience that exposed my adolescent spirituality, tested my faith, and equipped me for the journey ahead.

BIBLICAL INSPIRATION

The Composition of the Pentateuch

The authorship of the Bible—particularly of the Pentateuch—remains one of the Western world's oldest puzzles. For centuries, the question of human authorship rarely arose, and when it did, it was quickly suppressed. The Bible was understood to be divinely inspired, and whether that happened through dictation or some other form of divine direction seemed irrelevant. The task of Christians was to live according to its principles, not to question its authority.

Utilizing a contextualist approach, the consensus of biblical scholars locates the earliest written Old Testament material to the area of Jerusalem early in the reign of King Solomon (c. 950 BC). Behind the earliest written stages of the biblical story was probably a long period of oral tradition handed down by poets and storytellers. Even after it was given written form in court or priestly circles, the oral tradition persisted among the people. In antiquity only a few could read and write, and traditions were often passed on through oral performance on ceremonial or informal occasions.

The story of the composition of the Bible begins with the Pentateuch, five books traditionally attributed to Moses but written at least three hundred years after his death. Once we have a clear idea of the compositional history of the Pentateuch, our understanding of the composition of the rest of the Old Testament follows naturally.

There are two basic theories regarding the authorship and composition of the Pentateuch. The traditional view is that the primary author was Moses, who incorporated both written and oral material into the Pentateuch. This view affirms the basis unity of the Pentateuch. It is maintained by many Jewish and Christian readers, particularly those who assert the divine inspiration of this material. The proponents of this view recognize that, in accordance with the practice of Near Eastern scribes, a few details have been brought up to date, including names of cities and particularly the account of Moses' death (Deut. 34). In addition, editorial comments such as Numbers 12:3 are believed to have been added later. This view of the authorship and composition of the Pentateuch is supported by later biblical material (see 1 Kgs. 2:3; 2 Kgs. 14:6; Ezra 6:18; Dan. 9:11–13), including passages from the New Testament (see Matt. 19:8; John 5:46-47; Acts 3:22; Rom. 10:5).

The second view, known as the Documentary Hypothesis, states that the Pentateuch is a compilation of at least four different sources, none of which predates 950 BC. Each of these sources is said to preserve oral matter that may go back to the original time of the events. However, this oral material has been altered by the sources for political and theological reasons. These four sources are known as JEDP (or JEPD).

The first source, called J, was written about 950–900 BC by an unknown author in Judah identified as the Jahwist. He (or she) was interested in personal biography and in ethical and theological reflection. E, the second source, was composed between 850–750 BC in the Northern Kingdom of Israel by an unknown author identified as the Elohist. This source is more objective than J, being less interested in theological reflection. About 715 BC an unknown editor combined J and E into what is known as the Old Epic or JE.

According to the JEDP version of the hypothesis, a third source, called D, was composed in 621 BCE by someone identified as the Deuteronomist. It was composed to undergird the Deuteronomic Reform instituted by King Josiah (see 2 Kgs. 22:1—23:25). Its purpose was to show the necessity of Jerusalem as the only legitimate place of worship. The author is believed by scholars to have been the prophet Jeremiah or his scribe Baruch. The final source, according to JEDP scholars, was P, written by an unknown author identified as the Priestly writer. P is concerned with the systematic account of the origins and institutions of the Israelite theocracy. P is said to have been written in various stages, mostly during the Babylonian exile, beginning around the time of the prophet Ezekiel (580 BC) and completed about the time of Ezra (440 or 400 BC), the scribe who is said to have redacted (edited) the Pentateuch into the final version we have today. Richard Friedman reverses the order of D and P, arguing that P was pre-exilic and written before D. He places the date of P around 700 BC, during the period of the prophet Isaiah and the reform enacted by King Hezekiah. The debate concerning the authorship of the Pentateuch is ongoing.

The literary history of the emergence of the Documentary Hypothesis in modern times is fascinating and instructive. From time to time throughout history, isolated voices raised questions about the Mosaic authorship of the Pentateuch, but it took the rise of deistic philosophy in the eighteenth century to create the intellectual context to seriously question the possibility that Moses may not have been the author of the Pentateuch.

The critical study of the Bible[3] did not begin as an investigation into its authorship. It simply started with individuals raising questions about

---

3. In the realm of scholarship the word "critical" (as in biblical criticism or critical methods) need not imply disrespect or disagreement, but rather is an interpretive

problems that they observed in the biblical text itself. It proceeded like a detective story spread across centuries, with investigators uncovering clues to the Bible's origin one by one. Investigators began with questions about the first five books of the Bible, attributed to Moses, even though the text nowhere says that he was the author. But the tradition that one person wrote these books presented problems: "People observed contradictions in the text. It would report events in a particular order, and later it would say that those same events happened in a different order. It would say that there were two of something, and elsewhere it would say that there were fourteen of that same thing. It would say that the Moabites did something, and later that it was the Midianites. It would describe Moses as going to a Tabernacle in a chapter before Moses builds the Tabernacle. People also noticed that the Five Books of Moses included things that Moses could not have known or was not likely to have said. The text, after all, gave an account of Moses's death. It also said that Moses was the humblest man on earth; and normally one would not expect the humblest man on earth to point out that he is the humblest man on earth."[4]

At first the arguments of those who questioned Mosaic authorship were rejected. Investigators still accepted the tradition that Moses write the five books under inspiration, but they suggested that a few lines might have been added later, such as the naming of Edomite kings in Genesis 36, a list that includes kings who lived long after Moses. In a second stage of the process, investigators suggested that Moses wrote the five books but that editors later added occasional words or phrases of their own. The third stage of the investigation scholars concluded that Moses did not write the majority of the Pentateuch. In the seventeenth century the British philosopher Thomas Hobbes collected numerous facts and statements from these books that were inconsistent with Mosaic authorship. For example, the reference to something happening "to this day" indicates the presence of a later writer who is describing something that has endured over time. In Holland the philosopher Spinoza reviewed this information and concluded: "It is . . . clearer than the sun at noon that the Pentateuch was not written by Moses, but by someone who lived long after." His writings, like so many others that questioned the Bible's divine inspiration, were condemned by Jews, Catholics, and Protestants alike. His book was placed on the Catholic Index of Prohibited Books and attempts were made on his life.

---

approach meaning "method of analysis."

4. Friedman, *Who Wrote the Bible?*, 17–18.

Like skepticism questioning Mosaic authorship, the Documentary Hypothesis developed in various stages. In 1753 Jean Astruc, professor of medicine and court physician to Louis XV, published anonymously his findings. In his study of Genesis 1 and 2, Astruc noticed that God was referred to as Elohim exclusively in Genesis 1 and as Yahweh Elohim in Genesis. His explanation was that Moses had used two different documents that provided two accounts of creation. Out of fear of repercussion, Astruc waited until the age of seventy before publishing his findings secretly and anonymously. His results laid the foundation for the Documentary Hypothesis, based on the *criterion of divine names*.

In 1780 an academic, Johann Eichhorn, published a similar discovery, based on the *criterion of "doublets"* or "parallel accounts." A doublet is a case of the same story appearing with variations of detail in two different places in the Bible. For example, in Genesis there are two different stories of the creation of the world; two stories of Noah and the flood; two stories the covenant between God and the patriarch Abraham; two stories of the naming of Abraham's son Isaac; two stories of Jacob making a journey to Mesopotamia; two stories of a revelation to Jacob at Bethel; two stories of changing Jacob's name to Israel; and more.

Eichhorn divided the entire book of Genesis plus portions of the book of Exodus into two sources which he labeled "J" and "E," on the basis of doublets. At first Eichhorn assumed, like Astruc, that the two sources were pre-Mosaic; later he argued that the Pentateuch was written after Moses.

By the beginning of the nineteenth century, the two-source hypothesis was expanded. In 1806 Wilhelm De Wette, a young German scholar, concentrated his study on the book of Deuteronomy, particularly the book's obsession in chapter 12 with "the city which Yahweh shall choose." This obsession led De Wette to argue that "D" was not a desert treatise (presumably written at an early period in Israel's history by Moses) but a document reflecting concerns of an established central government trying to institute a reform. De Wette determined that the historical context for the authorship of Deuteronomy was found in 2 Kings 22, a passage dated to 621 BCE, when the book of the Law was "found" in the Jerusalem temple during the time of King Josiah's reform. Using the *criterion of centralization of worship*, De Wette viewed the book of Deuteronomy to be a "pious fraud," a propaganda document written in support of a reform movement whose primary purpose was to undergird a political and religious unification that would result in increased revenues for the Jerusalem priesthood. He also observed that the fifth book of Moses was strikingly different in its language from the four books that preceded it. Neither of the source documents previously detected appeared to continue into this book. De Wette hypothesized that Deuteronomy was a separate source.

By this time scholars had found in the first four books of the Bible not only doublets but triplets as well. This, together with evidence involving contradictions and characteristic language, persuaded them that they had found another source within the Pentateuch. In 1866 Karl Graf summed up the views of several scholars and gave the strongest argument yet for still another source, "P," the Priestly source. Using the *criterion of highly developed religious material*, Graf argued that any material in the Pentateuch that demonstrated highly legal and cultic concerns came after D, probably from the time of the exile. He believed that the P material was not found in the pre-exilic prophetic literature, meaning that it could not have originated in the time of Moses or even during the period of the United or Divided Kingdoms, but that it came into existence while the Jewish people were in exile in Babylon during the sixth century BC.

Having provided evidence that the Pentateuch had been composed by combining four different source documents into one continuous history, scholars had to determine the relative order in which they were written. Two figures approached the problem in different ways, but they arrived at complementary solutions. Graf examined the sources to see how they influenced one another. The other investigator, Wilhelm Vatke, examined the texts for clues as to whether they reflected early or late stages in the development of Israel's religion. Both concluded that the J and E documents were the oldest versions of the biblical stories and the P document the latest, for it referred to a variety of matters that were unknown in the earlier portions of the Bible and reflected the latest stage of Israelite religion. The attempts by Vatke to reconstruct the development of the religion of Israel and by Graf to reconstruct the development of the sources of the Pentateuch were greeted negatively. Conservative scholars criticized their scholarship as based upon the presupposition that supernatural events and revelation are impossible and on the belief that Israel's religion and theology developed along consistent evolutionary lines, from the primitive to the advanced. Critical scholars such as DeWette could not accept the idea that the great majority of laws and much of the narrative were written toward the end of the biblical period, later than the kings and prophets of Israel.

Despite initially negative response, Graf's and Vatke's ideas came to dominate the field of biblical studies for a century primarily due to the work of one man, Julius Wellhausen, a towering figure in the investigation into the authorship of the Bible and in the history of biblical scholarship in general. He accepted Graf's picture of Israel's documents as having been written in three distinct periods and Vatke's picture of the religion of Israel as having developed in three stages and combined the pictures, arguing that the stories and laws that appear in J and E (dated to the tenth and ninth century BC) reflect the way of life of the nature/fertility stage of religion, the stories and laws of D (dated to the seventh century BC) reflect the life of the spiritual/ethical stage, and that the stories and laws that appear in P (dated to the sixth century BC) derived from the priestly/legal stage. In 1878 Wellhausen wrote *Prolegomena to the History of Ancient Israel*, one of the seminal works in biblical analysis. Using the *criterion of evolutionary development*, Wellhausen examined the biblical stories and laws that appear in the four sources, arguing that Israelite religion evolved in stages from primitive animism to ethical monotheism.

Wellhausen's theories about the development of the Old Testament are for Biblical criticism what Einstein is to physics. Wellhausen devised a new paradigm which explained many of the apparent inconsistencies in the Biblical texts. In the process, he upset many traditionalists, who opposed the concept that the early portions of the Bible were the product of four separate authors, or that the Levitical code was redacted into the text by the priestly class at a very late date in the evolution of the Bible, or that the Bible even evolved. The current Christian fundamentalist movement emerged as a response to the Biblical criticism of Wellhausen and other nineteenth-century scholars.

Critics point out that Wellhausen wrote at a time when Darwinian scientific thought and Hegelian philosophy were in substantial vogue and were influencing economic, political, social and religious understandings of reality. They caution against applying an evolutionary straightjacket on cultural and religious history in general, including Israelite history. If evolution can work both ways, progressively and regressively, might it be possible to posit that Israel's religion "devolved" rather than evolved?

The four-document theory and the conclusions of the Graf-Wellhausen school of biblical scholars in the nineteenth century continue to be accepted widely by the scholarly community, despite internal disagreements by their proponents and the fact that no such source documents as J, E, D or P have ever been found. Some biblical scholars suggest that instead of fragmenting the biblical writings, students of the scriptures should focus on the literary strands that appear to underlie certain Old Testament writings, such as the "Book of Generations" (Gen. 5:1), the "Book of Wars of the Lord" (Numb. 21:14), the "Book of the Covenant" (Exod. 24:7), and the "Book of Jashar" (Josh. 10:13). However, these too have never been found, and in some cases appear to be stylistic creations by scribes or editors.

Whether one agrees with his conclusions, Wellhausen's meticulous scholarship, drawn from the Pentateuch as well as from other books of the Bible, tied the source documents to history. His reconstruction was sensible, articulate, and extremely influential. Wellhausen's model continues to dominate the field of biblical studies. During the twentieth century every major premise of his model, known as the Documentary Hypothesis, has been attacked piecemeal by critics, yet no systematic scholarly account of the origin and the development of the Pentateuch has been formulated to replace it. "To this day, if you want to disagree, you disagree with Wellhausen. If you want to pose a new model, you compare its merits with those of Wellhausen's model."[5]

The Composition of the New Testament

The formation of the New Testament was gradual, complex, and somewhat haphazard. Jesus had left behind no writings of his own. Furthermore, his disciples made no initial attempt to write down an account of his life or a summary of his teachings. In fact, the oldest Christian documents are not the Gospels, which tell the story of Jesus, but the letters of Paul, a Jewish convert to Christianity who had persecuted Jesus' followers before his conversion. These letters date from the late-forties to mid-sixties of the first century AD, some twenty to thirty years after the crucifixion of Jesus. Written to churches Paul had helped establish, these letters were saved and later shared with Christians in other places. By the end of the first century other documents were added to this collection, including letters written by others but ascribed to Paul. Around this time these letters began to assume the authority of scripture among many Christians.

Soon other documents joined this group, including four separate accounts of Jesus' story known as Gospels. The English word "gospel" basically means "good news." Each of the four gospel writers—or "evangelists," as

5. Ibid., 26–27.

they are known—sets out the basic events behind the Good News. Though scholars remain uncertain about the authorship of these narratives, they do not generally doubt the claims to apostolic origin made by them. The Gospels did not originally come with titles and authors appended. Whether individuals named Matthew, Mark, Luke, or John actually penned these documents matters less than the fact that four different early Christian communities saw fit to tell the story of Jesus from four distinct perspectives. Whether the Gospels represent eyewitness accounts or were redacted by second or third generation believers, these documents are not primarily historical narratives of the life of Jesus. They are essentially testimonies of faith, written to bolster the faith of those who believed that Jesus was the Messiah and to win converts to a community that believed Jesus to be the Lord and Savior of the world.

The books of the New Testament were written over a period of some fifty years. The earliest book is probably 1 Thessalonians, the first of Paul's surviving letters. It is usually dated about the year AD 49, that is, about twenty years after the death of Jesus. The latest book of the New Testament is 2 Peter, generally dated around the start of the second century AD. During this period the Eastern Mediterranean world, the region out of which these books emerged, was undergoing constant turmoil and change. Several events are critical, including the reputed expulsion or ban of Jews from Rome by Emperor Claudius around AD 49 (see Acts 18:2), the martyrdom of James the Just in Jerusalem in 62 (or 69), the persecution of Christians in Rome by Emperor Nero in 64, the four-year-war of the Jews against Rome (beginning in 66 and culminating in the destruction of the Jewish temple and of Jerusalem in 70), and the official split of Jewish Christians from Judaism in the 80s and 90s. Those tensions find expression throughout the New Testament writings.

As noted earlier, the first author to interrupt the literary silence following the death of Jesus is Paul, whose authentic letters cover a period of some fifteen years, approximately from the year 49, the time of the Apostolic Conference in Jerusalem, to 64, when Paul appears to have died by order of Nero. Yet not all of the books that bear Paul's name were written by him. New Testament scholarship numbers seven letters as actually authored by him (1 Thessalonians, Galatians, 1 and 2 Corinthians, Romans, Philemon, and Philippians). Colossians, Ephesians, and 2 Thessalonians appear to be post-Pauline, written by some of his disciples from the late 60s to the early 70s, with the so-called Pastoral Epistles (1 and 2 Timothy and Titus), the General Epistles (Hebrews, James, 1 and 2 Peter, 1, 2, and 3 John, and Jude), and the book of Revelation all dated generally between 80 and 100. These books were not written by disciples of Jesus, but by second and third generation Christians who followed the common practice of Jews and Christians of that time by writing pseudepigraphically, in this case, by attributing their writing to prominent Christian leaders.

Second Peter, said to be the final book of the New Testament to be written, is radically different from that of 1 Peter. In addition, the author has borrowed major portions from the book of Jude and incorporated it into chapter 2. By this time, the writings of the apostle Paul are evidently in circulation as a collection and even being considered as scripture (2 Pet. 3:15–16), a sure sign that the letter was written long after Peter's martyrdom in Rome sometime around 64, during the reign of Emperor Nero. This letter, believed to have been written early in the second century, was not widely accepted as Peter's or even known to exist for most of the first three Christian centuries. Curiously, the author goes out of his way to insist that he is none other than Jesus' disciple, a sure case of protesting too much.

Like the letters of Paul and the General Epistles, the Gospels do not appear in the New Testament in the order in which they were written historically. Having been written forty to seventy years after the death of Jesus, they represent not so much a composite history of Jesus' words and deeds as the Church's expanding understanding of Jesus. While they certainly contain accurate information, they should not be viewed as factual. Their intent was not primarily to provide factual knowledge but to enhance faith.

The first Gospel was Mark (written around AD 65 to 70), followed by Matthew (written in the early 80s), then by Luke (written in the mid- to late 80s), and finally by John (written in the early to mid-90s). The first three Gospels are not separate witnesses, since Matthew and Luke copied large portions of Mark into their works. John may have been familiar with some or all of these, but his version is clearly independent. When we understand the order in which the Gospels were written, we can see the developing story line more clearly.

The Canonical Process

Most religious communities have a list of scriptures that are considered binding or authoritative. Such a collection is often called a "canon," a concept derived from a Greek word meaning "measuring device" or "ruler."

As applied to religious literature, it refers to the rule or standard of authority for belief and practice. Arriving at a definitive canon or binding list of scriptures involved judging the authenticity, doctrinal soundness, and communal acceptance of texts. While Jews and Christians have a "closed" canon, meaning that no books may be added or deleted from that official collection of writings, this does not mean that their religious communities always agree about which books they include in their respective canons, the form of those books, or the order in which those books occur.

The Old Testament

Although the basic biblical story extending from the creation of the world to Israel's return from Babylonian exile seems to have received definitive literary shape by the fourth century BC, the present literary division of that account into the canons of Torah, Prophets, and Writings and the inclusion of various supplementary writings took many centuries. Certainly the Torah and the historical narrative known as the Former Prophets were revered as uniquely authoritative very early on. Because of their association with Moses, the five books of the Torah were the first to receive canonical status. This may have occurred as early as the fifth century BC, as suggested by the description of Ezra as "a scribe skilled in the law (Torah) of Moses" (Ezra 7:6). Because of their narrative quality, the order of these books never varies. By the second century BC, the Prophets had also assumed canonical status, as noted in the prologue of a work known as Sirach. The Writings were the final part of the Jewish canon to be collected and designated as authoritative, although this process was not finalized until the start of the second century AD.

Several overlapping criteria were used by Jewish authorities to determine the inclusion of a work in the canon. To be included, a work was judged on the basis of:

- *Date*: a work should have been written before the fourth century BC or attributed to an author who had lived before that date;
- *Language*: a work should have been written in Hebrew (although parts of Ezra and Daniel were written in Aramaic, they were largely in Hebrew so this did not exclude them);
- *Extent of use*: some books were read or associated with specific festivals in the liturgical cycle (Song of Solomon with Passover; Ruth with Shavuot [Pentecost, or Feast of Weeks], Lamentations with Tisha

B'Av [the day of the month Av when the temple in Jerusalem was destroyed], Ecclesiastes with Sukkot [Booths], and Esther with Purim).

Given the diversity of Jews in the post-exilic period, theologically, culturally, and linguistically, intensified by their dispersion across the Mediterranean world, where no authoritative religious or political institutions legislated on matters such as the nature and content of scripture, it is remarkable that any uniform collection of Jewish scriptures emerged at all. By the third century BC, Greek-speaking Jews in Egypt became so comfortable with the Greek culture that they began to translate the Torah and other Hebrew writings into that language. This collection, which came to be called the Septuagint, includes a number of works that are not part of the Hebrew Bible. However much these writings might have been valued by some Jewish groups of this period or by emerging Christianity, these extra writings eventually fell out of favor with Jews and were dropped from canonical consideration, whereas they continued to be read and used liturgically by Christians. The Roman Catholic Church, together with the Eastern Orthodox churches, eventually gave most of these books official canonical sanction, whereas the Protestants, since the Reformation, excluded those books as apocryphal (the term Apocrypha means "hidden" or "secret" writings, though sometimes mistaken to mean "spurious" or "false"), restricting the Old Testament to those books found in the Hebrew Bible. Christians agreed, however, following the Septuagint, in placing the prophetic writings last, unlike the Hebrew Bible, which concludes with the Writings (ending with 1 and 2 Chronicles).

The New Testament

By the start of the first century AD, when Christianity emerged, most Jews subscribed to the special authority of the Torah. Not all accepted the authority of the Prophets (for example the Sadducees did not), but most mainline Jews, including the Pharisees, certainly did. Jesus is said to have quoted from some of these books, as did Paul and other New Testament authors, so we can assume that all accepted them as authoritative. The third part, the Writings, was not yet completed in the first century, but one of its major components, the book of Psalms, was already in use in synagogue worship. Indeed, this book was so important that the third part of the Jewish canon could be referred to simply as "the Psalms." This usage is found in

Luke's Gospel, from the late first century, which refers to "the Law of Moses, the Prophets, and the Psalms" (Luke 24:44).

It should come as no surprise that a faith firmly anchored in the sacred texts of its parent religion would develop scriptures of its own. Christians did develop their own scriptures, but not immediately. The first generation proclaimed its message almost exclusively by word of mouth and saw no pressing need to assemble its own sacred tradition, since it expected Christ to return momentarily. As the expected return of Christ was delayed and as the number of believers continued to expand, the need for written documents became manifest. With the passing away of the first generation of Christians, the need arose to preserve those crucial stories and lessons that had given shape to their community; continuity and order were at stake.

Near the end of the first century AD, Christians were citing Jesus' words and calling them "scripture" (see 1 Tim. 5:18). Furthermore, some of Jesus' followers, such as the apostle Paul, understood themselves to be authoritative spokespersons for the truth (Gal. 1:8–12). Paul's letters, written occasionally to specific congregations and individuals, were reverently saved and shared with Christians in other places. Shortly thereafter they began to assume the authority of scripture, at least among some Christians (2 Pet. 3:16). In fact, Paul's authority was becoming so significant that some documents written by others were being ascribed to him (see 2 Thess. 2:2; also the Pastoral Epistles and other disputed letters including Hebrews, which the King James Bible and some Bibles still attribute to Paul). In the next century a host of additional gospels, epistles, and apocalypses appeared, vying for authenticity. The author of Luke's Gospel openly admits that "many writers" had preceded him in the attempt to "draw up an account of the things that have happened among us" (Luke 1:1).

By the third century, more than twenty gospels were in circulation, all claiming, like the Gospel of Peter or the Gospel of Philip, apostolic derivation. Notable among them was the Gospel of Thomas, consisting exclusively of isolated saying attributed to Jesus, some of them said to be older than Mark's Gospel. The abundance of gospels was due mostly to the growth of "gnostic" sects within Christianity, especially in the second century. The vast majority of gnostics were "dualists," believing that human beings were spiritual entities trapped in an evil material world and that they could be freed, or saved, only through secret knowledge. They shared in common a tendency to produce texts that claimed to distill new revelation. It is no coincidence that the first lists of scripture began to appear among orthodox scholars and theologians shortly after the emergence of gnostic sects. While many gnostic writings were deemed "heretical" (i.e. "false") early on, it is striking that the official canon of twenty-seven book was not finalized until the fourth century.

The process that led to the formation of the Christian canon is complex but fascinating. The four Gospels now found in the New Testament, together with the other canonical writings, may have been produced by diverse, even antithetical communities, but all were viewed to be sufficiently orthodox to make the final cut. However, during the second, third, and fourth centuries, Christians continued to debate the acceptability of certain writings. The arguments centered on three criteria:

- *Apostolicity*: the book in question had to have derived from the initial community of Jesus and his disciples;

- *Orthodoxy*; the book in question had to be valued as inspired and revelatory, that is, as derived directly from God and hence harmonious with the rest of the New Testament;

- *Catholicity*; the book in question had to be accepted and used by a wide range of communities, especially those viewed as those considered authoritative or apostolic.

At first a local church would have only a few apostolic letters and perhaps one or two Gospels. During the course of the second century most churches came to possess and acknowledge a canon that included the present four Gospels, the Acts, thirteen letters attributed to Paul, 1 Peter, and 1 John. Seven books still lacked general recognition: Hebrews, James, 2 Peter, 2 and 3 John, Jude, and Revelation. On the other hand, certain Christian writings, such as the first letter of Clement, the letter of Barnabas, the Shepherd of Hermas, and the Didache, were accepted as authoritative by several ecclesiastical writers, though rejected by the majority.

Paradoxically, Marcion (c. 140), a heretical Christian preacher in Rome, was responsible for the first canon of the New Testament. Unable to reconcile the Old Testament's portrayal of God as violent and vengeful with the New Testament's portrayal of God as good and loving, he created a restrictive canon that excluded all of the Old Testament and any Christian literature that had Jewish overtones. Marcion's teaching prompted a hearing before other clergy in Rome that resulted in his condemnation in 144. Soon afterward, other church leaders began to form their own canons or lists of approved books. The most famous of these was the Muratorian

Canon, dated to the church at Rome circa 190. It included the four Gospels, the Acts of the Apostles, thirteen letters attributed to Paul, Jude, and 1 and 2 John, as well some books that were later excluded, including the Apocalypse of Peter and the Wisdom of Solomon. What is unusual about the latter is that despite being a Jewish work, written prior to the birth of Christianity (in the first century BC), it was listed as a Christian text.

Strangely, the development of a definitive canon of scripture took orthodox Christians nearly four centuries to complete. The earliest surviving list to include all twenty-seven books now known as the New Testament is from the year 367, appearing in an Easter letter written by Athanasius, bishop of Alexandria, to congregations in the eastern section of the church. In the West, the twenty-seven books of the New Testament were accepted at the subsequent Councils of Hippo (393) and Carthage (397).

Chapter 3

Biblical Interpretation

The Science and Art of Reading the Bible

Christians have always affirmed a close relationship between the Bible and God, just as other religions affirm a close connection between the sacred and their holy scriptures. Foundational to reading the Bible is a decision about how to view its origin. Does it come from God, or is it a human product?

Building on the conviction that divine revelation and man-made religion are fundamentally irreconcilable, many conservative Christians believe that the only choice a person can make about the Bible is to view it either as the infallible, inerrant word of God or as a collection of fairy tales with little or no value for modern people. Since the latter is what unbelievers think, evangelical conservatives believe they must view the Bible as God's very word of truth, defending it in all respects, even on historical and scientific matters. For many, the Bible's reliability is so critical that they will argue, "If I can't believe the Bible when it speaks about creation or history, then how can I believe it about Jesus Christ and salvation?" To frame the question of the inspiration and authority of the Bible in this manner, however, is to do an injustice to the traditional doctrines of the inspiration and authority of scripture.

Acknowledging the obvious human element in the Bible, modern Christians generally take a both/and stance regarding biblical authorship: The Bible is both divine and human. However, this approach is also problematic. When the Bible is seen as both divine and human, we have two options. One is to say that it is all divine and all human. That may sound good, but no one maintains such an unworkable tension. The other, more typical option is to attempt to separate the divine parts from the human parts—as if some come from God and others are human. The parts that come from God are then given greater authority than the others. However, who's to say which parts are divine and which human? The Bible does not come with footnotes that say, "This passage reflects the will of God; the next passage does not." So those who take the entire Bible as divine are consistent, but they might be consistently wrong.

How, for instance, does one understand the Ten Commandments? Most Christians who think of the Bible as both divine and human would say that the commandments come from God. Does that mean that they are equally authoritative? If so, all Christians should worship God on Saturday, since that is the day clearly in mind as the day of worship. There is biblical evidence that the sanctity of the Sabbath was in effect among the Israelites prior to the revelation of the commandments to Moses on Mount Sinai (cf. Exod. 16:22–30). And if the Ten Commandments are divinely inspired, why are they written from a male point of view (for instance, they prohibit coveting your neighbor's wife but say nothing about coveting your neighbor's husband)? Furthermore, the commandments against stealing, adultery, murder, bearing false witness, and so forth are simply rules that make it possible for humans to live together in community. Biblical scholarship affirms that the pattern upon which these commandments are based is a treaty pattern devised by the Hittites, a powerful empire that predated Moses and came to an end prior to the time of Moses. Divine genius is not required to come up with rules like these. This is not to say that the Ten Commandments are unimportant, but rather that their origin is human.[1]

The perspective I am advocating does not see the Bible in its entirety as divine in origin, or some parts as divine and some as human. Rather I view the Bible as the product of two faith communities, each responding uniquely to divine revelation. The Bible, therefore, contains ancient Israel's perceptions and misperceptions, just as it contains the early Christian movement's perceptions and misperceptions.

---

1. Borg, *Reading the Bible*, 26–27.

Christian Interpretation of Scripture: An Historical Overview

The earliest Christians had no Bibles to study or read individually. It was the church, and more specifically the religious leaders of that community, that interpreted the scriptures. This was so not only because it had been the church and its leaders that had defined which texts were "scriptural," but also because the texts themselves were not intended as much for private reading as for their suitability for liturgical use. If a document was not considered revelatory, it was not to be read in church. Since most Christians were illiterate and copies of the scriptures were rare, the majority of the faithful could only hear scripture read to them in church, almost always as part of the ritual celebration of the Eucharist. It was principally through the mediation of the clergy and in the restricted context of worship that early Christians could approach scripture.

From the earliest days, Christian leaders formulated theories of biblical interpretation. By the fourth century, clearly defined interpretive theories were already widely accepted by Christian leaders, including that scripture contained four levels of meaning: literal (historical and literal level), allegorical (hidden mystical and spiritual truths), tropological (moral lessons), and anagogical (eschatological level, revealing secrets concerning the afterlife and Christ's future kingdom). While allegorical and other levels of interpretation provided Christian theology with flexibility, giving it the capacity to intertwine written and oral traditions and the ability to adapt to ever-changing situations, in the wrong hands it could be abused, leading to heterodox beliefs and practices. From the fifth through sixteenth centuries, scripture remained firmly in the hands of the church elites who had mastered the accepted exegetical methods. Major controversies were addressed by bishops through synods or councils.

The Protestant Reformers of the sixteenth century declared that the church had become corrupt because it had buried the truths of scripture beneath layers of humanly devised traditions. Claiming to base their reforms on scripture, the reformers encouraged the translation of scripture into the vernacular, a process aided by the invention of the printing press. Martin Luther (1485–1546), a first-generation reformer, believed that faith and the Holy Spirit's illumination were prerequisites for an interpreter of the Bible. He laid down the foundational premise of the Reformation, the principle of *sola scriptura* (scripture alone), the primacy of scripture above all other authorities. Asserting that the Bible should be viewed differently from other literature, he downplayed dependence on church authorities to understand the Bible. Luther also challenged the prevailing "rule of faith," maintaining that rather than the church determining what the scriptures teach, scripture should determine what the church teaches. He also believed that the Bible is a clear book (the "perspicuity" of scripture), in opposition to medieval dogma that the scriptures are so obscure that only the church can uncover their true meaning. He favored a literal understanding of the text, rather than the allegorical method of interpreting scripture, stressing that the interpreter should consider historical conditions, grammar, and context in the process of exegesis.

Probably the greatest exegete of the Reformation was John Calvin (1509–1564), a second-generation reformer. Agreeing in general with the principles articulated by Luther, he too believed that spiritual illumination is necessary and regarded allegorical interpretation as a deceptive device that distorted the clear sense of scripture. Assuming the divine authorship of scripture, he adhered strictly to the principle of harmony, meaning that scripture is its own best interpreter. No passage of scripture should be set up against another; secondary and obscure passages in scripture should always be subject to primary and plain passages. He placed importance on studying the context, grammar, words, and parallel passages, stating that the primary task of an interpreter is to allow the author to speak, rather than to import one's own meaning into the text.

Espousing the priesthood of all believers, the reformers believed every Christian capable of reading scripture, as guided individually by the Holy Spirit. Rather than leading to unanimity, however, that impetus resulted in further disagreement and fragmentation. Despite their emphasis on scripture as sole authority, the reformers could not agree with one another on the application of scripture to polity, social issues, and sacramental practices such as baptism or the Eucharist. The unraveling of Christian unity in the sixteenth century led to the emergence of rival communities, each claiming to be the "true" church and to have the correct understanding of scripture.

The Renaissance and the Enlightenment gave rise to ideologies such as humanism, rationalism, skepticism, scientism, and existentialism, each to varying degrees undermining the authority of scripture while simultaneously unleashing a monumental critical effort to ascertain truth in scripture. Searching for truth in scripture, biblical scholars increasingly detected the humanity of the authors who wrote the documents that together constituted the Bible. As Johann Gottfried von Herder argued in the late eighteenth century, the Bible was religious literature, a composite of fact and fiction that was to be analyzed just as one would study any ancient literature. This approach to the Bible came to be known as higher criticism.

During the nineteenth and twentieth centuries, various patterns of response countered biblical criticism. One response was the resurgence of *pietism*, a concerted effort to retreat from the chaos and complexity of modernity to a simpler, less rational approach, where scripture was encountered primarily through one's heart. A second response was that of Protestant *fundamentalism*, which countered modernism by reiterating supernaturalism and the inerrancy of scripture. Fundamentalism was joined by Pentecostalism and evangelicalism, movements that likewise embraced conservative biblicism. A third response, *liberalism*, stressed morality in religion and gave precedence to reason over supernaturalism. Liberalism attempted to redefine Christian tradition in such a way as to engage modernity directly. Embracing the discoveries of higher criticism, liberals replaced literalistic approaches to scripture with moral ones. A fourth response, that of *Roman Catholicism*, accepted religious pluralism and modern biblical criticism while encouraging Catholic laity to engage more directly with scripture, arguing that the Catholic Church was the ultimate interpreter of scripture, with the help of the Holy Spirit.

The Science of Reading the Bible

The Necessity of Biblical Interpretation

All literature invites interpretation; all important literature demands it. This is particularly true of scripture, its truth claims fraught with meaning and therefore open to investigation. As my colleague Dan Stinson notes, "Every passage of scripture begs for interpretation."

There is no such thing as a noninterpretive reading of the Bible. Reading the stories of creation or the stories of Jesus' birth literally involves an interpretive decision equally as much as does the decision to read them metaphorically. When we speak of meaning in relation to a biblical text, five levels come to mind: (1) what the divine author intended (while this concern is primary for conservative readers, it applies indirectly to all who read the Bible as scripture); (2) what the human author intended (this concern should be important to all readers, conservative, moderate, and liberal alike); (3) how biblical scholars and theologians interpret a particular passage or verse (their views, both ancient and modern, are readily available in commentaries, handbooks, Study Bibles, and other interpretive aids. While it is important to recognize the bias or perspective of one's resources, those interested in breadth of insight should consult works from across the denominational and theological spectrum); (4) how leaders in one's church or denomination interpret a particular passage or verse; and finally, (5) what the text means to you. This final level, while indispensable, should not be arrived at quickly. Without the corrective of the other levels, this approach to the Bible can result in as many meanings as it has readers. This postmodern approach, based on the belief that "the meaning of a text is what it means to me," lacks hermeneutical validity.

We who read the Bible need assistance, a method to help us discern how to hear and value its various voices. When we read scripture, we encounter historical, linguistic, social, and cultural gaps between the ancient and modern worlds, barriers we must overcome if we are to understanding the original meaning of the text. In addition, each of us approaches the text with some preunderstanding of the subject. Those who read the Bible only from the perspective of their immediate personal circumstances, who forget that the passage was originally written for someone else, can easily misunderstand what the text says. We all do this on occasion, but some, seemingly unaware, do so to an extreme, as the following example indicates. A woman once explained to her therapist that God had told her to divorce her husband and marry another man, with whom she was romantically involved. She cited Paul's command in Ephesians 4:24, "Put on the new man" (KJV), as the key to her divine guidance. As humorous as this sounds, she was absolutely serious. Although modern translations clarify that Paul was instructing believers to replace their sinful lifestyle with a Christian one, this woman read her own meaning into the passage. While our manner of twisting scripture may be less extreme, can we prevent such misunderstanding?

When meaning is sought, it is pursued through some cognitive structure, generally through some hermeneutical system. The word "hermeneutics," deriving from a Greek verb that means "to explain, interpret, or translate," is said to have its origin in the name Hermes, the Greek god who served as messenger for the gods, transmitting and interpreting their communications to recipients. In its technical meaning, hermeneutics refers to the art and science of biblical interpretation. Hermeneutics is considered a science because it has rules, and these rules can be classified in an orderly system. It is considered an art because human communication must be flexible and personal. To be a good interpreter one must learn the rules of hermeneutics as well as the art of applying those rules.

A Method for Studying the Bible

The Bible, viewed as God's Word, is said to provide us with unchanging values and eternal commandments. As scripture, the Bible holds answers to life's toughest questions: "Where did we come from? "Why are we here?" and "How will everything end?" Yet the Bible is also a book of bizarre events and strange mysteries, with references to angels and demons, giants and dragons, rivers turning to blood, fire and brimstone raining down on cities, ax-heads floating, people walking on water, and dead people coming back to life.

Also strange are certain commands in the Bible, such as offering animal sacrifices to the Lord, not eating foods like pork and shellfish, not wearing clothing made of more than one material, not tattooing one's body, and doing no work on Saturday. Even in the New Testament people are told to wash one another's feet, to sell everything they have and give the money to the poor, and to pluck out their eye or cut off their hand if they cause you to sin. Women are told to cover their heads with a veil, not to cut their hair or wear pearls or gold jewelry, and to keep quiet in church. Are these cultural matters that no longer apply? If so, what about passages that promote celibacy, discourage marriage, or forbid greed and homosexual behavior? Are these cultural as well? To navigate these challenging waters we need a method (a consistent approach that can be used on any passage), hermeneutical principles, and regular practice. The process of interpreting the Bible involves building a bridge over a chasm. We are separated from the biblical audience by linguistic, historical, social, and cultural gaps, differences that separate us from the text and that often prohibit us from grasping the meaning of the text. To span this chasm we must erect two pylons, one on either side of the gorge. The first pylon represents *the descriptive task* (discerning what a text *meant* to the original audience), and the second pylon represents *the application task* (discerning what a text *means* to me, in my current situation).

The method I use in biblical study and recommend to my students involves three stages: *exegesis* (what a text *meant* to the original audience;

in this phase the exegete [the person studying the Bible] is asked to bring out of the text its natural, intended meaning.), *synthesis* (where one asks particular questions of the text, gathering and surveying, in an historically integrated form, the fruits of exegesis into a meaningful whole), and *application* (what a text *means* to you the reader and to your religious community).

Step 1: Exegesis

The great Louis Agassiz (1807–1873), the Swiss-born and European-trained zoologist, was well-known for his method of teaching students at Harvard to observe fish. He left his students in front of their specimens for days and weeks with only one instruction: "Look! Look! Look!" And that's where we begin in our study of scripture, with in-depth observation. This phase, known as the exegetical or descriptive phase, proceeds along three lines, analyzing the text, its context, and the movement of the argument.

Textual analysis recognizes the importance of the original languages, including knowledge of (a) words (their etymology, historical usage, and biblical usage); (b) grammatical structure (for example, ability to identify the subject, object, and the main verb of a sentence, as well as familiarity with tenses); and (c) literary form. The Bible contains a wide array of literary forms, regularly ignored or treated alike by readers. There is a vast difference between Hebrew poetry and the tightly argued epistles of Paul, or between the sweeping narrative of the historical books and the poignant stories of the parables. There is allegory and love poetry, satire and apocalyptic, comedy and tragedy, and much more. The literary form governs the meaning of a passage. If you want to grasp the message of the Bible, you must read correctly each genre.

Contextual analysis involves an awareness of context. Each text has four contexts: (a) immediate context (verses that immediately precede and follow the text); (b) specific context (the book in which the passage occurs; this step includes awareness of author, audience, and genre); (c) biblical context (how the passage relates verbally, thematically, and theologically to other biblical passages); and (d) cultural context (this includes awareness of the background and the historical, geographical, social, and political setting of the text).

Lastly, the exegetical process involves *analysis of the movement of the argument*. Here students of the Bible examine the contours of the text under examination, outlining the passage and exploring the immediate context to determine key terms, themes, ideas, and doctrines. Finally, the exegete identifies the key verse or the core concept of the passage, that upon which all else in the passage depends. This part of the process is sometimes difficult and time-consuming, but the results are expansive, informative, and ultimately transformative. From there one can determine the key to the book in which the passage occurs, and perhaps even the key to the New Testament and the Bible as a whole.

Exegesis is only the first step in Bible study method, but it is an absolutely critical step. Taking this step means you are on your way to becoming a biblical scholar.

Step 2: Synthesis

Howard Hendricks, the Seminary professor known for his Bible-study method, was once asked to speak at a church. "Preach on anything you want," he was told, "except Ephesians." When he requested an explanation, he was told that their pastor had spent three years preaching on Ephesians, and that he had only recently begun the second chapter. While at lunch with members of the congregation, he asked, "What's the theme of the book of Ephesians?" and they had no idea. They had all kinds of details, but the pastor had never put the data together into a meaningful whole. After three years of teaching, the congregation had not discovered the meaning of Ephesians.[2]

That's what this second stage of biblical interpretation is about. Synthesis is the stage where you reconstruct the meaning of a passage after you have taken it apart to inspect the details. In this phase Bible exegetes consult biblical resources such as concordances,[3] Bible dictionaries, Bible handbooks, atlases, and Bible commentaries, taking the results of exegesis and beginning to construct a meaningful whole.

Following exegesis, Bible students often turn to the twin fields of biblical theology and systematic theology for a more comprehensive understanding of the text and its meaning. Biblical theology attempts to show the development of theological knowledge during the Old and New Testament era. In contrast to biblical theology, systematic theology organizes

---

2. Hendricks, *Living by the Book*, 43.

3. A concordance is like an index to the Bible, alphabetically arranged, with references for where verses appear in the Bible. Some Bibles include a limited concordance at the back. A concordance is like a Google search; it can help you locate a passage if you only know a word or phrase but can't remember its reference. Concordances are also useful in doing word studies.

the biblical data in a logical rather than a historical manner. Systematic theology attempts to place all the information on a given topic (e.g. biblical ethics, the doctrines of God, salvation, or the afterlife) together so that we can understand that topic in its totality. Biblical and systematic theology are complementary fields; together they provide a greater understanding than either does alone.

A third discipline, practical theology, completes the theological task by developing an effective strategy for Christian life and practice that speaks to the contemporary situation. Practical theology culminates in the final stage of the hermeneutical process, the application of exegesis and synthesis to religious experience.

Step 3: Application

Exegesis and Synthesis lead to the critical step of Application. The best place to start is with questions. If you want to understand a biblical text, bombard it with questions. The Bible demands questions because it demands honesty. It might not answer all of your questions, but you need to ask them to determine if they can be answered. The answers to your questions will come from steps 1 and 2. That is why the more time you spend in the descriptive and dialogical process (in exegesis and synthesis), the more authentic and practical will be your results.

As you examine the meaning of the text in your contemporary world, you will be guided by two questions: (a) what does this passage mean to me? (in other words, what does it say to me, how does it work in my life?), and (b) what implications does this passage have for others? In application, we begin with ourselves. If something doesn't work in my life, then what authority do I have to share it with someone else?

The Art of Reading the Bible

Nine Questions to Ask about Application

When it comes to application, it is important to ask questions of the text. The following nine questions are helpful to ask when you read a passage of scripture. To start, consider applying them to a passage from Luke, beginning in 14:25 and continuing through 17:10. Here Jesus gives a series of parables and instructions. Using the skills of Exegesis, Synthesis, and

Application that we have examined thus far, answer the nine questions, based on the passage from Luke:[4]

1. Is there an example for me to follow?
2. Is there a sin to avoid?
3. Is there a condition to meet?
4. Is there a promise to claim?
5. Is there a prayer to repeat?
6. Is there a command to obey?
7. Is there a belief to challenge?
8. Is there a challenge to face?
9. Is there a verse to memorize?

Principles of Biblical Interpretation

Hermeneutics places two controls upon the exegetical process: (1) use of the grammatico-historical method (in order to arrive at the intended meaning of a biblical passage or book, this control stresses the importance of approaching the Bible by the same rules as other literature, namely, by understanding its historical, social, linguistic, literary, and cultural background). While the content may be unique, the mode—human language—is the same; (2) observance of fundamental rules in biblical interpretation. The following hermeneutical principles should be adhered when interpreting the Bible:

1. priority of the original languages: this principle also stresses the importance of accurate translations of the Bible;
2. historical propriety; this principle stresses the importance of the original setting of a biblical passage or book, including its meaning for the author and the target audience;
3. induction (exegesis, not eisegesis): this principle stresses the importance of discovering the intended meaning of a passage (exegesis), rather than attributing one's own meaning to the text;

---

4. These questions are taken from Hendricks, *Living by the Book*, 338–42.

4. progressive revelation: this principle views the Bible canonically; accordingly, the Old Testament anticipates and is interpreted by the New Testament;

5. the checking principle: this principle affirms the value of non-biblical disciplines, secular and theological alike, both to enhance perspective and also to act as a check upon excessive or limiting subjectivity. As Charles Spurgeon put it: "it seems odd that certain people who talk so much of what the Holy Spirit reveals to them should think so little of what God has revealed to others";

6. preference for the clearest interpretation: acknowledging that in the Bible everything essential to belief and practice is clear, this principle subjects that which is secondary and obscure in scripture to the primary and plain.[5] This principle has three corollaries:
   a. the incidental should be interpreted by the systematic (for instance, Jesus' statement about "hating" parents in Luke 14:26 should be viewed in the context of Matthew 10:37 or in the broader context of loving neighbors and enemies);
   b. the local must be interpreted by the universal (for example, interpreting the prohibition of kosher food laws in light of Jesus' statement declaring all food clean in Mark 7:19);
   c. the symbolic must be interpreted by the didactic, that is, by instructive passages (such as interpreting Jesus' statement about plucking out an offending eye in Matthew 5:29 in light of Paul's statement about our body being a temple of the Holy Spirit in 1 Corinthians 6:19);

7. acknowledge ignorance on some areas of scripture: this principle affirms that the author's intention is not always clear to modern readers. Such passages should be devalued and not serve as the basis for belief or practice;

8. the principle of harmony: this principle affirms the harmony of scripture in fundamental points of faith and practice. If two doctrines are clearly taught but appear to be contradictory, such as predestination and free will, one should try to harmonize them;

---

5. There are times when the figurative sense is the intended meaning.

9. differentiate interpretation from application: this principle affirms that "interpretation (what a text meant) is one, but application (what a text means) is many."

Spiritual Factors in the Interpretive Process (Illumination)[6]

A controversial issue in contemporary hermeneutics concerns whether spiritual factors affect our ability to read scripture properly. On the one hand, if scripture is read like any other historical writing, two people who are equally prepared intellectually (that is, educated in the original languages, history, and culture) should be equally good interpreters.

On the other hand, scripture itself teaches that spiritual commitment, or lack of it, influences ability to perceive spiritual truth (Rom. 1:18–22; 1 Cor. 2:6–14; Eph. 4:17–24; 1 John 2:11). If, as asserted earlier, the meaning of scripture is to be found in a careful study of words and of the culture and history of its writers, how does that correlate with the added dimension of spiritual insight? If we rely on the spiritual intuitions of fellow believers, we often end up in confusion because we no longer have any normative principles for comparing the validity of one intuition with another.

One way to resolve this dilemma is to examine the term "know." According to the Bible, persons do not truly possess spiritual knowledge unless they are living in the light of that knowledge. True faith is not only knowledge but knowledge acted upon. The unbeliever can know something intellectually without truly knowing it morally and spiritually. Scripture warns against sin in a person's life, likening it to slavery or blindness (John 8:34; Rom. 1:18–22; 6:15–19; 1 Tim. 6:9; 2 Pet. 2:19). Thus spiritual truths become progressively less clear to one who continually rejects those truths. Just as the inspiration of the biblical authors is said to be the work of the Holy Spirit, so another ministry of the Holy Spirit is the work of illumination, helping believers understand more fully the meaning of the words of scripture.

Rather than give new meaning to scripture, a first-half-of-life understanding of the concept of illumination argues that the role of the Spirit is to enable the *original* meaning in the text to speak with power and conviction to each reader's circumstances (John 16:8–15). Quoting John 3:8: "The Spirit (wind) blows where it chooses," conservatives argue that the

---

6. The material on illumination is adapted from Virkler, *Hermeneutics*, 27–29.

text states only that the Spirit may blow *where*, but not *what* it chooses, meaning that the Spirit works *with* scripture and cannot be set in opposition to it. To that argument, second-half-of-lifers might add: "what if the traditional meaning of a passage is in error, or only captures part of the author's original intent? Should we prevent the Spirit from blowing once again, in freer and fuller ways?"

While hermeneutics cannot be limited to the use of only human faculties and education to discover the text's meaning, neither should it be a process that ignores a disciplined approach. That is to say, hermeneutics should be methodical but not mechanical. Hermeneutics involves a fourfold approach to scripture, valuing the student's pedagogy, insight, and circumstances while affirming the Holy's Spirit's role.

The Goal of Hermeneutics

We would be misguided if we limited hermeneutics to the factors and issues that concern our understanding of the ancient text. People do not usually seek to understand the Bible as a mere intellectual exercise. Certainly the biblical authors never intended their writings to be objects of such study. Christians study the Bible precisely because they believe it does have something to say to their lives. The goal of hermeneutics—of the exercise of historical and grammatical methods that disclose the original meaning of a text—must include how the scriptures can affect readers today. This means that true interpretation of the Bible combines an exercise in ancient history with the text's contemporary impact on our lives.

Part II

Theological Topics

Chapter 4

Biblical Theology

Humans as Related to God

When we examine the structuring theological elements in scripture, we discover that the basic symbolic vocabulary reflects on two axes of thought, one vertical and the other horizontal. The Bible links the people of God, whether Israel or the church, to the divine through the *vertical axis* of revelation, divine providence, and the created order. This stable relationship is supplemented with a *horizontal or historical axis*, characterized by loyalty to God, obedience to God's will, care for God's earth, and love for one another. This chapter investigates the vertical dimension by examining the development of the doctrine of God in the Old Testament. Chapter 5 continues the discussion by addressing the horizontal dimension.

The Bible addresses reality by speaking of God: "In the beginning . . . God created the heavens and the earth" (Gen. 1:1). Likewise, when the Bible speaks of humans, it describes them by speaking of God: "And God said, 'Let us make humans in our image'" (Gen. 1:26–27). When the secular world speaks of the divine-human relationship, it reverses the dynamic from divine to human initiative, inferring that because humans are meaning-seeking creatures, they are spiritual.

It is not my intention to offer a solution or even clarification on the distinctions between these perspectives, only to affirm that as soon as men and women became recognizably human, they responded to the human experience creatively, through religion and art. While there may have been some desire to propitiate powerful forces, these early faiths were more interested in expressing the wonder and mystery that seemed always to have been an essential component of the human experience. "Like art, religion has been an attempt to find meaning and value in life."[1]

Which God Do Christians Worship?

The principle figure in the Bible—as in life—is God, and the central theme of the Bible—as of all mystical experience—is the relationship between humans and God. But with which God? The radical God of Abraham, the capricious God of Sarah, the legalistic God of Moses, the nationalistic God of David, the exclusive God of Isaiah, the surprising God of Mary, the empowering God of Peter, the sentimental God of Mary Magdalene, the loving God of Jesus; the mystical God of Paul, the orthodox God of Augustine, the impassive God of Aquinas, the gracious God of Luther, the sovereign God of Calvin, the puritanical God of Jonathan Edwards, the just God of Martin Luther King, the redeeming God of Billy Graham, or the progressive God of Pope Francis? While the explanations for the varied views of God held by these individuals are historical, linguistic, social, cultural, and theological, they are also biblical.

When Karen Armstrong, former Catholic nun and now leading religious scholar, began to research the history of the idea and experience of God in the three Abrahamic faiths (Judaism, Christianity, and Islam), she was surprised to discover that eminent monotheists in all three traditions, instead of advising devotees to wait for God to take the initiative in the relationship, encouraged them to create a sense of God for themselves. Some spiritual masters discouraged believers from expecting to experience God objectively, as a reality "out there," suggesting that in an important sense God was a product of the creative imagination. A few highly respected monotheists, thinking philosophically, denied God's existence while emphasizing that God was the most important reality in the cosmos.[2] While ideas like these boggle Western rationality, such paradox is central to authentic spirituality.

Historically speaking, there is no one unchanging idea in the word "God"; instead, the word contains an entire spectrum of meanings, some of them contradictory and even mutually exclusive. Indeed, the statement "I believe in God' has no objective meaning, but like any other statement

---

1. Armstrong, *History of God*, xix.
2. Ibid., xx.

only means something in context. The same is true of atheism. Since one cannot logically say for certain that there is no God, people dubbed atheists usually deny particular conceptions of the divine. Had the notion of God not had sufficient flexibility, it would not have survived to become one of the great human ideas.

The Emergence of Monotheism in the Bible

Building on the contributions of dialectical philosopher Georg Wilhelm Friedrich (1770–1831), evolutionary scientist Charles Darwin (1809–1882), and cultural anthropologists Sir Edward Tylor (1832–1917), critical religious scholars of the nineteenth century considered it axiomatic that all religions go through evolutionary stages of development, moving from the simple to the complex. As noted earlier, when Julius Wellhausen (1844–1908) examined the stories and laws that appear in the Hebrew scriptures, he concluded that Israelite religion evolved in stages from primitive animism to ethical monotheism. Critical scholars have detected as many as five such stages:

- Animism—belief that all natural objects are inhabited by souls. While enhancing awareness, in this phase religious attention is directed toward appeasing these souls. Hints of this mindset have been found in the talking serpent of Genesis 3, in Abraham's conversing with angels by the oaks of Mamre in Genesis 18 (some scholars suggest that Abraham may have been communicating with spirits that inhabited the trees), in Jacob's visions of a heavenly ladder while sleeping on a stone pillow at Bethel (Genesis 28:18 suggests that the stone became a cult object), and in the commandment to make altars only from uncut stone (Exod. 20:25), supposedly to avoid offending the spirit within the stone.

- Totemism—a clan or group is represented by a particular animal; images (totems) of the animal are worshipped. Religious attention is focused on a few objects only. Critical scholars find an example of totemism in the making of a golden calf at Sinai (Exod. 32:4; cf. 1 Kgs. 12:28; Acts 7:41). Archaeological digs in Israel have unearthed a bronze bull in an ancient Israelite cultic site, dated from the period of the judges (c. 1200 BC). This figurine, symbolizing power and fertility, apparently was associated with the worship of Yahweh (Israel's deity) as well as Baal (a deity of the neighboring Phoenicians).

- Polytheism—recognition of many higher powers, friendly and unfriendly. All are ranked higher than humans and have designated functions such as deities of war, love, agriculture, rain, and so forth. Polytheism is alleged to exist in the Pentateuch, where the chief title for God was Elohim, a term with a plural ending.

- Henotheism (also called "monolatry")—one god in a certain territory. This transition stage between polytheism and monotheism, based on the idea that each tribe, clan, or nation is ruled by a single god, suggests there are as many gods as there are nations or ethnic groups. This is alleged to be evident in the Israelite religion, which pitted the national god, Yahweh, against the gods of surrounding nations such as Baal and Astarte, deities of the Phoenicians (Judg. 2:11–13) or Dagon, god of the Philistines (Judg. 16:23).

- Monotheism—belief in the existence of only one God. According to Wellhausen, this stage was not consistently reached until the period of Israel's classical prophets.

What are we to make of the presence of religious evolution in the Bible? Was there a time when the Israelites were animists, totemists, or polytheists? Of course, given what we know about biological, social, and cultural evolution, and if we go back far enough, say to the Paleolithic (Old Stone) Age, everyone's ancestors were animists to some extent. That, however, is not the question we are asking. Rather, what we want to know is, does the Bible provide evidence that at some point in biblical history, say during the patriarchal period, the Israelites were animistic, totemistic, or polytheistic?

Admittedly there are references to such beliefs and practices in patriarchal times, (otherwise how can one explain mention of "household gods" in Genesis 31:19–35?), but such references, including the examples given above about altars made out of unhewn stones, Jacob's stone pillow, and Abraham's residence by the oaks of Mamre, can be explained otherwise and need not be animistic. Nineteenth-century biblical scholars cautioned against applying an evolutionary straightjacket on cultural and religious history in general, including Israelite history. Some considered animistic references in the Bible to be holdovers from ancient times. And before we fault Wellhausen for arguing that Israelite religion had developed in five-stages, let us recall that he also espoused Vatke's notion that Israelite religion had developed in three stages: the nature/fertility stage, the spiritual/ethical stage, and the priestly/legal stage.

We need to remember several things about Wellhausen's theory of evolutionary development, namely, that (1) according to the romantic ethos of the nineteenth century, which Wellhausen inherited, to label something as "primitive" is to hold it in esteem; and that (2) progress is not always one way or in a straight line. There is regress and decay. Wellhausen admired the passion of the eighth-century prophets but disparaged the legalism of the Deuteronomic Reform and the ritualism of the priestly writers. For Wellhausen, the religion of Israel ended in decay, preparing the way for the new religion of Christianity.

A helpful place to start our discussion of the theology of ancient Israel is 1 Kings 19, a passage that records a memorable experience of the prophet Elijah on Mount Sinai. Elijah (his name means "Yahweh is my God"), persecuted by Jezebel (King Ahab's Phoenician wife) for his faithfulness to Yahweh, has fled to Mount Sinai, where he prepares for an encounter with the divine: "Now there was a great wind, so strong that it was splitting mountains and breaking rocks in pieces before Yahweh, but Yahweh was not in the wind; and after the wind an earthquake, but Yahweh was not in the earthquake; and after the earthquake a fire, but Yahweh was not in the fire; and after the fire a sound of sheer silence" (1 Kgs. 19:11–12; these last few words are traditionally translated "a still small voice").

This passage is often cited as a landmark in the history of Israelite religion, for it reveals an emerging distinction between polytheism and monotheism. In polytheism, the forces of nature may be inhabited by the gods, or loosely equated with them. But in the monotheism that was developing in Israel, there would be greater distance between nature and divinity.

Most Jews and Christians, whether observant or not, know that at the heart of the Torah lies the famous faith statement known as the Shema: "Hear O Israel: The Lord is our God, the Lord alone" (Deut. 6:4). While that translation, taken from the NRSV, neither affirms nor denies monotheism (the Hebrew words can also be translated: "The Lord our God is one Lord," or "The Lord our God, the Lord is one," or "The Lord is our God, the Lord is one"), when Jews recite these words, they are clearly affirming monotheism. We cannot assume, however, that such was their original meaning.

In its biblical context, the statement "Hear O Israel" (Deut. 5:1; 6:4) is proclaimed with great urgency. While Moses is said to be speaking at a time when the memory of the Exodus is still fresh and the people are faced with the hazards of entering Canaan, it is quite clear that the author has in mind another audience. Deuteronomy is primarily being addressed to a later generation, to "those who are not here with us today" (29:14–15). Biblical scholars tell us that the Shema—and its view of God—does not come from the eleventh century BC (the Mosaic period) but rather from the seventh century BC (the reign of Josiah and the time of the classical prophet Jeremiah), suggesting that monotheism, as we know it today, emerged relatively late in Israelite history.

The idea that other gods exist, but are not to be worshipped, is clearly evident in the Ten Commandments. Understood as having been given by God, they represent the very heart of the law of the Jews. They begin with an interesting statement: "I am the Lord your God, who brought you out of the land of Egypt, out of the house of slavery; you shall have no other gods before me" (Exod. 20:2). This text clearly presupposes the existence of other gods, but they are not to take precedence over the God of Israel. The text declares the God of Israel to be the only God for the Israelites, but it doesn't state that there are no other gods. Quite the contrary!

Eventually a strain of monotheism developed within ancient Israel, as is evident in Isaiah 45:5: "I am the Lord, and there is no other; besides me there is no god." But this passage is dated to the sixth century BC, long after Moses. Even as late as the time of Jesus, Jews who were monotheists also believed in divine beings such as angels and archangels, far more powerful than mortals. The basis for such beliefs is found in the Hebrew Bible, which mentions divine beings coming to earth as humans. Sometimes God also is said to appear on earth in human or some other form. Already in the book of Genesis Abraham is said to have an encounter with three "men"; later in the story, two are revealed to be angels and the third is God.

Another occurrence of an angel being identified as God occurs in Exodus 3, at the burning bush. Here Moses is addressed by the "angel of the Lord" (Exod. 3:2), who is later identified as "the Lord" (Yahweh) and as God ("Elohim"). Other passages of the Bible tell us that angels can be called sons of God (see Job 1:6) or God himself and that they become human. Perhaps the most famous instance of a "man" identified as God is the story of Jacob's wrestling match at Bethel in Genesis 32:24–30. Jacob's divine adversary had to vanish before sunrise, but not before giving Jacob a new name.

Viewing the doctrine of God as having changed through Israelite history contradicts what we were taught in church. Most of us never envisioned God as having evolved at all. We learned that God was there in the beginning, fully formed, that God gave form to everything else, and that the earliest humans, including Adam and Eve, the patriarchs, Moses, and Israel's religious leaders, were monotheists from the start. But that's not really the story in the Bible, at least not the whole story. "If you read the Hebrew Bible carefully, it tells the story of a god in evolution, a god whose character changes radically from beginning to end."[3]

The view that Israelite religion reached monotheism only after a period of henotheism (exclusive devotion to one god without denying the existence of others) is now widely accepted by biblical scholars, including by many practicing Jews and Christians, but things get more controversial when you suggest that there was a long time when Yahweh was ensconced in an Israelite pantheon, working alongside other gods. Let's examine the archaeological, biblical, and historical evidence, starting with the biblical account of the conquest of Canaan, to see if we can determine why a gap exists between scholars and rank-and-file Christians, most of whom believe monotheism was revealed to Moses, who then created a theocracy based on monotheistic faith.

The Archaeological Evidence[4]

According to the book of Joshua, the Canaanites, wicked polytheists, were conquered by monotheistic Israelites, led by Joshua: "Joshua defeated the whole land, the hill country and the Negeb and the lowland and the slopes, and all their kings; he left none remaining, but utterly destroyed all that breathed, as the Lord God of Israel commanded" (Josh. 10:40). Religious conservatives rely on the findings of William Albright, sometimes called the founder of biblical archaeology, for support of this scenario. In his book *From the Stone Age to Christianity*, published in 1940, Albright affirmed that artifacts unearthed in Palestine (today's nation of Israel) paint a clear picture: Israelites had marched into Canaan from Egypt and swiftly destroyed and occupied Canaanite towns, rapidly replacing indigenous paganism with a radically different Yahwism. In his estimation, archaeological excavations showed an abrupt break between the Canaanite culture first encountered by the Israelites and the culture they built to replace it. Albright was a devout Christian, something that clearly impacted his findings. His views now lack foundation.

3. Wright, *Evolution of God*, 101.
4. This segment is adapted from Wright, ibid., 106–9.

Recent decades of painstaking excavation and scientific archaeological research in the region supposedly conquered by the Israelites fail to provide evidence of a violent conquest by the Israelites. There isn't even much evidence to support a competing theory, that of a gradual, more peaceful influx of desert nomads gradually displacing Canaanites. While biblical archaeologists disagree about many things, there is now consensus that the Israelites who first settled in the highlands of Canaan were not foreign invaders but rather that they were Canaanites all along.

In the twelfth century BC, as the Bronze Age was giving way to the Iron Age, there was political and economic disruption across the Middle East. Amid this chaos, new settlements, clearly Israelite, arose in Canaan. In all likelihood, the Israelites emerged from a particular line of Canaanites, a group which may have absorbed exiles from Egypt. One of these early Israelite settlements yielded an artifact that illustrates the cultural continuity between Israel and Canaan. It artifact is a small figurine of a bronze bull, exactly the kind of "Canaanite" idol that the Bible condemns.

In addition to figurines of Baal, recent archaeological digs in Israel have unearthed in ancient Israelite settings testimony of extensive devotion to Asherah, the Canaanite goddess of fertility and the wife of El. In the late twentieth century archaeologists discovered inscriptions, dating to around 800 BC, at two different Israelite sites, one in the northern Sinai and another near Hebron in Judah. Both inscriptions invoke blessings "by Yahweh and his Asherah." In both cases the implication is that Asherah is a consort of Yahweh. The word "his" puts a suggestive spin, corroborated by a passages in 2 Kings 23:6, reporting that near the end of the seventh century (around 620 BC), Asherah was worshipped in Yahweh's temple in Jerusalem.

As one would expect, there are numerous references to Asherah in the Bible, all disparaging. Her symbol was a sacred pole in a grove of trees near an altar (1 Kgs. 16:33; 2 Kgs. 21:3). The biblical writings regularly command destruction of these symbols (Deut. 7:5; 12:3; 16:21). A crucial development in the evolution of monotheism occurred when a priest who didn't favor polytheism "brought out the image of Asherah from the house of the Lord, outside Jerusalem, to the Wadi Kidron, burned it at the Wadi Kidron, beat it to dust and threw the dust of it upon the graves of the common people" (2 Kgs. 23:6). These passages attest to the pervasive polytheistic practices of the Israelites, late in the prophetic period; the fate of monotheism lay in the balance.

Such finds would not have surprised William Albright, for the Bible indicates that the Israelites occasionally worshipped idols. But the biblical story views such episodes as lapses in monotheism, a belief system brought to Canaan by Moses. However, few biblical scholars today agree with this assessment. They do not view biblical accounts of Moses to be historically reliable. Rather these stories are believed to have been recorded centuries after the events they describe, and then further redacted later by monotheists who wished to give their theology greater authority.

Increasingly it is suspected that an early pure Yahwism may never have existed except among a small minority of Yahweh devotees, or perhaps only in the minds of later revisionists such as the Deuteronomistic historians. The evidence seems to point to later Yahwism having emerged out of a greater Canaanite religion or out of a Yahwism basically indistinguishable from the Canaanite religion.

How Yahweh Became Yahweh[5]

From an objective standpoint, there is no reason to assume that the advent of Israelite monotheism took place anywhere other than Canaan, after centuries of immersion in Canaanite culture. It is also possible that Yahweh, who in the Bible expends so much effort denouncing Canaanite gods, actually started as a Canaanite deity.

Such a hypothesis is helpful because it addresses numerous problems in the biblical text, including (a) references to God speaking in the plural (see Gen. 1:26–27; 3:22; 11:7. This use of the first-person plural by God, in both the P and J sources, seems to indicate that this language was originally part of the Israelites' tradition); (b) references to the "divine council" (Ps. 82:1. Traditional explanations suggest that this reference is to angels, the heavenly host, or other supernatural beings, but Psalm 82:1 and 6 refers to "gods," and none of the above qualify as gods); and (c) the many titles for Yahweh in the Bible that include the word El:

- Elohim ("God"; "gods");
- El Elyon ("God Most High"; "Exalted One");
- El Shaddai ("God Almighty"; "God of the Mountain");
- El Olam ("God of Eternity"; "The Everlasting God);

5. This segment is adapted from Wright, ibid., 110–15.

- El Roi ("God of Vision or Divining"; "God Who Sees");
- El Berith ("God of the Covenant").

Of these, the phrase El Shaddai is especially intriguing, for its meaning remains unclear; it seems to refer to mountains, not omnipotence. This name probably refers to El's localization in a mountainous region or to his theophany in mountain storms (cf. the "thunder and lightning" associated with the Sinai theophany, Exodus 19:16, and the "wind, earthquake, and fire in 1 Kings 19:11–12). In the time of the patriarchs the deity was identified with the storm god Hadad, often known as Baal among the Canaanites. After the patriarchal period, the original meaning of "Shaddai" was eclipsed, and the name occasionally was used as a synonym for "Yahweh." The author of Job favors this name, for it expressed the majesty and omnipotence of deity. The Septuagint renders "Shaddai" in the book of Job as Kurios ("Lord") or Pantocrator ("Almighty"), expressing aspects of God attractive to later Jews and Christians.

While El is the generic Semitic name for "God" or "deity," it was also the name for the Canaanite high god. "Given that the Canaanite El appears on the historical record before the Israelite god Yahweh, it is tempting to conclude that Yahweh in some way emerged from El, and may even have started life as a renamed version of El."[6] For instance, there are a few times in the Bible when the term El applied to Yahweh seems to be a proper noun. According to Genesis 33:20, Jacob "erected an altar and called it El-Elohe-Israel." This concept could be translated as "god, the god of Israel," but uncapitalized it wouldn't make much sense. Some English translations of Genesis render the expression as "El, God of Israel." Perhaps an even closer link between Israelite religion and El can be found in the word "Israel," which ends in "el" and means "El does battle," "El contends" or "El perseveres." In ancient times names were often inspired by gods, and names ending in "el" typically referred to the god El.

For present purposes, of interest is the way "El Shaddai" is used in Exodus 6:3, in a conversation between Moses and God. God says: "I am Yahweh. I appeared to Abraham, to Isaac, and to Jacob as El Shaddai, but by my name Yahweh I did not make myself known to them." Here even Yahweh claims to have started life in Canaan with the name El.

If you were crafting a history of your god, would you add such an odd twist, saying that he used to go by another name? Wouldn't such an oddity

6. Ibid., 111.

fit better if one were trying to convince two religious groups—one worshipping a god called Yahweh and another a god called El—that they actually worship the same god? This is precisely the suggestion of the Documentary Hypothesis, that at some point in Israelite history there were two geographically distinct traditions to reconcile, one worshipping a god named El (the E author lived in the north, closer to the heartland of El worship) and one worshipping a god named Yahweh (the J author lived in the south, in part of Israel known as Judah).

Certainly the Bible holds hints of once separate groups having united. It describes Israel at the end of the second millennium BC, before it evolved into a monarchical state, as a confederation of twelve tribes. The merging of Israel's tribes is also reflected in the patriarchal story: Abraham begat Isaac, who begat Jacob. Few scholars consider this lineage accurate, but most think it significant.

The idea that Israel coalesced near or in the region of El worship and only adopted Yahweh later, while absorbing tribes from the south, gains support from the famous Merneptah Stele, an ancient Egyptian stone inscription from 1219 BC, on which the name "Israel" first appears historically. The word clearly refers to a people, not a place, but the people seem to have been Canaanites. The stele does not mention Yahweh; its only possible allusion to any god is the "el" in Israel. And centuries would pass before a text would mention both Israel and "Yhwh" (the ancient spelling of Yahweh, before Semitic languages were written with vowels). Intriguingly, there are separate Egyptian references to "Yhw" even earlier than that first reference to Israel, but here "Yhw" seems to be a place, not a god. And that place "seems to have been somewhere around Edom, in southern Canaan, which makes sense if a Yahweh-worshipping people from the south eventually merged with an El-worshipping people to the north."[7] As the name Israel indicates, over time a group of Israelites transformed the concept "El the warrior" to Yahweh the warrior, styling itself nationally after this deity. At first Yahweh came to be regarded as Israel's God and only long afterwards as the God of the universe.[8]

Most of us grew up hearing stories about Elijah, a classic Israelite prophet who defended monotheism without compromise in his conflict with Jezebel and the prophets of Baal, but even this great hero cannot be considered a monotheist, since he advocated monolatry rather than true

---

7. Ibid, 114.
8. The biblical doctrine of creation is discussed in chapter 8 below.

monotheism. He didn't necessarily deny Baal's existence (the monotheistic position), just that Baal was not worthy of Israelite worship. The first "effective monotheist" seems to have been the prophet Amos, although later classical prophets developed his ideas further. It took an event and a person to develop monotheistic belief most thoroughly, an event known as the Babylonian exile and an unknown prophet called Second Isaiah. It was this event, called "the furnace of adversity" (Isa. 48:10), that led to the monotheistic standard the masses would accept.

Two themes catapulted Second Isaiah to popularity, first within Judaism and later in Christianity. The first theme is that God alone is the God of the whole earth: "I am the Lord, and there is no other; beside me there is no god" (Isa. 45:5); "I am the Lord, who made all things, who alone stretched out the heavens, who by myself spread out the earth" (Isa. 44:24). Biblical scholars cite Second Isaiah as a landmark, and deservedly so. Finally, after centuries of monolatry, monotheistic declarations come with clarity and force. The second theme, that God will "bring forth justice to the nations," gets as much attention as monotheism. What kind of God is this God? What is God's stance toward the world? The answer is inspiring: God is universal not only in power but in concern, and this gives God's people a momentous mission: "I will give you as a light to the nations, that my salvation may reach to the end of the earth" (Isa. 49:6). What this mission means for the world will be the subject of chapter 5.

Conclusion

While the cult of Yahweh is the principle concern of the Old Testament, it may not have been the principle religious concern of the Israelites. The common masses participated in syncretistic beliefs and practices throughout the pre-exilic period, while a small minority were monolatrists, belonging to what scholars call the "Yahweh alone" movement. This minority wrote the biblical texts and projected their beliefs into the distant past to give the impression their monotheism was the norm from which Israelites deviated.

In the early 1970s Morton Smith became the first biblical scholar to propose seriously that the Yahwism-alone movement was a minority religio-political movement in the pre-exilic period, in opposition to the royal cult and all popular or familial forms of religion. Smith traced the movement's development through five stages:

1. During the pre-monarchic and monarchic periods, Israel shared the common religious perspective of the ancient Near East. Each region had a national deity and Yahweh was the national god of Israel. Properly speaking, Yahweh was the deity of the dynastic rulers in Judah and Israel (his status was like that of Chemosh in Moab or Milcom in Ammon. Perhaps a few elements within Israel had a proclivity to worship one universal god, but their impact was minimal);

2. From the time of David (1000 BC), the court of Judah may have been responsible for popularizing the worship of Yahweh among the masses;

3. In the northern nation of Israel, a move toward monotheism began with the Omride conflict (850–840), when Jezebel persecuted and killed Yahwistic prophets. However, the overthrow of the Omrides (kings Omri and Ahab) resulted from their foreign connections rather than from a desire to elevate Yahweh monotheistically;

4. Classical prophets and the Deuteronomic Reform movement brought the message of practical monotheism to the masses. Amos and Hosea were forerunners among the prophets in 750 BC. Despite attempts at reform (probably more political than religious) by kings Hezekiah (c. 700 BC) and Josiah (621 BC), by 580 BC monotheism appears to have been in the minority once again;

5. In the exilic and post-exilic eras the people became monotheists, for by then people living under foreign rule and influence had to make a clear decision about participating in those cults. Restraint in the fact of such pressure makes people true monotheists.

The constant biblical rhetoric against syncretism and idolatry should not be seen as evidence of monotheism, but rather as admission that pure Yahwism was in the minority. During the pre-exilic period most Israelites were polytheists, worshipping Yahweh along other gods, and they saw this as perfectly acceptable. Initially, the elevation of Yahweh for exclusive veneration was an act of nationalistic expression, as one might find in a time of crisis. Ultimately, in the post-exilic era, priestly laws separated the Jews from others and encouraged pure monotheism.

Chapter 5

Biblical Anthropology

Humans as Related to Self, Nature, and Culture

Humans are made in the image of God. That is a biblical given, but it is only part of the story. The other part, which each of us must determine for ourselves, is this: in the image of which God? Perhaps we have no more important theological investigation than to discover in whose image we have been made. Our sociology—including our values, priorities, choices, and behavior—is derived from, legitimated by, and reflective of our theology.

Biblical Images of God: How Theology Impacts Anthropology

In his book *The God We Never Knew*, Marcus Borg examines images of God in the biblical and Christian traditions and discerns therein two primary "models":

1. the "*monarchical model*," which clusters images of God as king, lord, and father. This approach leads to what Borg calls a "performance model" of the Christian life;

2. the "*Spirit model*," which clusters images of God that point to intimate relationship and belonging. This model leads to a "relational model" of the Christian life.[1]

---

1. Borg, *God We Never Knew*, 57–83.

Both models, Borg discovered, are found throughout all periods of Christian history, though the first is more common. From roughly the fourth century—when Christianity became the dominant religion of Western culture—through the present, the monarchical model has dominated. But alongside it, as an alternative voice, the Spirit model has also persisted. These models reflect two different voices within the Christian tradition. They also embody first- and second-half-of-life attitudes, values, and perspectives.

The monarchical model portrays God as male, as all-powerful, as lawgiver, and as judge. Images of God in this model suggest that God is distant. Within this model, humans have offended divine majesty and deserve judgment. But because God loves his subjects, God creates a way for his people to escape the punishment they deserve: through appropriate sacrifice and true repentance. In the royal theology of ancient Israel, atonement was institutionalized in temple rituals. In the Christian version of the monarchical model, the king's (Lord's) love is seen especially in Jesus. Because God loves us, he sends his son into the world to die on a cross as the sacrifice that makes our forgiveness possible.[2] This model is well suited to the conserving tasks and preoccupations of first-half-of-life Christianity: establishing religious identity, creating identifying boundaries, and seeking security. Unfortunately, like the Precritical Paradigm, the monarchical model has contributed to racism, sexism, nationalism, exclusivism, and other harmful ideologies.

The Spirit model is more conducive to the progressive tasks and needs of second-half-of-life Christianity. It portrays God in culture and in nature, with us and in us. An ancient Hebrew word for God is *ruach*. Literally, the word means "wind," a natural and even an impersonal concept. The wind or *ruach* was observed not as a being, but as a vitalizing force. Among the Hebrews the *ruach* or wind of God was said to have brooded over the chaos in the story of creation in order to bring forth life (Gen. 1:2). Slowly this *ruach* evolved, became personalized, and was called "Spirit." The *ruach* or wind of God was not external. It rather emerged from within the world and was understood as its very ground, its life-giving reality. This *ruach* was also thought to be connected in some way to human *nephesh* or breath, also understood as impersonal. Breath was a force that wells up from within each of us and was thought in some sense to be identical with human life. *Nephesh* would later be translated "soul" or "spirit." Therefore, in Jewish

2. Ibid., 63–64.

thinking, spirit was conceived of externally as the wind, the *ruach*, and internally as the breath of life itself, the *nephesh*.[3]

The Spirit model, as used in the Bible, is broader than the specific Christian doctrine of "the Holy Spirit," which sees the Spirit as one aspect of God. In the Bible, Spirit is used comprehensively to refer to God's presence in creation, in the history of Israel, and in the life of Jesus and the early church. While the monarchical model also affirms that God is Spirit, of course, and that affirmation can be a source of confusion that limits our understanding of God, there is a difference. When Spirit is assimilated to the monarchical model, God is not Spirit but a spirit—that is, a spiritual being out there, not here. But when Spirit is set free from the monarchical understanding, Spirit retains the suggestive meanings associated with breath and wind: God is the encompassing Spirit both within and outside us.[4]

In addition to wind and breath, the Bible provides other non-anthropomorphic images for God as Spirit, such as God as rock (meaning a place of refuge and safety). Additional non-masculine images include mother, wisdom, lover, and shepherd. These metaphors for the Spirit affect our root image of God in quite obvious ways: (1) they emphasize *the nearness of God* rather than the distance implied by the monarchical model, thereby suggesting the language of relationship; (2) they utilize *both male and female metaphors* (as well as some that are neuter), rather than the exclusively male images of the monarchical model; and (3) they include *both anthropomorphic and nonathropomorphic images.*

Taken together, both models suggest that the relationship to God is personal, even as God is more than a person. The sacred is not simply an inanimate mystery but a presence. Using an ancient biblical analogy, these metaphors lead to a covenantal understanding of the divine-human relationship, which emphasizes belonging and connectedness. This model is intrinsically dialogical.[5]

The Spirit model of God affects the meaning of a number of central Christian teachings. It does so by changing the framework in which things are seen. Borg provides four examples:

    1. *Creation looks different.* According to the monarchical model, God's creation of the world is understood as an event in the distant past involving the creation of a universe separate from God. The Spirit model depicts

---

3. Spong, *Christianity Must Change*, 59–60.
4. Borg, *God We Never Knew*, 72.
5. Ibid., 75–76.

God's creation as an ongoing activity: in every moment God as Spirit (as the nonmaterial "ground" of all that is) is bringing the universe into existence.

2. *The human condition looks different.* The central human problem is not sin and guilt, as it is within the monarchical model, but "estrangement," meaning that humans are separated from that to which they belong. Blind to the presence of God, human beings are separated from the Spirit around and within them and to which they belong.

3. *Sin looks different.* For the monarchical model, sin is primarily disloyalty to the king, seen especially as disobedience to his laws. The Spirit model addresses "sin" in more profound ways: for the metaphor of God as lover, sin is unfaithfulness; for the metaphor of God as the compassionate one who cares for all her children, sin is failure in compassion. Thus sin remains, but as betrayal of relationship and absence of compassion. Repentance also remains, only now it does not require sacrifice and contrition but a turning and returning to that to which we belong. Judgment also remains, only now not as the threat of eternal judgment but rather as living with the consequences of our choices. To remain estranged from God is to remain unsatisfied and unfulfilled.

4. *God as king and lord looks different.* God as Spirit is glorious, radiant, and splendid, like the splendor of a king. In the Spirit model, God as king and lord is the subverter of systems of domination, not the legitimator of domination systems.[6]

The images of God associated with the Spirit model dramatically affect how we think of the Christian life. Rather than God as a distant being with whom we might spend eternity, Spirit—the sacred—is right here. Rather than sin and guilt being the central dynamic of the Christian life, the central dynamic becomes relationship—with God, the world, and each other. The monarchical model promotes stability, security, conformity, and uniformity, while the Spirit model promotes newness, growth, change, and transformation.

The mystics of every religious tradition, following the Spirit model rather than the monarchical model, have always spoken out against specific definitions of God. The Western mystics appear to have assumed that a personal God was only a stage, and an inferior one at that, in human religious development. The mystical portrait of God was first imaginative, and then ineffable. It involved an interior journey, not an exterior one. In the mystical tradition, no one can claim objectivity for his or her insight. Each

6. Ibid., 77–78.

person is called to journey into the mystery of God along the pathway of his or her own expanding personhood. Every person is thus capable of being a theophany, as sign of God's presence; but no one person, institution, or way of life can exhaust this revelation. God, for the mystics, is found at the depths of life, working in and through the being of this world, calling all nature to its deepest potential. It is a God concept better approached if we move from our perception of God to our experience of God.

So the call of this internal God found in our depths becomes primarily a call into being, a call that is not unique to religion. It is a call that refocuses what has been known as the religious dimension. In this scenario, the task of the church becomes less that of indoctrinating or relating people to an external divine power and more that of providing opportunities for people to touch the infinite center of all things and to fulfill all their potential. This understanding of God places a premium on the church's vocation to oppose anything that prevents us from the fullest expression of our humanity.[7]

We are learning that "meaning" is not external to life but must be discovered in our own depths and imposed on life by an act of our own will. We are being made aware that life is not fair and will not necessarily be made fair either in this life or in any other. So we have to decide how we will live now with this reality. One thing is certain: the journey of faith must go forward.

The Human Condition: Biblical Anthropology

Having examined elements of biblical theology, particularly the development of the Old Testament doctrine of God, we continue the discussion by addressing biblical anthropology, particularly the doctrines of sin and salvation.

Many Christians have been reared with the sin and salvation paradigm, a view prominently upheld in evangelical preaching and teaching.[8] This view compresses the overarching storyline of the Bible into a conversionist template. It begins with absolute perfection in the Garden of Eden, followed by a Fall into original sin (it is important to note that terms such as "Fall" and "original sin," while essential to this paradigm, are not found in the Bible). As a consequence of the sin of Adam and Eve, all humans

---

7. Ibid., 66.

8. This segment on sin and salvation is taken from my earlier book, *Beyond Belief*, 28–29.

find themselves in a state of condemnation. Unable to save themselves (that is, to be restored to proper relationship with God, others, themselves, and nature), they are dependent upon God's grace to provide a way of redemption. Because of God's great love for humanity, God sent Jesus to die in our place. God's gift, however, must be accepted by faith, and those who accept Christ as Savior are assured of eternity in heaven with God. Those who remain unrepentant or in a fallen state—which represents the vast majority of humans according to some versions of this conventional view— face damnation to hell, defined traditionally as banishment from God and eternal torment.

Traditional Christians sometimes modify this story line, but rarely do they question its trajectory as a whole, its morality, or even whether it is truly biblical. If it is biblical, did Abraham hold it, or Moses, or Isaiah, or Jesus? Is it explicitly taught in scripture? Was it held in the first three centuries of Christian history? Surprisingly, the answer to each question is "no."

While the Christian tradition tends to present the doctrine of salvation in terms of the ultimate destiny of the individual, this is not accurate, for as the etymology of the word demonstrates, "salvation" comes from the Latin words *salutas*, meaning "security, safety, or wholeness" and *salvus*, meaning something "whole, intact, or in good working order." In biblical times, as today, a viable religion must keep its social system intact, meaning it has to provide salvation at the social level. The majority of current Christian scholars are convinced that the modern evangelical emphasis on "being saved," which views salvation primarily as an assurance of entrance to heaven, is at best a rather recent emphasis in Christian tradition, going back no earlier than the nineteenth century.

In the Bible the concept of salvation had an essentially this-worldly orientation, meaning that the concept was used to assure believers of security from physical and external threats and to guarantee their place in the coming kingdom of God on earth. The paradigmatic model for salvation is the Exodus from bondage in Egypt. In the Song of Moses, a hymnic passage about the Exodus, God is proclaimed as the "salvation" of the Israelites (Exod. 15:2; see Ps. 106:21) because God was instrumental in their deliverance from oppression. They were later saved from various other oppressors, sometimes through a human being sent for that purpose: "The Lord gave Israel a savior, so that they escaped from the hand of the Arameans" (2 Kgs. 12:5). During the Babylonian exile, God is said to have prepared Cyrus of Persia to carry divine salvation to the Israelites yet again (Isa. 44:28—45:7).

Thus the prophet Jeremiah could call God the "hope of Israel, its savior in time of trouble" (Jer. 14:8).

The doctrine of salvation is complex, and different aspects of the Christian understanding of sin and salvation have been emphasized by theologians, teachers, or by different sects and denominations during different periods of church history or for specific situations. Recent studies of the biblical notion of salvation emphasize the importance of contextualization, meaning that because the Christian gospel always addresses specific situations, the doctrine of salvation should be contextualized in those circumstances. For example, to the oppressed—whether spiritually, economically, or politically—the gospel message is that of liberation; to those burdened by personal guilt, the message is one of forgiveness; to the despondent, the message is one of hope.

Christianity holds that the created order, particularly humanity, has fallen into disorder. Things are not what they were meant to be, and something needs to be done about this. The same God who made the created order must act to reorder it, something God accomplished through the life, death, and resurrection of Jesus Christ. In his widely used text *Christian Theology*, Alistair McGrath provides answers given by Christians throughout their history to the question, "*from* what are we saved?" In each case, the doctrine of sin provides an answer. Each model, in turn, also points to the doctrine of salvation, with its hopeful answers.[9]

From what, then, are we saved? McGrath provides six answers: Christians are saved from (1) their human condition, (2) their guilt, (3) their lack of holiness, (4) their inauthentic human existence (characterized by faith in the transient material world), (5) oppression, and (6) from forces that enslave humanity—such as satanic forces, evil spirits, fear of death, or the power of sin. In summary, the Christian doctrine of salvation deals with the restoration of all things, including humanity, to its proper relationship to God.

Salvation, consequently, represents new possibilities, a new state of being. McGrath provides models of salvation that correspond to the six models of sin. Together, they answer the question, "*for* what are we saved?" Christians are saved for (1) relationship with God, (2) righteousness in the sight of God, (3) personal holiness, (4) authentic human existence, (5) social and political liberation, and (6) spiritual freedom.

---

9. McGrath, *Christian Theology*, 339–42.

The understanding of salvation presented above exhibits a radical this-worldly orientation. The reason is clear: traditional Christians followed their Jewish counterparts in placing their faith into a historical context. The basic conviction of the Greeks was that truth was changeless and hence not tied to events. The earliest Christian creeds, such as the Apostles Creed, were composed to counter such views, which tended to overspiritualize Jesus and detach Christianity from history.

In his seminal work *Original Blessing*, Dominican scholar Matthew Fox distinguishes between the fall/redemption paradigm and creation spirituality. The former, akin to Borg's "monarchical model," is dualistic and patriarchal. It begins its theology with sin and original sin, and it generally ends with redemption. Unlike creation spirituality, which teaches about creativity, justice-making, and social transformation, the fall/redemption tradition has proven unfriendly to artists, prophets, and women. Because this tradition considers nature "fallen" and does not seek God in nature, it is frequently hostile toward science. If the fall/redemption paradigm is foreign to the story of Adam, Abraham, and their Jewish descendants, whence did it arise?

Brian McLaren, hailed widely as one of the most significant religious leaders of our time, argues brilliantly in *A New Kind of Christianity* that the fall/redemption paradigm is adapted from the ancient Greek philosophical tradition, a variant of "the descent into Plato's cave of illusion and the ascent into philosophical enlightenment,"[10] particularly as promoted by Plotinus, (204–270), the third-century father of Neoplatonism, which became dominant in the Greco-Roman world at precisely the time when Christians were constructing an identity first as a "third race" and later as holders of the "true philosophy" to which the Greeks had aspired. According to McLaren, the Christian religion in the West "unwittingly traded its true heritage through Jesus from Judaism for an alien heritage drawn from Greek philosophy and Roman politics. Through this profound and unconscious syncretism, biblical data was reframed by the Greco-Roman narrative."[11]

When we allow Genesis, Exodus, and Isaiah—rather than Plato, Aristotle, and Caesar—to set the stage for the biblical narrative, what emerges is a powerful, transformative story that resonates with the life and teaching of Jesus. This story invites our participation, not as pawns on the squares of a cosmic chessboard, but as creative partners and protagonists with God

10. McLaren, *New Kind of Christianity*, 37.
11. Ibid., 41.

in the story of creation. This story begins with original blessing, not Greco-Roman perfection, and this beginning is not complete; it is evolving into something better and more wonderful. All that we call human culture waits to be created in this "very good" world—music, science, art, literature, engineering, even theology. These things are to be created not by God but by humans, who, as image-bearers of the Creator, are themselves creative.

As Christians, our concern should be on the here-and-now, on our "this-worldly" task and journey. In my estimation, focusing on sin as a path to damnation and on salvation as a path to the afterlife is peripheral to Christianity and serves as a distraction from the urgent tasks at hand. Furthermore, to quote award-winning author Robert Wright, "religions that have failed to align individual salvation with social salvation have not, in the end, fared well. And, like it or not, the social system to be saved is now a global one. Any religion whose prerequisites for individual salvation don't conduce to the salvation of the whole world is a religion whose time has passed."[12]

Recapturing the Sacramental Sense of Reality

Religion is sacramental in the sense that it can speak of unspeakable mystery only through the use of symbols, or what theology calls sacraments. A sacrament, in its broadest sense, includes any object, person, or event through which religious consciousness is awakened to the presence of sacred mystery. Historically, most of religion's sacraments have been closely related to nature. The luminosity of sunshine, dawn, and dusk; the experience of wind or breath; the purifying power of clean water; the fertility of soil and life—such natural phenomena have been used by religions to symbolize the way in which ultimate mystery affects us.

Since nature provides many of the fundamental sacraments of human religion, it is easy to see how the conservation of nature is indispensable for the survival of religion. If we lose the environment, we lose God as well. And it is equally true that when religion loses touch with its sacramental origins, it begins to grow indifferent to the natural world. A sacramental vision makes nature transparent to divinity. In this sense it concedes to nature an inherent value without allowing it to become a substitute for God. According to this Christian perspective, nature is worth saving not because it is sacred, but because it is sacramental.

12. Wright, *Evolution of God*, 430.

BIBLICAL ANTHROPOLOGY

Like McLaren, Matthew Fox argues that the fall/redemption paradigm, based upon the doctrine of original sin, developed during medieval times and is essentially foreign to scripture. This tradition, dualistic and patriarchal, considers all nature "fallen" and does not seek God in nature. Creation spirituality, on the other hand, begins with original blessing, embodying the biblical emphasis on the goodness of creation. Fall and Redemption theology begins with original sin and ends with redemption. Creation theology begins with original blessing and flows to all subsequent blessings, including those we share with our loved ones and those we affirm in creativity, compassion, birthing, and justice-making; all are prefigured in the grace of creation. Creation spirituality does not ignore sin, but views it differently. Boredom, depression, arrogance, violence, addictive behavior—these occur when we get cut off from the sense of grace and blessing. Original sin is not "original" or primary in time or in biblical theology, but derived. Evil is conceived as neither original nor eternal, but rather as something good gone bad.

Hope for humanity and the future of our planet must be based on a proper understanding of the doctrine of creation, one that is not antithetical to science but rather is the subject of the scientist's search, the source of the prophet's vision, and the subject of the mystic's commitment. According to Fox, the universe loves us every day, and the Creator loves us through creation. The following quotation captures his perspective:

> Creation is the source, the matrix, and the goal of all things—the beginning and the end, the alpha and the omega. Creation is our common parent, when 'our' stands for all things. Creation is the mother of all beings and the father of all beings, the birther and the begetter. It is all-holy; it is awe-filled. . . . Creation is never finished, never satisfied, never bored, never passive. Creation is always newly born, always making new. . . . How can such a drama be jeopardized as it is today? Only because our species, with its religions, education, moralities, governments, and economics, has lost the sense of creation. When that happens, nothing is holy; nothing seems worth the struggle for justice that is necessary to preserve it. Community dies, and relations no longer exist.[13]

In his writings on creation spirituality, Fox describes spirituality as a way of life characterized by four paths: (1) The Via Positiva: Befriending Creation; (2) The Via Negative: Befriending Darkness; (3) The Via Creativa:

---

13. Fox, *Creation Spirituality*, 10–11.

Befriending Creativity; and (4) The Via Transformativa: Befriending New Creation. For each path he provides a signpost or commandment (italicized below):

- Via Positiva: *Thou shalt fall in love at least three times a day.* This applies to human beings, to nature in all its magnificence, and also to activities such as music, poetry, and dance. Creation has much to do with falling in love. The first commandment, one of praise, flows from the awe of being alive.

- Via Negativa: *Thou shalt dare the dark.* Every spiritual journey moves from the surface to the depths, and there is no moving from superficiality to depth without entering the dark. "Daring the dark" means entering nothingness and letting it be nothingness while it works its mystery on us. "Daring the dark" also means allowing pain to be pain and learning from it. Being at home in the dark involves relinquishing control—letting go and letting be.

- Via Creativa: *Do not be reluctant to give birth.* Spiritual discipline in the creation tradition is focused on the development of the aesthetic. Beauty, and our role in co-creating it, lies at the heart of the spiritual journey. Such creativity wrestles with the demons and angels in the depths of our psyches, embracing our "shadow" side as well as our visions and dreams. "To give birth" is to enter the Creator's realm. The work of co-creation engages the image of God (*imago dei*) that is in every person, essential for assisting nature and history in carrying on the creativity of the universe.

- Via Transformativa: *Be compassionate, as your Creator is compassionate.* This commandment, the summation of Jesus' ethical teaching, corresponds in meaning to Matthew's passage from the Sermon on the Mount, translated "Be perfect, as your heavenly Father is perfect" (Matt. 5:48). A better rendition of Matthew's Greek word *teleios* is: "Be mature" or "Be complete." As Luke's version makes clear, for humans to be perfect or complete is for them to be compassionate to all creatures: "Be merciful, just as your Father is merciful" (Luke 6:36). In this understanding, compassion is not about the actions that flow from a superior to an inferior, but as a result of our interdependence. True compassion, therefore, involves a deep respect for other cultures and traditions and the willingness to work together in our need for mutual wisdom.

If spirituality can be defined as "meeting with God in history," as Leonardo Boff defined it, and if a new spiritual era is emerging, then a new meeting with God is also upon us, providing a self-disclosure of God that is less warlike, less patriarchal, and more concerned with compassion, justice, celebration, beauty, and creativity.[14]

14. Ibid., 18–23, 31.

Part III

Literary Topics

The Essential Message of the Hebrew Bible

Chapter 6

Covenant

In *The Covenant*, a novel on South Africa, James Michener introduces a thought-provoking concept: "Often in the biographies of important women and men," he writes, "one comes across the phrase, 'Like a burst of light, the idea which would animate her life came upon her.'" In our examination of the first five books of the Bible, our animating concept is this: *covenant precedes creation*, and redemption precedes covenant. Affirming this literary sequence will revolutionize your reading of the biblical text, including your understanding of the biblical doctrine of creation (see chapter 8).

When we seek to understand the meaning of our individual life stories, we do not actually begin with birth or infancy, even though a written autobiography might start there. Rather, we view our early childhood in the light of later experiences that are impressed deeply in memory. Analogously, Israel's life story did not begin with Abraham or even with the Creation, although the Old Testament in its present form starts there. Rather, Israel's history had its true beginning in an historical experience so crucial that earlier happenings and subsequent experiences were seen in its light.

This decisive event—the great watershed of Israel's history—was a redemptive event, the Exodus from Egypt. This note is struck again and again in the Old Testament, particularly in the prophets and the psalms. For the pre-exilic prophets, the Exodus marks the beginning of the Israelite people, not the earlier migration of Abraham or even the Creation. In the eighth century BC, Hosea traces Israel's formation, calling, and knowledge of God to the Exodus event: "out of Egypt I called my son" (Hos. 11:1), and "I have been the Lord your God ever since the land of Egypt" (Hos. 13:4).

The theme still reverberates in literature composed late in the Old Testament period, such as Daniel 9:15 (see also the deuterocanonical Wisdom of Solomon 15:18—19:22, dated to the first century BC).

The same accent is found, though not so obviously, in the five books of Torah called the Pentateuch, the section of the Hebrew Bible regarded as most authoritative by Jewish tradition. There, the account of primeval beginnings (Gen. 1–11) and the stories of the Israelite ancestors (Gen. 12–50) function as prequels to the Exodus story. Strange as it might seem, "when we begin with Genesis and read to the book of Exodus, we are reading the story backward, as it were, for the period before Moses was remembered and interpreted in the light of the Exodus event."[1] Even in the earliest period, long before Israel's history was composed as a written epic, Israelites celebrated the Exodus story in poetry and song. An excellent example is the ancient poem found in Exodus 15:1–18, the "Song of Moses." In this poem, which displays the influence of Canaanite style and mythology,[2] the poet extols "the glorious deeds" of the God of Israel, who liberated a fugitive people from Pharaoh's army and guided them into the land of Canaan. Here we find Israel's primary confession later elaborated in epic narrative and poetry (see Pss. 77, 114).

Considering the impressive evidence of the importance of the creation-faith in pagan religions during the second millennium BC, it is curious that in Israel's faith during its formative and creative period the belief in God as creator was not stressed. For example, the "Song of Deborah" (Judg. 5), which displays striking affinities with Canaanite style, fails to mention Yahweh's power as creator in connection with his epiphany in a mighty storm for the purpose of delivering the Israelites. Here, however, the poet highlights the saving deeds ("triumphs") of Yahweh on behalf of Israel in a critical hour of history. This reticence about Creation does not downplay God's role in creation so much as shift the center of Israel's early faith from Creation to historical redemption in the cultic life of the nation. When periodic covenant renewal ceremonies were held and the tribes of Israel were asked to reaffirm their loyalty to Yahweh, these became occasions for shifting the focus from the creation-faith of Canaanite cults to historical redemption. If creation-faith was given a secondary place in Israel's liturgy, this helps explain the silence about Creation in ancient creedal confessions (e.g. Deut. 26:5–9). In Israelite festivals, Creation was a central theological

---

1. Anderson, *Understanding the Old Testament*, 11.
2. Cross, *Canaanite Myth and Hebrew Epic*, 112-44.

concern not in the sense of the creation of the world but only in the sense of the creation of the people, that is, creation as an historical event. Before creation in the cosmic sense could become a central concern for Israelite worship, creation-faith had to be related to the soteriological drama of Exodus theology.[3]

Throughout the generations Israel praised God as the Holy One who brought a band of slaves out of Egypt, formed them into a people, and gave them a future (Exod. 20:1–2). The Exodus is the central moment in Israel's history, its true beginning, the time of Israel's creation as a people. Here began the purposive movement of events that later made it possible to see all history and nature embraced within the divine design.

The Centrality of Covenant

In 1933 Walther Eichrodt published in Germany a groundbreaking polemical work in which he took aim against the entire nineteenth-century historical-critical movement. Published in English decades later under the title *Theology of the Old Testament*, Eichrodt sought to articulate what was constant and therefore normative in the Old Testament, and he determined that all of the variations and developments of Israel's religion could be seen to be in the service of a single conceptual notion: Covenant (commonly expressed by the Hebrew word *berith*). To subsume all of the Old Testament under one idea seemed risky, but to Eichrodt's credit he made an excellent choice in noting that what most characterizes Israel's vision of reality is that all things—God, Israel, humanity, the world—partake of relatedness. The implications of this insight are enormous, not only for divine-human interaction, but for the relation of God and the world. Eichrodt's readiness to relate "cosmology and creation" to covenant suggests that even "the world" is to be understood not as an independent system, but as a creature and partner to God.

This is an enormous claim when viewed in the context of Enlightenment thinking about the autonomy of the scientific world. To subsume creation under the rubric of covenant directly nullifies any attempt to understand the world either autonomously or pantheistically. Thus Eichrodt's capacity to treat creation in this way was an extraordinary insight in his time and place. Moreover, as interest grows in the relation between ecology

---

3. Anderson, *Creation versus Chaos*, 49–55.

and biblical faith, this covenantal interpretation of world reality is likely to continue to be important.

Because of the centrality of the concept of covenant, not only in the Pentateuch but throughout all scripture, we need to define the concept and place it in its historical and literary setting. As in a marriage or a business contract, a covenant describes a binding relationship between two parties (nations, individuals, or a person and God), based on commitment. The Old Testament speaks of covenants established by God with Noah (Gen. 6), Abraham (Gen. 15 and 17), Moses (Exod. 20 and Deut. 5), David (2 Sam. 7 and Ps. 89), and Israel (Jer. 31:31–34 and Ez. 36:22–38). In reality, these are differing views of the covenant between God and Israel.

In antiquity, secular covenants could be divided into two main types: (a) *parity treaties* governed relationships between equal parties, and (b) *suzerainty treaties* governed relationships between unequal parties. In the second type of covenant, the superior was known as the suzerain and the inferior as the vassal. In the Bible, God is the suzerain and humans are the vassal. This covenant agreement involves certain obligations, with sanctions (blessings or curses) to follow, depending upon the carrying out of the obligations. Often a solemn oath gives force to the covenant.

Two forms of the suzerain-vassal treaty are found in the Old Testament, depending on whether the text emphasizes God as being bound to Israel unconditionally or Israel being bound to God conditionally: (1) In a *promise covenant*, God swears an oath of unconditional loyalty to Israel. In this case God assumes the responsibility and obligations set down in the agreement. A prime example is Genesis 15, where God promises to give posterity and land to Abraham. In the account Abraham prepares the ritual of the covenant, dividing sacrificial animals into two pieces with the intention of walking through them to seal the treaty. A deep sleep, however, overcomes Abraham and God alone passes between the parts, thereby assuming full responsibility for the covenant and its promises.

(2) In a *law covenant*, both parties swear to uphold the terms of the treaty. God establishes the laws (stipulations) by which Israel is to live. Because both God and Israel are required to fulfill certain covenantal demands, both stand under what is known as the "sanction," which describes the results of obedience or disobedience to the stipulations. In conditional covenants with Israel, such as the Mosaic covenant at Sinai, God enacts the sanctions, which can be either positive (a reward or blessing) or negative (a punishment or curse).

A seal or ritual sign of blood confirmed the agreement. The significance of using blood in the ritual is important, for the Israelites believed that blood was the key to life. To seal a covenant with blood expressed the primacy of the commitment between God and Israel: it implied blessing and curse, life and death. In fact, the terminology used in the Old Testament for sealing a covenant agreement is "to cut a covenant," implying blood. The best examples are the "cutting" of the animals by Abraham in Genesis 15:10 and the "cutting" of circumcision in Genesis 17:9–14. Exodus 24 portrays the ceremony of covenant-making where the entire assembly of Israel ratifies the covenant by participating in a sacrifice. Half the blood is dashed against the altar as a symbol of God's participation in the rite, while the other half is poured into basins. Acting as covenant mediator, Moses then reads to the people "the book of the covenant" (Exod. 24:7), which the people pledged to accept and obey. Moses then dashes the blood upon them as a symbol of their participation in the rite.

The two understandings of the covenant—conditional (law) and unconditional (promise)—stood in tension with one another throughout the history of Israel's traditions. While the Old Epic tradition (which combined the earlier J and E traditions) insists that the covenant contains a conditional element that the people must take with utmost seriousness, the Priestly writers viewed the covenant as unconditional and everlasting.

Exodus Theology

Exodus 1–24, a passage that speaks of the Exodus and the birth of the nation of Israel, is less concerned with what happened historically and more concerned with the meaning behind these events. This is not to say that the narrative does not describe actual events, but to emphasize that it describes them theologically. While providing interesting stories about Moses and the Israelites, the Exodus account focuses not so much on Moses as liberator of the people but on God's redemptive role. God, not Moses, is the primary actor. Hence the Exodus story, the paradigmatic pattern of deliverance from Egyptian slavery, including the covenant enacted on Mount Sinai and the subsequent wilderness experience that led to the conquest of the Promised Land, is not recorded for its own sake, but rather as a clue to who God is and how God acts toward humanity, particularly toward those who are downtrodden and oppressed.

Despite his upbringing in Pharaoh's court, Moses identifies with the Hebrew slaves, an impulse that led to his slaying an Egyptian taskmaster. Forced to flee, Moses took refuge in "the land of Midian," an area of the Sinai Peninsula occupied by shepherds. There he marries the daughter of a Midianite priest. While tending the flocks of his father-in-law, Moses came upon "the mountain of God." Moses's encounter with the God of the ancestors (Exod. 3:13) in that sacred place and his role in the ensuing encounter with the Pharaoh is one of the masterpieces of religious literature. It was in the Midianite wilderness that God discloses essential aspects of the divine nature, including (1) God's personal name (Yahweh), which, literally untranslatable, has come to be associated with *God's creative activity* ("I am", "I cause to be") and (2) *God's redemptive activity* ("I will be with you"; see Exod. 3:12) on behalf of Israel.

Yahweh appears to Moses with memorable words: "I have observed the misery of my people . . . I have heard their cry . . . I know their sufferings, and I have come down to deliver them . . . and to bring them to a good and broad land, a land flowing with milk and honey . . ." (Exod. 3:7–8). In a fundamental declaration of faith, the ancient Israelites affirmed that their history originated in a marvelous liberation from oppression, declaring climactically the mighty deeds of God on their behalf. The verbs of the narrative sweep to a climax: God heard, God saw, God rescued.

The primary purpose of the Exodus narrative is to glorify the God of Israel, the "divine warrior" whose strong hand and outstretched arm wins the victory over Pharaoh and his armies. The text heralds five interlocking biblical themes: (1) *divine love* (when things on earth get bad, God's love is greater still); (2) *divine mercy* (God's is always "for us," never "against us"); (3) *divine initiative* (God always takes the initiative in restoring that which is broken, forgotten, or lost); (4) *divine sovereignty* (God is completely in control, even to the point of hardening Pharaoh's heart); and (5) *divine freedom* (while disclosing the divine name, God nevertheless retains the divine freedom that eludes human control: "I will be gracious to whom I will be gracious, and will show mercy on whom I will show mercy. But you cannot see my face; for no one shall see me and live"; Exod. 33:19–20).

As we learn from the third commandment, God's name is not to be taken in vain (Exod. 20:7), meaning that God cannot be manipulated or influenced magically. This commandment, read contextually, is less a prohibition against using God's name as a curse and more against attempting to use worship or religious ritual to manipulate or control God in a possessive sense. The God who speaks to Moses is the Lord, not the servant of the people. From this time forward, the question "what is God like?" would be answered in concrete historical events. That is precisely the point of the conquest with Pharaoh, the plagues against Egypt, the crossing of the sea, the guidance through the wilderness, and the conquest of the Promised Land. Because God is sovereign, God controls history, the powers of nature, and on occasion, even the human heart. In describing the Pharaoh, the text states repeatedly that God hardened Pharaoh's heart, but also that Pharaoh hardens his own heart. The narrator tells the story in a way that allows for human obstinacy while ultimately glorifying the God of Israel. Pharaoh is given freedom, but not so much that he can exceed the bounds of God's sovereign control (see Rom. 9:17–18).

The Covenant at Sinai

The Exodus account is firmly embedded into the story of Israel's theological history. It is part of the narrative that runs from Genesis 12 to 2 Kings 25. The first nineteen chapters of Exodus tell the story of the Israelites' bondage in Egypt and their deliverance by Yahweh. It describes the call of Moses and his powerful encounters with Pharaoh. It presents the story of the plagues on Egypt, culminating in the visit by the angel of death and the institution of the festival of the Passover. Next, Moses leads the Israelites out of Egypt and through the sea. The book of Exodus then describes their journey in the wilderness until, in chapter 19, the Israelites arrive at Mount Sinai, where God calls them into covenant relationship. The Ten Commandments in Exodus 20 and the laws that follow are part of this story.

The book of Leviticus records additional priestly legislation, presented as part of a dialogue between God and Moses. The book of Numbers picks up the narrative in the second year after the Exodus (Numb. 1:1) and describes the Israelites' journeys and wanderings for the next forty years (Numb. 33:38). Central to this story is the forty years of wandering that result from Israel's fear of entering the Promised Land, based on a negative account by ten of twelve spies sent to report on the land (by comparison to the Canaanites "we seemed like grasshoppers"; Numb. 13:32–33). The book of Deuteronomy records a series of speeches attributed to Moses just prior to Israel's entry into Canaan. In the overall story, a new generation has replaced the fearful generation punished by God for their refusal to enter the land. Deuteronomy (the word means "second law" or retelling of the law) represents a restatement of the covenant God made with the previous generation on Mount Sinai forty years earlier. The events of Deuteronomy flow into the book of Joshua, where the story continues without interruption.

Exodus 1–24 deals with two series of events: the deliverance from Egypt and the making of the covenant at Sinai. These two accounts are intertwined, the first a preparation for the second (see Exod. 3:12), and the second based theologically on the first. A small literary unit at the beginning of Exodus 19 stresses the essential connection between these traditions. This passage (Exod. 19:4–7), occurring right after the notice of Israel's arrival at Sinai, portrays God as carrying the people, like an eagle lifting its young, toward the mountain rendezvous: "I bore you on eagles' wings and brought you to myself. Now therefore, if you obey my voice and keep my covenant, you shall be my treasured possession out of all the peoples. Indeed, the whole earth is mine, but you shall be for me a priestly kingdom and a holy nation."

The restrained and rhythmic style of the passage suggests that this unit may have circulated independently, shaped possibly by catechetical usage, perhaps in connection with services of covenant renewal. At Sinai the people of Israel experienced what Moses had sensed earlier at that same sacred mountain—that God wished to relate to humanity through a covenant community, a people with a special vocation: the ordering of life according to God's sovereign demands. Here we find a unique characteristic of Israel's faith: the strange combination of the universal and the particular. God's sovereignty knows no limits ("the whole earth is mine"; Exod. 19:5), yet out of many peoples God singles out one people, not for privilege but for a task. They are to be a "priestly kingdom" (Exod. 19:6), that is, a community separated from the world and consecrated to the service of God (see 1 Pet. 2:5, 9–10).

The covenant at Sinai is generally understood to exemplify a law or conditional covenant, since the covenant rite includes the assent of the people: "if you obey my voice and keep my covenant . . ." (Exod. 19:5). This tradition, in contrast to the Priestly tradition, emphasizes the voluntary acceptance of the covenant by the people ("The people all answered as one: 'Everything that the Lord has spoken we will do'"; Exod. 19:8), and places severe consequences upon the covenant-breaker. This view is expressed by later Israelite prophets who announced the people's failure to obey God's voice and threatened them with divine judgment for breaking the covenant.

The present diverse form of the Pentateuch shows how successive generations continued to respond to the demands of the covenant under changing historical circumstances: The Priestly legislation found in Exodus 25–31 bears the stamp of later times; the Covenant Code (Exod. 21–23) betrays the interests of an agricultural rather than a wilderness environment; and a group of ritual laws in Exodus 34:10–26 reflects a Canaanite background. By a process of reduction, not much is left that comes from the time of Moses. Nevertheless, studies of the form and content of laws in the Pentateuch—particularly the Ten Commandments (the Decalogue)—indicate that the Jewish tradition tracing the covenant law back to Moses is fundamentally authentic.

A study of international treaties or ancient covenants that governed the relationships between peoples during the period before David has thrown light on the relationship between covenant and law. Among the archives of the ancient Hittites (a people who ruled in Asia Minor, now modern Turkey, from 1600 to 1200 BC) archaeologists have found copies of treaties between the Hittite suzerain and vassal states. The treaty form includes several major elements:

1. *Preamble*: the parties are identified; the purpose is to inspire awe for the suzerain.
2. *Historical prologue*: the suzerain rehearses benevolent deeds performed on behalf of the vassal; the purpose is to inspire gratitude.
3. *Stipulations*: the duties and obligations of the vassal are listed.
4. *Documentary clause*: provisions are made for deposit of copies of the treaty in the temples of both parties and for periodic public reading by the vassal.
5. *Witnesses to the treaty*: the gods of both parties are listed; included among the witnesses are forces of nature such as heaven, wind, mountains and rivers.
6. *Dual sanctions*: this is the binding element. Blessings are bestowed on the vassal who obeys the terms of the treaty, but curses await the vassal who is unfaithful. The threat of judgment, even total destruction, falls upon a vassal people that violate the treaty.

The striking correlation between this treaty form and the Mosaic covenant in Exodus 20–24 leads many scholars to argue that it must have been influential for the biblical portrayal of Yahweh's relationship with the

Israelites. Compare, for instance, the preamble and the historical prologue with Exodus 20:2; the stipulations with the Decalogue; the documentary clause with the tablets of stone upon which the commandments are recorded, or "the book of the covenant" which is written down by Moses and read in the hearing of the people (Exod. 24:4, 7; see also the Shema in Deut. 6:4-9 and 11:18-21); and the sanctions in the Second Commandment (Exod. 20:5-6.

In Deuteronomy 11 and 28 Israel is reminded that its future depends on the response of God's requirements. The people confront a crucial decision, with the alternatives of blessing or curse (see 11:26-29; 27:15-26, an ancient list of twelve curses; 28:1-14 [blessings] and 28:15-68 [curses]; notice how 30:15-20 combines the fifth and sixth elements of the treaty pattern: "I call heaven and earth to witness against you today that I have set before you life and death, blessings and curses. Choose life so that you and your descendants may live..."). The governing purpose of Deuteronomy is to summon Israel to a renewal of its covenant with God.

An important feature of the Suzerainty Treaty, associated with the fourth element (documentary clause), is the covenant renewal ceremony. This annual ceremony, held first at Shechem (see Joshua 24) and later at other central sanctuaries such as Shiloh, was an occasion for the recitation of laws and narratives binding on all Israel. Here the covenant would be read and the Israelites would respond with a pledge of allegiance. The covenant renewal service described in Joshua 24 contains features that are strikingly similar to the Suzerainty Treaty, including a preamble (24:2); a historical prologue (24:2-13); stipulations (24:14-24); documentary clause (24:25-26); witnesses to the treaty (24:22, 27); and dual sanctions (24:20). The parallel is almost exact if one associates this ceremony with other passages describing ritual acts that took place at Shechem, such as Joshua 8:30-35 and Deuteronomy 27.

History in the Old Testament is the history of a covenant relationship. This relationship is initiated and established by God, the sovereign Lord (Suzerain); as vassals, humans respond to it and bind themselves in obedience. The covenant involves not only obligations toward God but obligations toward the other members of the community. The legal stipulations are binding, yet not static. They can be adaptable to new cultural circumstances, but the basic principle remains constant: persons are absolutely responsible to one another (Second Table of the Law, commandments 5-10) because they are absolutely responsible to God (First Table of the Law, commandments 1–4).

Ethical responsibility is motivated by gratitude for what God has done. Nevertheless, the Mosaic covenant contains a conditional element: "*If* you will obey my voice and keep my covenant . . ." (Exod. 19:5). Faithfulness to the covenant yields blessing, betrayal brings judgment. This element of the covenant would become central to the great prophets of Israel, for despite God's faithfulness, Israel would be unfaithful. While there are consequences for betrayal, the biblical story places the accent on divine grace. The following biblical pattern unfolds: God establishes the covenant; humans break the covenant; God restores the covenant. Hence the covenant is re-enacted and re-established.

The Prophetic Task: The Call to Covenant Loyalty

The most fully developed law covenant in the Old Testament is the Mosaic covenant described in Exodus 19–23. This covenant provided the laws and ordinances by which Hebraic society was to function. It governed the relationship between God and the Hebrews and determined the code of conduct with the Israelite society. Although covenant law at times was altered, the basic principles upon which it rested did not. In the Old Testament, covenant statutes were based upon justice, righteousness, and steadfast love.[4]

In the Old Testament, the term justice (*mishpat*) denotes the rights and duties of each party to fulfill their obligations under the covenantal law. These laws, however, refer not only to the vertical relationship with God, but also to the horizontal relationship between humans, that is, to society as a whole. The Old Testament articulated the administration of legal justice under the concept of Lex Talionis, meaning that punishment or restitution should be in proportion to what a person deserves. This law of retribution, known popularly as "life for life, eye for eye, tooth for tooth" (see Deut. 19:19–21), means that the community would not tolerate retaliation greater than the actual injury done.

Whereas the Hebrew word for justice refers to the rights and duties of covenant participants, the Hebrew word for righteousness (*zedek*) pertains

---

4. The segment on justice, righteousness, and steadfast love is adapted from Bowne and Currid, "Biblical Society," 158–60.

to the conduct or attitude of the covenant people. It is often used of God and man having the right and consistent conduct in all matters of life, social and religious. Ultimately, righteousness is an attribute of God, namely, God's perfection in all areas of covenantal conduct. Because humans are not perfect or consistent in their conduct, the Old Testament understands human righteousness not as a human attribute but as a human response. Noah "found favor in the sight of the Lord" (Gen. 6:8) and Job was "blameless and upright" (Job 2:3) not because they were perfect but because their lives largely reflected the righteousness of God.

If justice and righteousness were the only covenant principles, the relationship between God and humanity would remain strictly legal. The divine-human relationship, however, transcends impersonal legal and moral codes of conduct, for it is based on the concept of *hesed*, a Hebrew word usually translated as "loving-kindness" but better understood as steadfast love or loyalty, a covenant love that presupposes the mutuality of relationship: "For I desire steadfast love and not sacrifice, the knowledge of God rather than burnt offerings" (Hos. 6:6). The covenant love of Yahweh is a faithful love, a steadfast unshakeable maintenance of the covenantal relationship. Both parties must have a deep love and loyalty for the other. As with the other principles discussed, human beings are to build a *hesed* relationship not only with God but with each other as well.

These principles, and their accompanying laws and application, provide the basis for Israelite society. The Hebrews, both individually and communally, were to abide by these principles and regulations in order to maintain a proper relationship with God and with one another. The Israelites' failure to live by these basic principles, however, led to injustice at all levels of society, a state of heart and mind that resulted in prophetic condemnation.

The task and vocation of biblical prophets are today greatly misunderstood. Popularly viewed, the role of the prophet is to predict future events. Modern scholarship downplays this understanding of the role of prophets. Biblical scholars now understand the prophetic role as having involved three distinct yet related tasks, each with a different temporal focus: (a) they were predictors of the future (*foretelling*); (b) they were reformers who kept alive the Mosaic past through continuous appeal to the theocratic ideals expressed in the covenants (*retelling*); and (c) they were social critics who spoke out boldly and without compromise against current disobedience and disbelief within the social, religious, and political establishment (*forthtelling*). Of the three tasks, the most significant was forthtelling and the least significant was foretelling. Biblical prophets rarely, if ever, made open predictions about the future, and when they did so, the predictions were linked to their role as social critics, which focused on the consequences for unrepentance. The prophet's futuristic role was associated primarily with the certainty of the coming of the Lord, a coming to make things right through judgment and reward.

The key to understanding the Old Testament prophets is their relationship to the covenant. Of special importance in understanding the prophets is what can be called the "covenant lawsuit," a concept related to the ancient Hittite suzerainty treaties. There we find a provision related to covenant disloyalty. In cases where a vassal failed to fulfill the stipulations of a sworn treaty, the suzerain would institute a lawsuit, a procedure carried out through messengers and consisting of two distinct stages: The first stage consisted of *warnings*, delivered by the messenger, reminding the vassal of the suzerain's benefits and of the stipulations agreed upon. In addition, the vassal would be reminded of the curses or sanctions of the covenant. Using interrogation, the messenger would require an explanation of the vassal's offenses against the suzerain, charging the vassal with a change in behavior and warning of the vanity of appealing to alien help as a means of escaping the consequences. Finally, the messenger would issue an *ultimatum*: "if you continue, the curses will go into effect." If the messenger of the suzerain was rejected, the legal process moved into the second distinct stage: *declaration of war* as an execution of the sanctions of the treaty.

Like messengers of the Hittite suzerain, the mission of the Old Testament prophets was to serve as Yahweh's messengers to enforce the covenant mediated to Israel through Moses. Amos, the first of the classical writing prophets, was a vigorous upholder of the Mosaic tradition. The keynote of Amos's prophecy is struck in Amos 3:1–8, a passage that begins by recalling the crucial event of Israel's history: the Exodus from Egypt. Through God's action in this event, Israel had become a "family" bound together by religious loyalty. Through this event God had entered into a covenant relationship with Israel: "You only have I known of all the families of the earth; therefore I will punish you for all your iniquities" (Amos 3:2).

This passage, marked by solemnity, raises immediate questions: In what sense is it true that Yahweh has known only Israel, and why the "therefore"? What is the logical connection between God's knowledge of Israel and her fate? The passage makes little sense unless we know that we have here a usage of "know" borrowed from international relations. Hittite and other ancient Near Eastern texts reveal that "to know" in this technical legal sense means to recognize treaty stipulations as binding. In this context the term could be translated "recognize" or "be loyal to" a suzerain.[5] This clarification makes Amos's terminology understandable. Yahweh had recognized only Israel as legitimate servants, "therefore," since this sort of covenant involves obligations that were not fulfilled, "I will punish you for all your iniquities."

Other prophets speak in the same way. Jeremiah uses "know" in this way when describing a future repentance of the people: "I will give them a heart to know that I am the Lord; and they shall be my people and I will be their God, for they shall return to me with their whole heart" (Jer. 24:7). That this kind of knowledge is closely related to the people's conduct is evident from another passage in Jeremiah, where the prophet indicts the reigning monarch for thinking that being king is a matter of privilege rather than of justice: "Are you a king because you compete in cedar? Did not your father eat and drink and do justice and righteousness? . . . He judged the cause of the poor and needy . . . Is not this to know me?" (Jer. 22:15–16).

Hosea, best known for his extended use of the marriage metaphor to describe the relationship between Yahweh and Israel, makes the same connection. "Hear the word of the Lord, O people of Israel; for the Lord has an indictment [lawsuit] against the inhabitants of the land. There is no faithfulness or loyalty, and no knowledge of God in the land. Swearing, lying, and murder, and stealing and adultery break out; bloodshed follows bloodshed. Therefore the land mourns . . ." (Hosea 4:1–3a). In addition to using the technical Hebrew term meaning "covenant lawsuit" (*rîb*), Hosea provides a list of specific words very much like the Ten Commandments.

Along with Hosea 4, various additional texts in the prophetic literature contain references to the covenant lawsuit literary form, including Isaiah 1 and Jeremiah 2, but the classic passage is Micah 6:1–8, often cited as the sum and substance of Old Testament ethics. Like the book's opening oracle, this passage employs the imagery of a controversy in a law court. Notice the dramatic structure of the lawsuit pattern:[6]

A. *Summons* (Mic. 6:1–2): the trial opens with a summons by the prophet, who acts as God's prosecuting attorney. As we find in Hittite and other ancient international treaty patterns, the mountains serve as witnesses, before which Israel must present its case.

5. Hillers, *Covenant*, 121–22.
6. Anderson, *Understanding the Old Testament*, 311–12.

B. *The Plaintiff's Charge* (Mic. 6:3–5): Here God, through the prophetic attorney, interrogates the people, appealing to Israel's historical traditions rather than to specific laws recorded in a treaty. The appeal is based on events that displayed *hesed* or covenant love toward the people, beginning with the Exodus from Egypt and culminating in the occupation of the Promised Land. The prophet is appalled at the incongruity between God's benevolent deeds and Israel's disloyalty.

C. *The Defendant's Plea* (Mic. 6:6–7): Finally Israel speaks, but finds no case to plead save to confess betrayal of the covenant. Empty religious ritual does not satisfy the covenant demands, but seemingly adds to the offense.

D. *The Indictment* (Mic. 6:8): The passage reaches a climax as the prophet proclaims the essence of the covenant stipulations: "to do justice (*mishpat*), to love kindness (*hesed*), and to walk humbly with God." This simple statement expresses the prophetic demand for justice, righteousness, and steadfast love. Is this not to know God?

The prophets predict that in the end there will only be a remnant who will be faithful, hence only a portion of the people will experience covenant blessing. The prophets are often considered to have been messengers of doom, because they proclaimed a message of judgment. The truth is that before there can be good news, there must be truthtelling. Like God's *opus alienum* ("strange deed") in Isaiah 28:21, where God judges by fire his own people as a means to judge their enemies, the redemptive work of God is alien, more like the work of a surgeon—who uses a scalpel to cut living tissue, even stuffing gauze into the wound to keep the incision open until the blood flows red and the poison is gone—than like a parent, who uses "tough love" to discipline a child. The analogy applies to John 3:16, which can be revised to read: For God so loved the world that he bled—until his blood flowed red—that whosoever accepts this love may live in God's presence eternally.

The story of the Old Testament is the record of Israel's failure to live by covenant principles. Because God's people broke their covenant with God, they were eventually conquered by an invading nation, Babylon, and were taken into exile. But all hope is not lost. In the latter years of Israel's history the prophet Jeremiah promised that God would do something new in the future, once again restoring the people to proper relationship with God and one another.

Chapter 7

Community

As it now stands, the Pentateuch begins with an extended prologue to the Exodus story: the account of primeval beginnings (Gen. 1–11) and the stories of the Israelite ancestors (Gen. 12–50). As previously noted, when we begin with Genesis and read to the book of Exodus, we are reading the story backward, as it were, for the period before Moses was remembered and interpreted in the light of the Exodus event. In a later time of theological reflection, Israel would trace its self-understanding back beyond the Exodus to the first Hebrew, Abraham (see Gen. 14:13), portraying its election (its "call" by God) in the election of Abraham.

As the Exodus story models the covenant of law, the Abraham story (see Genesis 11:31—25:10) models the covenant of promise. Both covenantal models, the Mosaic and the Abrahamic, are foundational for understanding Israel's identity as community of faith. The first elucidates Israel's legal dimension as people of God (Israel as theocratic community), the second Israel's social dimension as people of God (Israel as collective community). In the Bible, when God calls an individual to faith, God is not so much interested in singular faith but in collective witness. Hence the provisions for land and posterity (see Genesis 12:1–2), both necessary for social stability. The role of community, as of authentic religion, is to unify people, not to divide them (see Ps. 133:1). While not a biblical text, a motto for community might well be "united we stand, divided we fall."

The general theme of the patriarchal period is "the promise to the ancestors." We will discuss this motif under three subheadings: (1) election, (2) the covenant with Abraham, and (3) the testing of faith (the delay of the promise).

The Election (the "Call") of Israel

Election, the idea of being "called" or chosen by God, is an essential biblical motif, indispensable to Israel's identity and later to Christian self-understanding. As we saw in the Mosaic tradition, God takes the initiative in establishing the covenant relationship. God enters the historical situation in an act of self-giving (disclosure of the divine name) and in acts of benevolence toward a people in distress. Israel does not first choose God, but rather is chosen by God.

Scholars emphasize that the underlying significance of the patriarchal stories in Genesis is not so much the stories of the patriarchs but the story of Israel's self-understanding. At the time this material was put into writing, the main question was not, "Who are Abraham, Isaac, Jacob, and Joseph?" but "Who is Israel?" Israel was grappling with her identity, her self-understanding as a people called by God. The theological answer was found in the doctrine of election.

What does election mean? The biblical answer is given in the portrayal of Abraham, Isaac, and Jacob, patriarchs whose lives were characterized by the following traits:

a. They *lived by faith in God*. In Abraham, Israel understands something about herself, that she has been called into existence by God himself, that she has been created by God's initiative and preserved by God's grace. The story of Abraham becomes the prototypical model for the journey of faith.

b. They were *called to be a servant people*. Election does not mean that one people is chosen because they are better than others, but rather that they are called to spread God's grace. God's purpose is seen in Genesis 12:3 ("in you all the families of the earth shall be blessed"); it is a universal purpose, one that moves from particulars to universals, from individuals to communities and nations. In Abraham, God brings one person of faith into existence in order that God's blessing might be extended to all humanity. This is the Bible's stress on election, that when God calls a people, they are called to service, and the rest of the Old Testament, and then the Gospels and Epistles, show what it means to be a servant people. The Bible makes it clear that Israel's calling is part of God's healing intention (the biblical word for healing, health, wholeness, and goodness is "salvation," similar in meaning to the Hebrew word *shalom*). In the Bible, the election of a people becomes the basis for good news, what the New Testament calls "gospel."

c. They were *called to pilgrimage*, namely, to a life of mobility, movement, and change. Biblical faith is a calling faith, a calling to go forth, to be on the way, to be moving in God's direction, to be pioneers of faith. Abraham was told to break his ties with his land and his former security, a way of life that up to that point had been deeply rooted to the land. Like Abraham, God's people are called to a nomadic consciousness. We see that clearly in the prophetic consciousness, a stance counter-cultural in the sense that one could be both an agent of change and a critic of the established order. The prophetic message was that God was doing a new thing. As we see in Abraham, faith is not so much consent or agreement as something dynamic, manifested in movement. So Abraham is the ancestor of a pilgrim people, and his story highlights the themes of mobility and change, meaning that when faith becomes lifeless, stagnant, or frozen, whether in institutions with superiority complexes or in self-serving lifestyles, God breaks them down and forces his people into radical recommitment. The story of Abraham and the patriarchs is the story of God on the move with his people.

The Covenant with Abraham

The divine address in Genesis 12:1-3 provides the theological foundation for interpreting the Ancestral tradition. Here God singles out one individual and opens an expansive horizon before him. The passage consists of three elements:

- *The command* (12:1): with the word "Go," God initiates the relationship. This corresponds to the beginning of Israel's national history in Exodus 1.

- *The promise* (12:1-2): under the promise of land and posterity God guides the patriarchs and Israel into the future. The promise is repeated to each patriarch, reinforcing the element of hope.

- *The blessing* (12:2-3): the promise of blessing unfolds in three stages, from those close at hand to all the races of the world.

From the broad beginning of the Primeval tradition (Genesis 1-11), the scope narrows until it concentrates upon the figure of Abraham, the ancestor of the people chosen for a special task in God's purpose for humanity. Coming almost immediately after the story of the Tower of Babel (Gen. 11:1-9), which presents a dark picture of human pride and ambition, the story of the call of Abraham establishes a new beginning for humanity. Whereas the builders at Babel failed in their ambition to make a name for themselves (to establish genuine community, Gen. 11:4), by contrast, God promises to make Abraham's name great (Gen. 12:2), that is, to bless Abraham with posterity and land and through him to model the meaning of community. Israel's greatness will lie not in its ambitions or achievements, but in its corporate witness to the God who acts to overcome the confusion, disharmony, and violence perpetrated by covenant-breakers. To possess a land, to become a great nation, to be a blessing to the peoples of the earth—this threefold divine promise punctuates the patriarchal narrative.

In Genesis, the covenant with Abraham is a doublet (narrated twice), combining the accounts of the Yahwist (chapter 15) and Priestly (chapter 17) writers. Theologically, chapter 15 is pivotal for the Abrahamic tradition. Many scholars judge this passage to be the oldest statement of Abrahamic faith. In the archaic covenant ceremony described in the J passage in 15:7–21, the covenant is ratified by Yahweh. God imposes no conditions upon Abraham, binding himself unconditionally to the covenant promise. Similarly, the P version of the Abrahamic covenant found in Genesis 17 is unilateral. It is unconditional, based solely upon the word of El Shaddai (God Almighty). Although Abraham binds himself to God by the act of circumcision, that ritual is understood as the external sign of membership in the covenant community, not the conditional basis of the covenant, which is described as everlasting (17:7).

The Testing of Faith (Delay of the Promise)

In Israel's ancestral period, a blessing or curse was believed to have immediate effect. Israel's Old Epic narrative, however, institutes a major change. The blessing is postponed to the future, beyond the lifetime of the original recipients. Hence the blessing becomes a promise. Postponement of the promise means that the whole ancestral period becomes an interim between promise and fulfillment, with the resulting tensions and anxieties of faith. This is a lesson not only for the patriarchs or for Israel, but for all people of faith. When the interim seems unbearably extended, people raise cries of lament, as in Psalm 13:1 ("How long, O Lord? Will you forget me forever?") and Psalm 22:1 ("My God, why have you forsaken me?").

An initial answer appears in Genesis 15:6: "And [Abraham] believed the Lord, and the Lord reckoned it to him as righteousness." The root of the

Hebrew word "believe" is "amen," meaning that Abraham trusted in God's faithfulness. While the word "faith" is sometimes taken to mean "belief in certain doctrines as true," that is not the connotation here. Unlike belief, which can be abstract, trust is relational. Whereas other nations lived in fear and uncertainty, Israel was to rely upon God's faithfulness. The concept of promise, coming from a trustworthy God, is hopeful, as we are reminded by an unknown poet encouraging exiled Jews in Babylon: "those who wait for the Lord shall renew their strength, they shall mount up with wings like eagles, they shall run and not be weary, they shall walk and not faint" (Isa. 40:31).

As we know from the biblical narrative, Abraham did not always respond to his circumstances with trust and hope. As all biblical personalities, indeed as people of faith in general, Abraham is a flawed individual with a steep learning curve. He encounters the tension in God's promise almost immediately, beginning in Egypt, where he attempts to deceive the Pharaoh in order to keep the promise alive (see Gen. 12:10–20). Deceit is followed by distrust in chapter 16, where he tries to force God's hand by cohabiting with Sarah's servant Hagar. Once again God intervenes, for Ishmael, the child born of Hagar, is not to be the child of promise. When Abraham is ninety-nine years old, God repeats the promise that Sarah will conceive, and Abraham responds with laughter (17:17); the promise has become absurd. Later, after Isaac's birth, Abraham's faith is taken to the limit.

The moving account of Abraham's testing in Genesis 22 brings to a climax the history of God's promise to the patriarchs. Here we are told that Abraham is commanded by God to sacrifice his only son, whom he dearly loved. Isaac was the child of the promise, and God now asks Abraham to sacrifice the only means by which the promise can be fulfilled. Abraham undergoes the supreme trial as he prepares to slay Isaac, thereby sacrificing the future of Israel on the altar. Only when the knife is upraised does God intervene. In that critical moment Abraham spies a ram caught in a thicket, which he offers in place of Isaac. Once again the promise is renewed (see Gen 22:16–18).

On almost every level, this story is disturbing. It raises questions that border on the absurd. How could Abraham agree to such a command? How did he know the command was from God? And if he could be sure, how could God make such immoral demands of Abraham? Is God's word to be obeyed even when obedience is contradicted by reason? Is faith the triumph of obedience over conscience? If so, what is the role of conscience in religion?

Verse 8, which seems to be structurally central to the narrative, merits special attention. There, in a statement of utter trust and confidence, we are told that God will provide. The statement, of course, is open-ended, for we are not told all that we want to know. Abraham cannot tell Isaac all he wants to know because Abraham himself does not know. He does not know if Isaac is God's act of provision or whether God will provide a rescue for Isaac. Abraham does not know, but he trusts God unreservedly. The narrative leads to a new disclosure of God. At the beginning, God is the tester (Gen. 22:1); at the end, God is the provider (Gen. 22:14). The fundamental issue at stake here, as in all scripture, is the faithfulness of God.

Søren Kierkegaard (1813–1855), the noted Danish Christian existentialist, made an important contribution to the religious journey in his formulation of three levels of existence or stages through which humans go in their ascent toward God. On the first level, which he labeled the aesthetic stage, individuals are ruled by their senses. Such persons live solely for the present, and particularly for self-gratification. The second level, the ethical stage, requires that one abandon attitudes of selfishness and embrace universal standards, making commitments to others. Here moral standards and obligations are adopted as dictated by reason. The third and final stage, which he called the religious stage, entails a life of faith. In each stage, Kierkegaard selected a figure from literature or history as an example. For the model of the religious stage of life, the highest level through which humans go in their ascent toward God, he selected Abraham, whose trust of God and unwavering obedience led him to choose to sacrifice his only son Isaac, even in the face of absurdity, for to question God would be to place reason over faith. In selecting this example, Kierkegaard was not denying the validity of ethics. He stated that the individual who is called to break with the ethical must first be ethical, that is, must first have subordinated to universal morality. The break, when one is called to make it, is made in "fear and trembling" and not arrogantly or proudly. In this final stage, the ethical is not abolished but dethroned by a higher purpose or end, a phenomenon he described as the "teleological suspension of the ethical." The key to this final stage is not the commendable humanistic goal of universal duty to others, but the unqualified giving of oneself to God. If one doesn't go beyond the ethical, beyond moral obligation, one cannot properly say that one is related to God, or obedient to God. Ethical duty, he believed, must ultimately lead to God, but since it usually leads to humanity (i.e. to humanism), then this stage must be transcended. An absolute relationship to an absolute (God) requires a relative relationship to relative ends. And for Kierkegaard, everything other than God is relative.

In the nineteenth century Kierkegaard was a voice crying in the wilderness of a complacent civilization, for his one passion was to show what it meant to be a Christian. The church in his day was so institutionalized, he argued, that it was no longer Christian; in fact, it had become "impossible to be a Christian in Christendom."

While Kierkegaard concluded that individuals were obligated to obey divine commands even if they knew the command to be immoral, others have questioned Abraham's compliant obedience. The following interpretations of Abraham's faith reflect two divergent views of religious duty.

1. Kierkegaard views Abraham as a religious hero, whose fidelity to God transcends his love of his son. In his willingness to sacrifice Isaac, Abraham passes the test of unconditional obedience. In the Jewish liturgy, Abraham is honored for his willingness to sacrifice the promised future of his people out of trust in God. In Christian theology, Isaac is viewed as a prefiguration of Christ and Abraham typifies God, who so loved the world that he gave his only son, sacrificing him vicariously as the perfect substitute for humanity. From that point of view, believers should obey the directives of divine authority without question. Conscience cannot be allowed to contradict the divine imperative.

2. An alternative interpretation of the biblical account emphasizes the role of the angel of the Lord. On this reading, the angel who stays Abraham's hand in Genesis 22:11–12 symbolizes Abraham's moral conscience, and Abraham's acceptance of the voice of the Lord's angel over God's commanding voice expresses his faith in a moral God who could not will the death of an innocent. Earlier in Genesis we read about God's threat against Sodom and Gomorrah, at which time Abraham challenged the morality of God's plan: "Will you indeed sweep away the righteous with the wicked?" (Gen. 18:23). Neither the biblical nor the theological tradition regards Abraham's rhetorical opposition to God's intention as a treasonable act against divine sovereignty. On the contrary, Abraham's dissent is grounded in God's goodness and fairness: "Shall not the Judge of all the earth do what is just?" (Gen. 18:25).

Which is needed today? Is it blind allegiance, such as might be commanded in the first approach, or do we need individuals with the courage to pursue the heroic role of moral conscience in religion, challenging mortal authorities when they contradict fairness and goodness? Holy dissent against God and in the name of God is a unique Judaic feature, one that Christians and Muslims are exhorted to emulate. In the Bible, Moses is depicted as rising on several occasions to challenge God's decision, and each time Moses succeeded in overturning God's judgment (Exod. 32:32; Deut. 9:19–20; 10:10). According to Rabbi Harold Schulweis, "Far from being considered acts of insubordination, these acts of dissent testify to the high status accorded to human conscience."[1] Although rebellion against God is certainly not condoned in the Bible, the name "Israel"—the name given to Jacob and to his posterity—is said to mean: "those who strive with God . . . and win."

This understanding of the role of conscience in religion challenges traditional views of revelation. If conscience is the hyphen in the human-divine covenant, revelation becomes "a dialogue of reciprocal covenant, an ongoing process of listening and interpreting, of receiving and giving. Awareness of having entered the covenant makes it impossible to separate the divine and human element in the encounter of revelation . . . The test of the believer is not whether he believes or whether he obeys, but what he believes and what he will not believe, what he obeys and what he will not obey."[2]

The story of Abraham sheds valuable light into the biblical vision regarding social relations and the establishment of community. Whereas secular models of society declare human beings to be the center and focus of culture, biblical theology argues that all culture building and social progress depend on God's character and norms. As modern individuals, should we pick one view and discard the other? I suggest that they are not mutually exclusive. Society does begin with individuals, but with individuals guided through conscience by God.

The message of Israel's ancestral accounts is summarized magnificently in the words of Joseph to his brothers: "Even though you intended to do harm to me, God intended it for good, in order to preserve a numerous people, as he is doing today" (Gen. 50:20). This passage encapsulates the patriarchal and Exodus narratives: Human affairs are not governed by the evil designs of human beings, or by economic and political forces, but by the overruling providence of God, who works for good in all things

---

1. Schulweis, *Those Who Can't Believe*, 85.
2. Ibid., 87–88.

(compare Gen. 45:5–8). As these stories make clear, the promise made to Abraham—that through Israel all nations would be blessed—was moving toward fulfillment.

The Deuteronomistic History

The Pentateuch ends with Moses dead and Israel camped on the east bank of the Jordan, poised to conquer the land of Canaan. A central theme of the J tradition is the promise that Israel would soon possess that land. While it is likely that J originally included an account of how the promise of the land was fulfilled, the J source ends abruptly, as do E and P, at the end of the book of Deuteronomy. The narrative of the books of Joshua, Judges, Samuel, and Kings (these books make up the "Former Prophets" in the Hebrew Bible) are part of a larger work called the Deuteronomistic history because of their close connection with the book of Deuteronomy, which functions as a sort of theological and thematic preface to that historical narrative.

Covering Israel's history for over six centuries, the Deuteronomistic history is the earliest extended historical narrative known from ancient times. Three themes are prominent in that account: (1) the exclusive worship of Yahweh as a prerequisite for Israel's continued possession of the Promised Land (idolatry will result in divine punishment); (2) the centrality of the city of Jerusalem as the only legitimate place of worship; and (3) the unconditional covenant with David, whereby Yahweh establishes the dynasty founded by David.

The Tribal Confederacy: The Period of the Judges

The books of Joshua and Judges continue the Deuteronomistic presentation of Israel's history in the Promised Land of Canaan, but they do so from differing perspectives. The book of Joshua presents an ideal picture of Israel united in worship of Yahweh alone, united also under the leadership of a divinely designated successor to Moses in fighting against their enemies. The book of Judges provides a more realistic assessment of life in Canaan, relating how the Israelites repeatedly failed to live up to the ideals of monotheism and the confederacy, while providing a less militaristic and more incremental approach to territorial acquisition.

The period of the judges follows a neat pattern that illustrates a basic theological conviction: Incomplete obedience yields incomplete victory. This cycle or pattern, repeated seven times throughout the book of Judges, consists of four elements that follow one another consecutively, as outlined in Judges 2:11–-3:16: (1) Disobedience (idolatry); (2) Punishment (oppression by enemies); (3) Repentance (remorse); and (4) Deliverance (God raises a judge and the land enjoys rest).

The pattern usually begins with a formulaic introduction: "Then the Israelites did what was evil in the sight of the Lord" and ends with "So the land had rest _____ years." In each instance the Israelites tended to move away from Yahweh during times of relative prosperity. While the pattern does not do justice to the complexity of events in the period of the judges, it is instructive, for history teaches that the downfall of a people often begins not with external military pressure, but with internal moral and spiritual decay. The Deuteronomistic historians emphasized the central truth that Israel's vitality and solidarity lay in a united loyalty to their God. When their covenant faith was strong, Israel was in a better position to cope with the inrush of foreign ideas and armies. In like manner, when their covenant faith was weakened under pressure from the surrounding culture, Israel became easy prey to economic, political, and military crises.

In addition to their focus on the consequences of worshiping other gods, another topic of the Deuteronomistic historians in the book of Judges is kingship, which they disparage. In the earlier part of the book kingship is experimented with and divinely rejected (see the story of Abimelech in Judges 9), and four times in the book, including its final verse, we are told: "In those days there was no king in Israel; every man did what was right in his own eyes." Rather than human kingship, the book of Judges advocates divine kingship: "The Lord will rule over you" (Judg. 8:23). One would be correct to call this a theocracy, but that term, meaning "rule by God," is extremely elastic, so flexible as to be relatively meaningless unless accompanied by some account of what practical shape the divine rule takes. The term theocracy can refer to a society controlled by a caste of priests; it can refer to divine rule; or it may be reduced to a vague notion of "one nation, under God." The particular shape which the rule of Yahweh took under the judges was none of the above but was in part determined by the pact between God and the Israelite tribes.

The negative judgment about human kingship is correct, at least politically. Because there was no king in Israel, there was no court, no courtiers, no extensive trade with other lands, no standing army, no tax-collecting, no royal decrees, and no royal judges—in short, none of the discipline and complexity that monarchy would one day provide.

But what does it mean to say that God is king? And if God is king, then how does God give orders? We might start by revisiting Joshua 24, a chapter that describes a great convocation at Shechem, an important Canaanite city-state located strategically on a narrow pass between Mount Gerizim and Mount Ebal. Shechem was an important religious center, not only for the Canaanites but also the Israelites, who associated it with Joseph's grave (Josh. 24:32) and Jacob's well (John 4:6). According to Joshua 24:1, Joshua assembled the Israelite tribes for a covenant renewal ceremony at this spot, but scholars suggest that the intent may well have been to enlarge the covenant community to include additional Hebrews new to the community. To them Joshua's words would have had special force: "Choose this day whom you will serve." If they chose to serve Yahweh, they had to put away all foreign gods, whether retained from the ancestral period or adopted from the Canaanites.

One of Israel's preeminent features was its organization into twelve tribes. This pattern, read back into the ancestral period, became fundamental to Israel's understanding as a worshiping community. Other groups in the area, such as the Ishmaelites (Gen. 25:12–16) and the Edomites (Gen. 36:10–14) apparently followed similar tribal organization. Such a league of tribes may have had a practical reason for adherence to the number twelve. For instance, this number made it possible for each tribe to bear the cost of maintaining a central shrine for one month of the year. Roughly similar institutions existed among the ancient Greeks, where separate city-states joined themselves by pact to support the shrine at Delphi. Such a league was called an amphictyony, from the verb meaning "to live in the neighborhood" of a shrine, and this term is now widely used to describe Israel in the days of the judges. It appears that a confederation of this sort was instituted at Shechem, which for a while seems to have been the center of the Israelite confederacy. Later the central sanctuary was located at Shiloh, some ten miles to the south of Shechem, where the ark was kept and where the tribes assembled for religious festivals. Throughout the biblical period the tabernacle (the shrine of the covenant) was the center of Israel's religious life, for it contained the ark of the covenant, a box-like object that contained various cultic articles, including a copy of the Ten Commandments inscribed on tablets of stone. And it is the presence of this ark that answers our previous questions about how God's will was made known to the people.

The Bible indicates that the ark was considered the point at which the heavenly and earthly spheres intersected. Apparently the ark played a key part in making known the will of God, as we learn from Numbers 7:89. Here we learn that Moses went into the tabernacle (tent of meeting) to speak with God, and he would hear the voice of God speaking to him from the top of the ark. It was here at the ark that God occasionally issued orders. Though the exact means of this disclosure is never mentioned, this seemed unproblematic for the writers of our texts. This association of revelation with the ark continues from the period of wilderness wanderings until the end of the period of the judges. Scholars indicate that the tradition of a portable shrine, with the ark as its most holy object, goes back to earliest times and even has a prototype in the mythology of the Canaanites.[3]

To say God communicated with Israel at the ark is not to say that Israel was controlled by the priests who officiated at the tabernacle. During this period, the prophetic office had not yet been instituted, the priests were primarily officiants, and no shrine had a monopoly on divine oracles. However, while God could not be controlled, the divine sovereign was believed to be present, and present for communication, at the place where the covenant tablets were preserved.

While Israel was unified by the worship of Yahweh at central sanctuaries and shrines, the unifying factor was not the league or confederacy between the tribes but their common association with the covenant. How close was this federation? How much unification of action did it bring about, and how were inter-tribal affairs regulated? While the evidence is scanty, we know that the tribes had chiefs, and it is likely that from time to time, perhaps at religious festivals, these chiefs and other tribal leaders met to discuss matters that involved more than one tribe. But this organization was hardly elaborate. When Joshua addresses the assembly at Shechem, we see that he speaks "for me and my household" (Josh. 24:15) and addresses those present as individuals and heads of families. The league with God is directly with the smallest social units. In the days of the judges, then, freedom of action and responsibility before God was in the hands of families, clans, and tribes.

What then of the status of the individual Israelite under the covenant? The above information leads us to believe that there was a fundamental equality of status so far as Yahweh is concerned, or to put it more accurately, an equality of responsibility. This egalitarianism is also reflected in the economic status of the people: The typical Israelite lived in a village and worked his own few acres. Land was held as a direct fief from Yahweh and

---

3. Hillers, *Covenant*, 74.

was inalienable, meaning that it was an act of impiety against God and one's ancestors to sell or trade one's inheritance. Israel's social system was radically different from the Canaanite and Syrian city-states in the Late Bronze Age, ruled by kings and maintained by a wretched class of serfs. In early Israel there is a deliberate rejection of the rigid social order that oppressed the poor to maintain an elite.

Democratization of religious responsibility meant that covenant traditions were kept alive in the individual family. This is a feature so characteristic of modern Jewish and Christian life that it takes an effort to recall that in the ancient Near East much of religion was a matter for the state: the gods were the gods of the city and priestly specialists preserved the liturgy and mythology of the temple. From earliest times, of course, there were shrines in Israel with specialist priests and even a central shrine that had special functions in preserving and transmitting the covenant. But along with this, the head of the individual family was charged with teaching his son the sacred statutes and ordinances (Deut. 6:6; 6: 20–24).

This decentralization had its advantages, but without modification it would have left Israel at a disadvantage in two important activities: in war and in the exercise of justice. Ultimately the tribal league failed over these two problems, but in the two centuries or so of its existence it developed a characteristic way of dealing with war and wrongdoing through the figure of the judge. The title derived from the type of leadership that characterized the Israelite theocracy between the death of Joshua and the establishment of the monarchy. The title "judge," though we retain it because it is tradition, is misleading. The term might be rendered better as "savior" or "deliverer." The judges were charismatic individuals who arose during time of crisis. While they were primarily military figures, who led pan-tribal armies against common enemies, some also had judicial functions, adjudicating conflicts and resolving problems in the absence of a king. There was no process by which one ran for judge, nor did one succeed a parent, though there were experiments along that line. Instead, it was a matter of a person's character. On the whole, the way the judges functioned reflects Israel's basic religious and social convictions: The person who is followed is the one in whom Yahweh's spirit has manifested itself.

The idea that Yahweh was the divine suzerain, for whom Israel was to do battle as a loyal vassal, determined the theory and practice of war. Two passages reflect the underlying theory that the victory belongs to Yahweh. Deuteronomy 20:1–9 lists provisions and exemptions from battle, including those who have recently built a house, planted a vineyard, or entered into betrothal. There is even a provision that exempts those who are fearful: "He should go back to his house, or he might cause the heart of his comrades to melt like his own" (Deut. 20:8). These provisions are not simply humanitarian but are intended to ensure that there will not be anyone in the ranks who does not rely wholly on Yahweh. According to the story of Achan's theft in Joshua 7, the spoils belong to Yahweh also. Because of a disaster in war, Joshua and the elders seek the reason at the most holy object, the ark of the covenant. There they determine the cause of the defeat—the theft of spoils from Jericho, dedicated to Yahweh in advance—and the guilty party, a warrior named Achan, who has stolen various items and concealed them beneath the floor of his tent. The punishment is severe, but the crime is capital. Achan's sin became Israel's. Achan had put Israel in the position of having broken the covenant with Yahweh, the divinely instituted constitution of early Israel, thereby unleashing its curse.

The legislation in the Book of the Covenant (Exodus 20:22—23:33) is said to reflect our earliest body of Israelite law. It cannot be dated as early as Sinai, because it is framed to fit a settled community living in villages and carrying out farming, but its antiquity is shown by its language and by the fact that Deuteronomy (seventh century BC) presupposes it. There is general agreement that the collection as a whole comes from the first years of the monarchy or even earlier, though individual laws may have a prehistory that can be traced in Mesopotamian law a thousand years earlier. If this material functioned as a law code, we would immediately recognize its inadequacy from the point of view of completeness and precision of formulation. However, as our knowledge of other collections of Near Eastern law makes clear, these bodies of law served educational purposes and gave expression to what was regarded as fair in typical cases, but they left considerable latitude to local courts for determining the right in individual suits. Thus the laws aided local courts without controlling them.

"In those days there was no king in Israel; all the people did what was right in their own eyes" (Judg. 21:25). These ambiguous words have a positive sense, if the picture drawn here is correct. The sovereign kingship of Yahweh exercised a loose but effective rule through the central shrine and oracle, through inspired heroes and arbiters, through a recognized form for the conduct of war, and through the pressure of Yahweh's covenant terms on the shape of Israel's laws. At the same time, Israelite tribes, clans, families, and individuals enjoyed the maximum freedom of action. This lasted for perhaps two hundred years, yet the Israelites came to regard the theocracy as a failure, partly for military reasons, and because justice was not always served. Peace, justice, and safety were dependent on the willing submission of the tribes to the covenant. Where this was lacking, where a tribe was willing to harbor rapists and murderers (see the dangerous case of the Levite and his concubine in Judges 19–21), the only recourse was to a blood feud that hurt the innocent along with the guilty and threatened to destroy all Israel.

The Transitional Rule of Saul

Israel's last judge was Samuel, whose farewell address to Israel (1 Sam. 12) concludes the biblical survey of the period of the judges. Samuel took leadership at a time of internal weakness. The Israelites were at war with the Philistines, a people of military superiority allied with Egypt who dwelt in city-states by the Mediterranean Sea, in the southwestern portion of Canaan. The battle was going against Israel, and out of desperation Israel's elders removed the ark from Shiloh, the central sanctuary of the Israelite confederacy, to the battlefield. The result was disastrous. The Philistines decisively defeated Israel and captured the ark as a trophy of war. Eventually the ark was returned, but not to Shiloh, which was destroyed by the Philistines.

A reformer, Samuel transformed the Israelite faith by de-emphasizing the priesthood, which had become corrupt, and by organizing a guild of young prophets to teach and interpret God's covenant law to the people. This marked the beginning of conflict between priestly and prophetic elements in the society. The priestly office, representing the people to God, would be subject to the cultic and religious institution that developed around the temple in Jerusalem, whereas the prophetic office, representing God to the people, would remain free from institutional constraints.

Few parts of the Bible are as dramatic as the accounts of the establishment of the monarchy in the books of Samuel and the beginning of 1 Kings. These chapters narrate how Israel transformed itself from a loose confederation of tribes into a nation with a dynastic monarchy and a permanent temple in Jerusalem. The narrative is advanced by accounts of a series of personal conflicts between Samuel and Saul, the first king of Israel; between Saul and David, who succeeded him as king; and between David and his sons. Together with the books of Kings, the books of Samuel record the history of the kingdoms of Israel and Judah from the beginning of the monarchy until the fall of Jerusalem in 587 BC. In their current form they are part of the larger work of the Deuteronomistic historians. As such, they include traditions shaped and edited with a distinct theological perspective, viewing the vicissitudes of the people not from the interplay of social or political activities but from the action of the divine covenant partner, who either rewards or punishes Israel in accordance with its observance of the law given to Moses.

First Samuel views the establishment of the Israelite monarchy in an ambivalent light; two sources represent two traditions, one critical, the other hopeful. First Samuel 8:7, representing the Samuel Tradition, provides an antimonarchical slant. This tradition regards the people's demand for a king as an affront to Yahweh, who ultimately acquiesces to their demands (see 8:22), after instructions are given on selecting the king and instituting the kingship. First Samuel 9:16, representing the Saul Tradition, portrays the monarchy in a positive light, as a new possibility graciously offered by God to the people's demand. Samuel thus represents both continuity with the past and innovation, even if that innovation was one over which he presided reluctantly. Despite textual ambivalence, Samuel is presented as crucial for the institution of kingship, functioning both as king-maker, anointing first Saul and then David, and as king-breaker, in the case of Saul.

Saul is a complex and ultimately tragic figure. Although he begins his career as a successful military leader, he is a flawed leader, psychologically and spiritually. Rejected by Samuel and forsaken by Yahweh, Saul suffers from extreme depression. Despondent, he commits suicide during a rout of his army by the Philistines, his decapitated body impaled on the walls of Beth-shan, a nearby city under Philistine control.

The Covenant with David: Royal Theology

Unlike Saul, 1 Samuel portrays David as an heroic figure, viewed as the legitimate successor to the divinely rejected Saul. David comes to prominence as a court musician (1 Sam. 16:17–23) and then by slaying the Philistine giant Goliath (1 Sam. 17). Anointed king by Samuel, David took Saul's daughter Michal as his first wife in order to establish a claim upon Saul's throne. He began his reign in the southern city of Hebron, ruling there for seven years. Desiring a greater centralization of power, he captured the old fortress of Jerusalem, a neutral site bypassed by Israelite forces during the earlier occupation of Canaan, and made it into his capital. The city, naturally fortified and ideally located on the boundary of the Southern and Northern tribes, came to be known as "the city of David" (1 Sam. 5:9).

In order to capture the allegiance of all Israel, David brought to Jerusalem the ark of the covenant, shifting the religious center of Israel from the confederate sanctuary of Shiloh to the royal shrine in Jerusalem. Establishing his throne on the religious sanctions and Mosaic traditions of the tribal confederacy, David laid the groundwork for the theocratic fusing of religion and politics. With the ark stationed in the tent of meeting, David joined together the two major cultic objects inherited from Mosaic times. Thus the city of David became Zion, the city of God.

His defeat of the Philistines, followed by successful wars against Moab, Ammon, Edom, Amalek, and Aram (Syria), led to a treaty with the Phoenician king, Hiram of Tyre. David came to be recognized as the ruler of an empire that stretched from Phoenicia (southern Lebanon) to the borders of Egypt, and from the Mediterranean Sea to the desert of Arabia. Never before or after did Israel exceed this zenith of political power.

Having established his capital, David designated Abiathar and Zadok as chief priests and guardians of the ark, appointing some of his sons as priests to work with the Levites in administering Israel's religious rituals. David also called upon the guidance of the seer Gad, who advised him to purchase the threshing floor of Araunah on which to build an altar to God. This property, adjacent to his palace, would become the site of Solomon's temple. To help govern, David also selected Nathan the prophet, adding the prestige of the prophets to his cabinet.

In managing his kingdom, David built on the foundations that had been laid by Saul, beginning with a professional army. Second Samuel contains two lists of David's appointees, in 8:16–18 and 20:23–26. In addition to prophets and priests, David centralized authority through commanders, secretaries, and cabinet members, probably according to Egyptian standards. He appointed Joab commander over the army, Jehoshaphat as "recorder" (perhaps the equivalent of a prime minister), and Seraiah as "secretary" or scribe. The second list includes a new official, Adoram, responsible for the "forced labor," a group consisting of war captives, subjugated populations, and perhaps Israelites. He would also have been responsible for public building projects.

Another monarchic innovation is the census (2 Sam. 24), its purpose being to ascertain the number of males to be drafted into the army. The census also demonstrates a royal attempt to impose further centralization on the kingdom by assessing the population's resources for taxation and labor. The census was opposed by the Deuteronomistic historians as sinful (even David is said to have regretted this decision; see 2 Sam. 24:10), probably because it implied a lack of confidence in God, who should have been trusted to provide for Israel.

David's innovations marked the beginning of "royal theology," the view that God had made a special covenant with David, promising to establish David's throne securely though all generations (2 Sam. 7:1–17). This passage, placed immediately after the establishment of the capital in Jerusalem and the ark's transfer there, sets forth for the first time the Deuteronomistic ideology of kingship. It opens with David's desire to build a temple (a "house") for Yahweh. The prophet Nathan expresses his approval, but Yahweh has other plans, which are transmitted to David through the prophet: Yahweh does not want a temple, but rather wishes to establish a covenant with David and Israel, guaranteeing the security of Israel and the dynasty ("house") of David unconditionally and in perpetuity. According to the prophetic word, a temple will be built by David's successor (Solomon), who will be regarded as God's son, punished if he "commits iniquity" but never to lose God's "steadfast love" (*hesed*), phrases that reflect a covenant relationship.

Because royal ideology (God's covenant with David) is so pervasive in the Bible, especially in the historical books, the prophets, and the Psalms, it is appropriate to summarize its main features. God's covenant with David:

1. Establishes a permanent dynasty (2 Sam. 7:13, 16; 23:5; see Ps. 89:4, 29, 36–37; 132:12); the covenant is said to be unconditional and everlasting (a covenant of promise, not law). David's dynasty would remain unbroken in Israel (the United Kingdom) and in Judah (the Southern Kingdom) for some four hundred years.

2. Guarantees Israel land, security, and stability (2 Sam. 7:10).

3. Centralizes worship in a temple (2 Sam. 7:13; Ps. 132:1–5).

4. Establishes the king as covenant mediator, with whom God has a special relationship (2 Sam. 7:14–15; Ps. 2:7; 89:27–33).

Royal Theology in Context

Like the twenty-first century, the period of David and Solomon (the tenth century BC) was a time of upheaval and uncertainty, caused by rapid growth and expansion. Vast changes, akin to secularization, were occurring in society, and the old theological formulations seemed inadequate. Saul, unable to keep up, was the last of the old order, whereas David, the first of the new order, would survive through innovation, combining elements of the sacred Israelite past— nomadic faith and theocratic rule (exodus theology)—with pagan and secular politics.

As the Mosaic covenant was influenced by the Hittite suzerainty treaty, the Davidic covenant was influenced by Canaanite and other Near Eastern models of kingship and temple. Kingship itself was pagan in origin, although Egyptians, Mesopotamians, and Canaanites based it upon religion. Pagan kinship ideology regarded the king as mediator between the divine and social order. Indeed, divine blessing was said to flow through him. In Mesopotamia the king was seen as divine, the son of god by adoption. In gratitude, the king was a temple builder. The temple, seen as the center or "navel" of the world, was the meeting place of heaven and earth, where creation was renewed annually in a ritual drama in which the king was the main participant, mythically acting out the victory of divine forces over the powers of chaos. While most of these elements are present in the Davidic covenant, the setting and function change.

The Davidic covenant was probably at first conditional, as the following passages indicate:

- "*When* he commits iniquity, I will punish him with a rod such as mortals use, with blows inflicted by human beings . . ." (2 Sam. 7:14);
- "*If* his children forsake my law and do not walk according to my ordinances, if they violate my statues and do not keep my commandments, *then* I will punish their transgression with the rod and their iniquity with scourges . . ." (Ps. 89: 30–32);
- *If* your sons keep my covenant and my decrees that I shall teach them . . . (Ps. 132:12a).

But soon the agreement came to be expressed in unconditional terms:

- ". . . But I will not take my steadfast love from him, as I took it from Saul, whom I put away from before you. Your house and your kingdom shall be made sure *forever* before me; your throne shall be established *forever*" (2 Sam. 7:15–16);

- "... but I will not remove from him my steadfast love, or be false to my faithfulness. I will not violate my covenant, or alter the word that went forth from my lips ... [David's] line shall continue *forever*" (Ps. 89:33–34, 36);

- "... their sons also, *forevermore*, shall sit on your throne" (Ps. 132:12b).

An important direction Israel's theorizing took was the development of a different view of the covenant with God. It was not invented at this time, for there were existing traditions of God's accord with the patriarchs and with Moses on which David's priests and prophets and hymn-writers could draw. Some scholars see Israel's theology of sacral kingship beginning with the kingship of God, already present in exodus theology: "The Lord will reign forever and ever" (Exod. 15:18). Like the Sinai covenant, the pact was between Yahweh and the Israelites, in which God took the initiative. But unlike Sinai, there is no obligation on David's part. There is simply a unilateral promise of God: to build David a dynasty unconditionally and in perpetuity. Like the covenant with David, that with Abraham binds only God. It is God who participates in an oath ritual, promising Canaan to Abraham and his descendants. Both covenants, the Davidic and the Abrahamic, are perpetual covenants of grace, for the security rests with the covenant maker.

It should not be imagined that the extremely high view of the monarchy presupposed in the covenant with David was held always, everywhere, and by everyone. During his reign David occasionally fell short of the ideals, enacting harsh economic practices that forced his subjects into work camps. Such practices, coupled with personal indiscretions like his affair with Bathsheba, caused his popularity to wane and led to a revolution by his son Absalom. In time, however, his weaknesses were forgotten and his greatness extolled.

Solomon's reign was a different matter. He is remembered for his wisdom, which enabled Israel to attain its greatest outward splendor, resulting in strong foreign relations, commercial growth, and an elaborate building program, including the erection of the lavish temple in Jerusalem. However, the last days of Solomon also began a period of inward decline, characterized by complacency, religious apostasy, and indulgence in polygamy (Solomon erected shrines for his seven hundred wives and three hundred concubines, many of whom were non-Israelites, and he is said to have participated in idolatrous practices). Despite his accomplishments, Solomon's reign is presented by the Deuteronomistic historians as a moral disaster, a primary example of failure to live up to Israel's theocratic ideals. After Solomon's death the ten northern tribes seceded and became a separate kingdom. In particular, these northerners did not favor a hereditary principle, for though Judah was ruled throughout her history by one dynasty, no royal line managed to maintain itself for more than a couple of generations in the north. For the Deuteronomistic historians (the writers responsible for most of the Old Testament's historical books), the Davidic monarchy was responsible for its own destruction. While recognizing the divine choice of the house of David, these writers maintained the priority of the Sinai covenant.

Periodically throughout Judah's history, particularly in times of national crises, two different but related hopes would emerge from royal theology: (1) *Kingdom hope*: the hope for rule by God, so important in both the Old and New Testaments, and (2) *Messianic hope*: the hope for a Davidic ruler that would guarantee the promissory terms of the Davidic covenant. After the end of the Davidic dynasty in 587 BC, elements of the royal ideology continued to play an important role in later Jewish and Christian traditions. The earliest Christians applied the language of divine sonship to Jesus. One of the titles used for him was "Christ," a Greek term that translates the Hebrew *mashiah* ("messiah," meaning one who was "anointed" or consecrated for an exalted office such as prophet, priest, or king). Royal theology also survives in the hope for a restored or new Jerusalem, in which the promises attached to the city would be fulfilled.

Corporate Personality

The Bible portrays Israel as God's people, not simply a collection of persons but a divine company ("a priestly kingdom and a holy nation"; Exod. 19:6; 1 Pet. 2:9). Out of families, clans, and tribes God formed a nation, with a corporate personality: When one person suffered, everyone suffered; when one person was blessed, the people enjoyed the benefits; when one person sinned, the whole nation participated in the judgment; when one person received a promise, he or she did so on behalf of the nation.

Americans today live in a pluralistic society, with diverse cultures, religions, and societal values, and we are taught to be tolerant. Ancient societies were quite the opposite; they were homogeneous, with little tolerance or diversity, and with no such thing as freedom of religion. The concept of corporate personality provided Israel with stability, solidarity, and unity during the period of its ascendency. These qualities enabled Israelites to maintain social and religious cohesion in a sea of paganism. Their laws, rituals, and values provided them with a distinctive way of life, which has preserved them to this day. In order to be a community the Israelites needed land—physical and geographical space where they could carry out their theocratic uniqueness—and a temple—where they could make their pilgrimage, bring their tithes and offerings, and celebrate their festivals.

To understand the biblical concept of community one must go back to the story of Abraham: God started with one family, declaring a promise so wondrous yet absurd as to engender laughter, creating something in Sarah's womb when she was unable to conceive: "Is anything too wonderful for the Lord?" (Gen. 18:14). From Isaac came Jacob and from him the twelve tribes of Israel. They took his name, his personality, his style of life, and the covenant he had with God. They would call themselves "*bene* Israel," sons of Israel. The doctrine of election was not arbitrary. Rather it reminded them that they were beloved, God's intentional creation. They were not one nation *out of* many, but one nation *for* many. In such unity there is resolve, resilience, and strength.

The basis of all societal views in the Bible is the covenant treaty God establishes with Israel through individuals such as Abraham, Moses, and David. The covenant relationship serves to reveal God's nature, purpose and, more importantly for this chapter, how God's people are to live. The covenant is the means by which God regulates biblical society, establishing statutes, laws, and principles. Biblical stories about Adam, Noah, Abraham, Moses, David, as about judges, priests, kings, prophets, and sages, are accounts about community writ large.

Chapter 8

Creation

As previously noted, the first biblical epic, that of the J writer, was essentially composed backward, beginning with the People's History, followed by the Ancestral History, and ultimately back to the Primeval History. In the previous chapters we have traced the movement of the biblical drama through the first two acts. Act I addresses the Mosaic period, when God called Israel and began to lead the Hebrew people into a deepening understanding of the covenant of law, including the consequences of disobedience and disloyalty. Act II addresses the Abrahamic period, when God called one family, Abraham and Sarah, into a covenant relationship based upon the promise of land and posterity, a relationship renewed with David and through him the nation of Judah. Act III addresses creation, where God establishes a covenant with the cosmos and all humanity.

In the Old Testament, the movement is not from creation to history, but vice versa. Encounter with Yahweh, who is mighty to deliver, leads to faith that this deity, the God of Israel, is Creator. Israel understood herself as fashioned by God (see Jer. 18:1–6), and from this understood God to fashion the world and to predetermine the nation's history (see Ez. 37:26). The Yahwist presents the acts or stages of Israel's life, not from the standpoint of history, but rather from the standpoint of faith in Israel's God. The Mosaic tradition introduced the sacred name as the root experience of the Mosaic period. The Ancestral History tells us it is Yahweh who initiates Abraham's migration and gives promises to each of the patriarchs, and in the Primeval History Yahweh is creator of the world and director of human history.

The Primeval History (Gen. 1–11) deals with fundamental human experiences such as the place of humans in the natural order, guilt and punishment, broken relations, the struggle for power, the search for security, and the powers of chaos that threaten society and the cosmic order. There is no mention of Israel, the people of God, only individuals and groups struggling for survival. For the most part the stories presuppose a Mesopotamian setting: the motifs of creation, paradise, the flood, and the deliverance of humanity from evil and extinction are common in myths and legends of the ancient Near East. There include striking parallels between the biblical creation account and the Enuma Elish and between the biblical flood story and the famous Gilgamesh Epic. The Enuma Elish, often called the Babylonian creation epic, is both a theogony and a cosmogony, for it describes how the gods emerged from nature and how the god Marduk became the king of the gods and the chief god of Babylon. The Gilgamesh Epic, one of the oldest and most popular tales in the ancient Near East, tells how Gilgamesh, a legendary ruler of the Mesopotamian city of Uruk, set out on a quest to discover the secret of immortality from Utnapishtim and his wife, survivors of the flood and the only humans whom the gods had made immortal. His long journey across the ocean and beyond the waters of death brought him to Utnapishtim, who explained that his attainment of immortality was a one-time event. Gilgamesh departed, but only after receiving directions about how to attain a plant from the bottom of the sea, which would restore youthful vigor. Gilgamesh retrieved the plant, only to lose it in an unguarded moment to a sly snake, who stole the plant and thereby shed its skin, having restored its youth. Gilgamesh returned to Uruk, a sadder but wiser ruler.

The Biblical Doctrine of Creation

The doctrine of creation is central to all biblical faith traditions. The doctrine affirms that God created all things, meaning that the world and everything in it depends on God for its existence. Whereas prominent Greek thinkers such as Plato and Aristotle virtually ignored origins, accepting the explanation that matter, and therefore the world, was eternal, the Bible presents an external force that created and continually sustains the cosmos.

In the Bible, however, the doctrine of creation does not stand alone but depends upon and elaborates on the redemptive activity of God in history. In the Old Testament, creation is viewed in the light of Israel's covenant faith; in the New Testament, creation is viewed in the light of Jesus Christ and the "new creation" that through him became a historical reality. In both testaments, the doctrine emphasizes the sovereignty of God, the goodness of creation (that the cosmos and everything in it is characterized by design, that is, by a divinely decreed order), the supreme position of honor and responsibility that God has given to human beings, and the divine purpose that undergirds and controls history from its beginning to its consummation.

Creation faith, particularly as affirmed in the historic creeds of Christianity, represents a repudiation of metaphysical dualism, which might suggest that the created world is evil, and a repudiation of metaphysical randomness, which might suggest that life is essentially meaningless. Creation faith is what American Christians overwhelmingly affirm when they profess: "I believe in God the Father almighty, maker of heaven and earth."

Seven Keys to Interpreting the Biblical Doctrine of Creation

As we examine the stories in Genesis 1–11, we need to give attention to several general observations.

1. *Literary Sources*: The first observation concerns the literary sources said to underlie the text. Scholars accept that Genesis 1–11 come from two different traditions, commonly called J and P, which were combined, expanded, and redacted over time, a process completed around 400 BC by Ezra, an influential scribe called "the founder of Judaism." The J material (found in Gen. 2:4b—4:26; 11:1–9; in parts of the flood narrative; and in the genealogies) is taken to be earlier. This source, said to represent a critique of royal autonomy (perhaps Solomonic), may be viewed as a polemic against the willful pride of the creature who will not live in harmony with the creator but craves autonomy (see Gen. 3:5 and 11:6). The P source, commonly dated to the Babylonian exile (587–539 BC), deals with the problem of hopelessness. This tradition is found in Genesis 1:1—2:4a; in parts of the flood narrative; and in the genealogies. While the former tradition is concerned with prideful self-assertion, the latter deals with despair. Against despair, it asserts not only humanness in the image of God (1:26), but that this image endures after the expulsion from the garden (5:1) and after the flood (9:6). These two literary sources and their competing theological agendas live in uneasy tension.

CREATION

2. *Symmetrical Structure*: While the structure of Genesis 1–11 is difficult and admits various interpretations, scholars have detected various symmetrical correlations in this unit, including:

- Two basic creation accounts: pre-flood (1:1—2:24) and post-flood (9:1–17).
- Two stories of disobedience: pre-flood (6:1–4) and post-flood (9:18-28).
- Two genealogies of continuity: pre-flood (5:1–32) and post-flood (10:1–32; 11:10–29).
- Two major traditions of sin and judgment: pre-flood (3:1—4:16) and post-flood (11:1–9).[1]

According to this interpretation, the carefully structured flood narrative stands at the center, having as its main counterpoint the creation of the world in chapter 1. These two narratives provide the main dynamic of the unit: creation; uncreation; new creation. Because Genesis 1–11 as presently shaped ends with the genealogy of Abraham, Genesis 12:1–4 completes the symmetry, its theme of promise the counterpart of chapter 1.

Symmetry appears in Genesis 1, the Priestly account of creation, particularly when the poetic and literary elements of the passage are emphasized. This perspective interprets the Hebrew word *yom* (translated "day") figuratively, not literally, and the six-day pattern topically, not chronologically. Viewed in this way, the six-day pattern contains two sets of triads. The first triad (days 1, 2, 3) establishes three spheres or realms, and the second triad (days 4, 5, 6) names various subjects that inhabit those realms. A direct correspondence is portrayed between days 1 and 4, 2 and 5, and 3 and 6. The topical structure of the narrative is as follows:

Spheres	Subjects
Day 1. Light (Gen. 1:3–5)	Day 4. Light Bearers (Gen. 1:14–19)
Day 2. Sea, Sky (Gen. 1:6–8)	Day 5. Fish, Birds (Gen. 1:20–23)
Day 3. Land, Vegetation (Gen. 1:9–13)	Day 6. Land Animals, Humans (Gen. 1:24–31)

Day 7. Sabbath (Gen. 2:1–4a)

---

1. Brueggemann, *Genesis*, 14–22.

According to this third option, the function of the creation narrative is to focus on the centrality of the Sabbath and on worship. The text is only secondarily about creation, which should be understood as unfolding according to a meaningful pattern.

Symmetry is further enhanced by the presence in this unit of two overarching cycles: The Adam Cycle of Genesis 1–4, which asserts God's intention for the creation, and the Noah Cycle (Genesis 6–9), which presents the tragic account of the old creation followed by the start of a new creation. The Adam Cycle begins with affirmation, followed by a pattern of indictment and sentence. This cycle is completed in chapter 5 with a genealogy of the generations. The genealogy is idealized and symmetrical, consisting of ten generations, the last (Noah) having three sons. The Noah Cycle is structured in the reverse order from the Adam Cycle. This cycle begins with indictment (6:5–8) and ends in resolution (8:20–22). The decision to destroy in 6:11–13 is resolved in 9:1–17. This cycle is completed with another genealogy in chapter 11. Like the genealogy in chapter 5, the tenth generation also results in three sons.[2]

3. *View of History*: Unlike the cyclical pattern of nature, which guided both agrarian and nomadic peoples in antiquity, the biblical authors maintained a linear view of history, bracketed by a beginning and an end. Unlike their neighbors, who viewed life as repetitive, biblical writers viewed history as purposive. The very idea of purpose, however, implies both the initiation of purpose (a beginning) and the attainment of purpose (an end). Purposive history moves forward in the direction of the realization of a goal. Therefore, the Bible deals with "first things," that is, with God's initiation of the drama of human history, as well as "last things," the conclusion of the historical drama in the purpose of God. "Beginning and end are the terminal points of an interpretation of history which measures time according to the realization of God's purpose."[3] In other words, the biblical

---

2. The use of the number ten in these genealogies is a way to show completion, namely, that an era of human life has run its full course. The New Testament Gospel of Matthew famously provides a genealogy of Jesus (1:1–17), dividing the list into three groups of fourteen, based on a principle called gematria, the number fourteen being the numerical equivalent of the word "David." Using numbers symbolically, the author attempted to prove that Jesus was a descendant of David and therefore the long-awaited Messiah. Genealogical lists in the Bible are often selective and are not meant to be taken literally. In the seventeenth century, Bishop Ussher erroneously calculated the date of creation by using genealogical figures in the Bible as literal historical records. Reading the Bible this way is misguided and ultimately futile.

3. Anderson, *Rediscovering the Bible*, 239.

drama, both at the beginning and the end, is bounded by and part of the incomprehensible mystery of "eternity," that is, by "God's Time." Clearly we are dealing here with an interpretation of history that lies beyond the scope of science.

Accordingly, it is wrong to suppose that the biblical authors were primitive scientists who speculated on the origin and dissolution of nature. The very fact that Genesis includes two strikingly different accounts of creation indicates that the authors of the Pentateuch were concerned with the religious meaning of the stories, not with scientific or even consistent accounts of the way nature evolves. When the P writer arranges his story into six creative days, he is not doing so for historical or scientific reasons but for a religious one, namely, to show the sanctity of the Jewish Sabbath. The pattern: six days God "labored" and on the seventh day God "rested" also emphasizes that from the very beginning, God established a pattern to guide Israel's national life.

4. *Universality of Scope*: The fourth observation concerns the universal scope present in the biblical depiction of creation. These stories not only place history within God's timespan, but they emphasize that the whole creation is included within God's redemptive purpose. The biblical stories of the beginning and the end have a universal range of interest; they concern all humanity and not merely Israel narrowly. Of course, this perspective is dependent upon a biblical teaching we discussed in an earlier chapter, namely, the doctrine of election: God's special revelation to a chosen people. By starting with the creation story, the Bible seemingly "puts the cart before the horse," for Genesis would not have been written had it not been for the patriarchal, Mosaic, and Davidic traditions and other interpretations of Israel's history. So the stories of Genesis 1–11 indicate that the God of Abraham, Isaac, and Jacob is the God of all nations; the whole human drama having its beginning (and its ending) in the creative Word of God: "And God said . . . And it was so."

5. *The Language of Myth*: The fifth observation concerns the language of creation. The Bible speaks of the eternal boundaries of the human drama metaphorically, in the language of myth. The term "myth," understood literarily, does not refer to something purely fictitious, but rather is a way of thinking that transcends reason. Mythology, Karen Armstrong reminds us, "is not about opting out of this world, but about enabling us to live more intensely within it."[4] The dictionary defines a myth as a story dealing with

4. Armstrong, *Short History of Myth*, 3.

the actions of the gods, in contrast to a legend, which deals with the actions of humans. This is a helpful distinction, in part because it puts the accent upon divine action. Dismissal of myth and other types of religious symbolism usually rests upon the belief that the meaning of life can be defined by reason and that truth can be measured by the scientific method. Yet most of us realize that there are areas in which the most important truths have an immeasurable quality, as in the case of falling in love, and that we must turn to poetry, song, and art for the expression of life's deepest experiences.

About one third of the Hebrew Bible is poetry. Awareness of this feature of Israel's liturgical and literary expression is invaluable for reading and interpreting scripture. As artists communicate life's deeper dimension by transforming the things of the everyday world into the language of symbol and imagination, so also the biblical writers use myth and symbol to communicate the faith that human history, as the arena of God's purposive activity, reaches backward and forward into the endless Time of God.

We know that many myths circulated in the ancient world and that this mythology profoundly influenced the biblical tradition. The biblical writers borrowed freely from the common fund of mythology, though purging the myths of their polytheism and other archaic features. According to Babylonian mythology, Marduk slew the watery monster of chaos, Tiamat, and made the earth and firmament by splitting the goddess's body in half. Reminiscences of this myth are scattered throughout the Bible. For instance, the Hebrew word "deep" (*tehom*) in Genesis 1:2 is cognate with Tiamat. Other poetic passages in the Bible, such as Job 26:12-13, Psalm 74:13-14, Isaiah 27:1, and Isaiah 51:9, magnify God's power not only by extolling God's first and most marvelous work but also by reflecting upon the wonderful order and regularity in the universe. They do so by drawing upon the old Canaanite myth of Baal's triumph over the forces of chaos and evil, embodied in the primeval serpent Leviathan and the sea dragon Rahab. Such passages also anticipate the biblical hope for the New Creation, as we shall see. To be sure, the details of the myths reflect the archaic views of the ancient world; indeed, they are absurd if we literalize them. But when read in the framework of the biblical view of history, these myths set forth a conviction that is basic to biblical faith: God's action inaugurates the historical drama, and God's action brings it to completion.

6. *Creation and Worship*: In a real sense analysis destroys myth, just as the beauty of a poem or the mystery of love vanishes when it is dissected. A myth must be viewed in its totality, every part blending into a poetic

whole. This is as true of the Priestly story of creation (Gen. 1:1—2:4a) as of the Yahwist story of the Fall (Gen. 3:1–24), which was intended to be read aloud or heard to be appreciated. The original setting of these passages, widely gleaned in modern times for historical and scientific truths, is not a laboratory or a classroom but rather corporate worship. The setting of the creation-faith within worship is clearly evident in Psalm 24, a three-part liturgy once used during great pilgrimage festivals celebrating Yahweh's kingship. The Psalm was undoubtedly used originally in connection with a processional bearing of the ark of the covenant into Jerusalem. The opening word of the Psalm, which announce that Yahweh is creator, functioned as an introit: "The earth is the Lord's and all that is in it, the world, and those who live in it; for he has founded it on the seas, and established it on the rivers" (24:1–2). The second part, in question-and-response format (24:3–6), is a liturgy for admission to the temple, and the third, an "entrance liturgy" (24:7–10), was sung antiphonally in the presence of the ark, understood to be Yahweh's throne-seat. In this liturgical setting, the function of creation language is to set the stage for praising God. Thus in the book of Psalms, known as the hymnbook of Judaism, the affirmation that God is the creator is a call to worship.

Back in the 1920s, when a storm of controversy broke out in the United States over the doctrine of evolution, people passionately took sides in the "science versus religion" battle, some attempting to demonstrate that the biblical doctrine of creation is good science and others rejecting it as bad science. That conflict continues today between evolutionists (theistic and atheistic) and anti-evolutionists like Young Earth Creationists and Intelligent Design proponents. Fortunately, as many now realize, the conflict resulted from a failure to understand the intention of Israel's language of worship. The word "creation" is neither scientific or philosophical; rather it is theological, a language whose affirmations should not be confused with statements made in the context of secular or scientific thought. In the Bible, the announcement that God is the creator primarily concerns the source and basis of life's meaning. Negatively, it counters the notion that the world is at our disposal, to use or misuse as we please. To understand the creation stories at the beginning of the Bible we ought to divest our minds of scientific and philosophical preconceptions and begin with the Psalms, which praise God as the creator. While the position of the Priestly story of creation is the opening of a cosmic drama, the prelude of the story of God's special dealings with humanity, the form of the story suggests that it was shaped by liturgical usage over a period of many generations, perhaps in connection with one of the great pilgrimage festivals of Israel, and thus it is told confessionally to glorify the God of Israel.

This leads to an important point. When creation-faith is interpreted within the context of worship, there is a tendency to shift the accent from creation as the event at the beginning to a relationship in the present, from the horizontal dimension (the movement of events from beginning to end) to the vertical dimension (the relationship between God and humanity). In our time the existentialist interpretation of creation has found wide support. In his commentary on Genesis 1–11, Alan Richardson suggests that we consider these stories as "parables," to be read as poetry, not prose. The parables of Genesis, he says, contain a special kind of truth: "not the truth with which history and geography, astronomy and geology, deal; it is not the literal truth of the actual observation of measurable things and events; it is ultimate truth, the truth which can be grasped only by the imagination, and which can be expressed by image and symbolism."[5] Such truth, "the truth of religious awareness," cannot be expressed in philosophical, theological, or psychological terms, for that would be to depersonalize it. You are Adam, I am Eve; this is our story!

Psalm 8, related to the Priestly creation account in Genesis 1, is an eloquent witness to the meaning of creation-faith in the liturgy of Israel's worship. This hymn begins and ends with an exclamation of praise to God's glory and majesty, which, to the eye of faith, are evident in nature. The psalmist knows that we sometimes take this world for granted, and yet he knows too that praise is the sign that we are alive, that we are fully heaven. Creation-faith focuses upon the relationship between God and humanity: "When I look at your heavens, the work of your fingers, the moon and the stars that you have established, what are human beings that you are mindful of them, mortals that you care for them?" (Ps. 8:3–4). It is not simply that humans, in contrast to God, are finite. As the book of Ecclesiastes shows, the awareness of the gulf fixed between creature and creator can prompt a feeling of futility and desolation (Eccl. 1:12-14; 3:16–22; 6:1–2). Rather, creation-faith provides context for understanding existence, the awareness that our relationship with God is one of incomprehensible grace. As we see also in the Priestly creation story, where humans are said to be created "in the image of God" (Gen. 1:27), praise rises to a climax as the psalmist draws upon the old cultic tradition: "You have made [humans] a little lower

---

5. Richardson, *Genesis I–XI*, 30.

than God, and crowned them with glory and honor. You have given them dominion over the works of your hands; you have put all things under their feet" (Ps. 8:5–6).

7. *Stewardship*:[6] Our final observation concerns the creation mandates given to humans in Genesis 1:28—2:3. Though the word "covenant" does not appear in the creation narrative, theologians speak of God's relation with Adam and Eve prior to their departure from the Garden as the covenant of creation. Like God's call (election) of Abraham, basic to the covenant of creation is the cultural mandate God gives to Adam and Eve, whereby they were to be God's servants on earth. Unlike the Enuma Elish, where humans are depicted as servile by nature, creating society to protect themselves from capricious gods, in Genesis 1 humans are depicted as divine image-bearers, vice-regents with God, and God institutes creation ordinances for their wellbeing. These ordinances include family (procreation and marriage; 1:28), labor (work is not a curse but a blessing; 1:28), and worship (the Hebrew verb for "rest" [*shabath*], is the basis of the word "Sabbath," the day of rest. As God rests from the labor of creation, so the Sabbath completes the workweek, thereby establishing a pattern of work followed by rest. As this passage suggests, duty and pleasure are complementary, not antithetical; 2:1–3).

The concept of realizing and acting upon one's ordained position as God's co-worker (vice-regent) is called stewardship. The covenant of creation binds all humans to God and to one another. It entails that, as image-bearers, humans are to reflect God's concern for all of life. That includes using wealth and property for the benefit of the entire community. The Bible provides many examples of how this occurs, stressing the welfare of the poor (the fatherless, widow, and sojourner; the book of James in the New Testament powerfully summarizes this concept in 1:27: "Religion that is pure and undefiled before God, the Father, is this: to care for orphans and widows in their distress . . ."). In Deuteronomy 24:19–22 God instructs the Israelites to harvest their fields only once a season; what remains is reserved for the needy. Leviticus 23:22 commands farmers not to harvest their land to the borders, but to leave the produce at the edges for the poor. The Bible also contains strict regulations regarding lending practices (Exod. 22:25–27), provides for an impartial judicial process (Deut. 16:18–20), and for paying the poor and needy worker on the day they earn

---

6. This segment on stewardship is adapted from Bowne and Currid, "Biblical Society," 160–61 and 166–68.

their hire (Deut. 24:14–15). Partiality and bribery are denounced, and the Hebrews are warned to protect strangers and foreigners in their midst, for God protected them while they were strangers in Egypt (Exod. 22:21–24). As Deuteronomy 16:20 makes clear, the concept of stewardship embodies the principle of justice, and, indirectly, of righteousness and steadfast love: "Justice, and only justice, you shall pursue, so that you may live and occupy the land that the Lord your God is giving you."

The institution of marriage stands at the center of biblical society. In ancient Israel and among its neighbors, marriage was a religious affair, a transaction between two families bound by a covenant agreement and sealed with an exchange of gifts. The Israelites viewed marriage as a religious rite because God had ordained marriage at the creation: "Therefore a man leaves his father and his mother and clings to his wife, and they become one flesh" (Gen. 2:24). Though the Israelite system of marriage recognized the practice of polygamy and placed no restrictions on the number of wives a man could have (provided he could financially support them), the ideal was unmistakably monogamous marriage (Gen. 2:24).

The belief that marriage was ordained by God and existed under the covenant illustrates further the Hebrew conviction that all of life lies under God's sovereignty. Furthermore, the Old Testament upholds the sanctity of marriage as a religious ritual by frequently using marriage as a metaphor to depict the relationship between God and the Hebrew nation.

As we examine the biblical covenant of creation, particularly its universality, we need to take inventory. How well are human beings doing in the area of stewardship? If Christians fail to lead the way in justice, righteousness, compassion, and stewardship, does God have a back-up plan?

The "Imago Dei": Made in the Image of God

Despite the differences between the two accounts of creation, in these chapters it becomes clear that God personally chose to create, and that creation is an act of love. Although Christians disagree as to how God created, they affirm that human existence is due to the personal and purposeful involvement of God. The creation accounts in Genesis, as statements of faith, portray in narrative form three grand themes: (a) God as Creator, (b) Humans as Creatures, and (c) the meaning of the relationship between God and Humanity.

The first chapter of Genesis reaches a climax in these words: "Let us make humankind in our image, according to our likeness; and let them have dominion over . . . the earth" (Gen. 1:26). While it is not clear what it means to say that humans are made in the "image" of God—that idea is never systematically explained in any one place in the Bible—it clearly cannot refer to physical likeness, for the Priestly writer takes pains to stress the holiness and transcendence of God. With regards to the phrase "image of God" (often referred to by the Latin phrase *imago dei*), the following meanings have been suggested:

- Humankind's nature: Because humans are created in the image of God, they have a moral and spiritual nature. Having a God-given freedom provides both dignity and responsibility.

- Humankind's position: Being made in the image of God implies personhood and attributes to human beings a unique relationship with God. As persons, humans are related to God in a manner different from anything else in the created order.

- Humankind's function: Since human beings are uniquely related to God by creation, the Old Testament states that their primary function is to worship and serve the Creator in every aspect of life. Furthermore, as God's vice-regents, they are given ecological responsibility over nature.

- The universality of the image: We are told in Genesis 1:27 that both male and female are created in God's image. In the creation account, Adam and Eve represent all humanity. Indeed, the word "Adam" is not a proper name in Hebrew, but merely a word meaning "humankind." Likewise, the word "Eve" is the Hebrew word for "life" or "living." The *Imago Dei* is not the sole possession of one tribe or race or nation. Its potential applies to every human being without exception.

According to this understanding, while we humans are *in* nature, we stand *above* nature, for we have the freedom to acknowledge the claims of the Creator upon us and, within that relationship, to exercise dominion over the earth. Because they stand in a personal relation with God, humans are the crowning glory of God's creation (Ps. 8:5–8).

The Yahwist story (Gen. 2:4b–3:24) states the same truth, only less theologically. We are told that humans, like the animals, are made out of dust (2:7) and return to dust (3:19). While human life is depicted as part of the natural cycle of birth, decay, and death, the J story discloses that humans are more than natural creatures, for unlike the animals, into them is infused the life-giving breath of God (2:7).

Hebrew anthropology does not divide human nature into mutually exclusive parts. The Hebrew word for "breath" (*nephesh*), sometimes mistranslated as "soul," refer to one's life, desire, or individuality. Likewise, when "heart" is mentioned, biblical writers are pointing to the will, the conscience, or the intellect. There is no dualism to speak of in Hebrew anthropology. Humans with *nephesh* are creatures who are responsible. They have the capacity to hear the Word that God addresses to them, and to respond to that Word with obedience or disobedience, with devotion or disdain.

The Temptation

The account of the expulsion from the Garden of Eden, traditionally called "The Fall of Man" or Paradise Lost, is one of the best known, yet most baffling portions of scripture. The story takes place in an idyllic setting: peaceful, relational, harmonious, and free. The J writer portrays the relationship between humans and God in the Garden as intimate, that is, until their disobedience (3:8). What happened? What does this story mean? Theologians and commentators differ widely on their interpretation. Are they about sexuality and the loss of innocence? About gaining a conscience? About moral knowledge, evil, or original sin?

The story of Adam and Eve in the Garden, filled with images found in ancient folklore, evidently once circulated as the answer to perennial human questions such as: Why are the sexes attracted to each other? Why is life so difficult and childbirth so painful? Why are humans afraid of snakes? Why do we wear clothing? Scholars call these stories etiological, because they answer important sociological questions. But these stories are also theological, addressing profoundly existential questions regarding what it means to be human; the nature of evil and temptation; why we feel guilt, shame, and alienation; why we fear God; and why we die.

In his commentary on Genesis, Walter Brueggemann identifies five misunderstandings that need to be dismissed before we can interpret the J account of creation in context. I will simply list them, including Brueggemann's assessment of each in parenthesis.[7]

---

7. Brueggemann, *Genesis*, 41–42.

1. That this is a decisive text for the Bible in that it states the premise for all that follows. (This text may have been important for Paul and St. Augustine, but in terms of biblical significance, it is marginal).

2. That this text is about "the fall," understood as "original sin." (This text makes no general claim about the human condition. While some traditions, such as found in Hosea, Jeremiah, and Ezekiel, contain a pessimistic view of human nature, in general the Old Testament does not assume such a "fall," but rather assumes that humans can indeed obey the purposes of God).

3. That this text explains how evil came into the world. (In fact, the narrative gives no explanation for evil, and there is no hint that the serpent is the embodiment of evil. The Old Testament is not interested in speculation or in abstract thought; it's approach is more existential and pastoral).

4. That this text explains the origin of death. (It is worth noting that no one dies physically in this text. The reference to death in 2:17 is spiritual and psychological rather than physical. While some biblical passages affirm a "doctrine of retribution" [cause and effect, disobedience and punishment], the Bible contains various explanations for death, most often assuming that while certain forms of death may be punishment, death itself belongs properly to the human condition).

5. That popular references to "apples and snakes" have to do with questions of sex and the evil said to be associated with sex. (While there is mention of nakedness [2:25; 3:7], the connection between sex and sin is not faithful to the narrative. Insofar as the text reflects on gender [Gen. 3:15–17], its concern is with the political dynamics of power, control, and autonomy).

The J text, like so much else in the Bible, is not interested in theoretical or abstract questions about sin, death, evil, and fall. While abstraction has its place in the classroom, such questioning is often false, futile, and escapist. The Bible is not an answer book to the myriad questions we may ask. The J text, viewed historically (dating it as early as 950 BC, the period of Solomon, or around 850 BC, about the time of Elijah), could be interpreted as prophetic writing. A review of the prophetic message supports this correlation. According to the prophets, Israel's life was corrupted by henotheistic or even polytheistic practices, specifically by refusal to acknowledge the sovereignty of Yahweh. Economic, social, and political calamities were traced to the autonomous will of the Israelite people, who regularly turned from God to pursue their own ends. The prophets claimed that God had created Israel in order that she might live in harmony with God, nature, others, and self. But Israel's history was the dismal story of disloyalty and disobedience; Israel was a rebellious son, an adulterous wife, a traitor to Yahweh. Israel was a "fallen creature"—the object of God's judgment, though also the recipient of divine mercy.

As Bernhard Anderson indicates: "From this understanding of Israel's history the J narrative looks backward to the very beginning of things, in such a way as to suggest that this is actually the inner character of all human history."[8] While the "Fall" may be said to describe the "beginning of history," it also describes the human situation at any moment in time. Through literary counterpoint, J blends together two familiar prophetic themes: (a) the corruption of human history owing to human rebellion against the Creator (see Is. 1:2–9; Jer. 8:7) and (b) God's intervention into human affairs in acts of judgment and mercy.

That is the picture dramatized in Genesis 2 and 3, a drama in four scenes:

- Scene 1 (Gen. 2:4b–17): Placement of Adam in the garden.
- Scene 2 (Gen 2:18–25): Formation of a "helper" (Eve).
- Scene 3 (Gen. 3:1–7): Disruption of the garden.
- Scene 4 (Gen. 3:8–24): Judgment and expulsion.[9]

In Scene 1, everything is preparatory to verses 15–17. Here we learn that God's will for humans is threefold: (a) there is a *vocation* (v. 15); From the beginning, the human creature is called, given a vocation, and expected to share in God's work; (b) there is a *permit* (v. 16); regarding food, everything is permitted; (c) there is a *prohibition* (v. 17); what counts is the authority of God and the unqualified expectation of obedience. These three, taken together, constitute the meaning of human life. The primary human task is to find a way to hold the three facets of divine purpose together; one facet without the others is surely a perversion. While readers and commentators have focused on the prohibition, the divine will for vocation and

---

8. Anderson, *Rediscovering the Bible*, 249.
9. Brueggemann, *Genesis*, 44–50.

freedom has been lost. The prohibition makes sense only in terms of the other two.

Two agendas appear in the J account: theological (issues related to the vertical relationship, that between humans and God), and sociological (issues related to the horizontal relationship, that between human). The primary thrust of the story is vertical, having to do with the rule of God and the nature of human destiny. They both belong together. The pattern is in Scene 2: vocation, permission, and prohibition. Scene 4, traditionally understood, shows the distortion of human community that comes from a fundamental disobedience of the prohibition: disharmony with God, nature, others, and self. Disobedience (the pattern of the fall) represents a reversal of the pattern of creation: harmony with God, nature, others, and self.

There is a pathetic grandeur in the picture of Adam reaching to taste the fruit of the tree of knowledge of good and evil. Knowledge is humankind's capacity. Freedom to leave the innocence of nature is precisely what elevates humans above the animals. But when humanity's capacity for knowledge becomes the occasion for arrogant power and self-exaltation, inevitably it results in a fall from the life of trust and goodness that God intends. We cannot recover the mythological innocence of Adam, nor can we return to a Garden that is a figment of the religious imagination. Nevertheless, through imagination humans know there is a better way, the way life should be, even though we cannot fully attain it.

While the pattern of the fall ends with the expulsion of Adam and Eve from the Garden, there is good news here. Graciousness appears in the narrative in verse 21, where God clothes the hapless couple, mercifully shielding them from their shame, but also in the judgment, for the couple get to live and try anew. The ending is hopeful as well, for it is a new beginning. God pushes the couple out of the nest, the idyllic garden in which they have lived. Having tasted of the tree of knowledge, they will no longer have access to the tree of life, meaning they will someday return to the dust from which they were originally created. Their expulsion is the first stage of ascent as human beings progress through the stages of civilization into an unknown future, filled with weal and woe, in the company of the God who promises never to fail or forsake them (Deut. 31:6; Josh. 1:5; Heb. 13:5). So we can say with confidence: "The Lord is my helper; I will not be afraid. What can anyone do to me?" (Heb. 13:6; see Ps. 118:6).

Excursus: Rethinking The Tree of Life and the Tree of Knowledge

Instead of focusing on the details of the J account, as if it were an allegory, I suggest that we examine one aspect of the story—the two trees in the Garden—and consider these as two types of existence possible for humans in a universe provided by God.[10]

The first type of existence, symbolized by *the Tree of Life*, represents plateaued existence in a garden of bliss; a gilded-cage existence somewhat like the pleasure-palace into which the young Siddartha (later to become the Buddha) was placed by his father so that he might control the destiny of his son and keep him on the path to becoming a powerful ruler rather than a compassionate healer. In a universe of aggressive Providence, God is everywhere present and everywhere active. Under the dynamics of a Tree of Life existence, the needs of humanity and the vicissitudes of nature are handled by a hands-on God, who like a helicopter parent hovers over humans as though they were infants in a comfortable home. All is lush and relatively problem-free. Human growth and dignity are sacrificed on the altar of bliss. All is taken care of.

By contrast, the second type of existence, symbolized by *the Tree of Knowledge*, represents a quite opposite set of dynamics, including: a life of challenge, freedom of choice, and responsibility; the reality of temptation; an aggressive pursuit of knowledge; pain and joy in great extremes; a life of independence and risk; mortality by virtue of natural and moral evil; a higher potential for moral good and for moral evil; diminished Divine Providence; and the possibility of a lifestyle based on faith.

According to this scenario, human individualism, creativity, and capacities for good and for growth will have a greater arena for expression but so also human cruelty and natural calamity. By seeking to manage their environment and to nurture it, rather than to have it handed to them on a silver platter, humans living in the Tree of Knowledge type of existence come closer to a true image of God than they do in the Tree of Life scenario. Biblical support for this understanding comes from the syntax of Gen 2:9, where the phrase commonly translated as "and the tree of the knowledge of good and evil" literally reads: "and the Tree of Knowledge, (comma) good

---

10. The segment on the trees in the Garden is adapted from my book, *Dark Splendor*, 135–40.

and evil," or it could very well be translated: "and the Tree of Knowledge; (semicolon) consequently good and evil."

So we have two ways of life; two complete sets of dynamics: the dynamics of the Tree of Life and the dynamics of the Tree of Knowledge. And these sets are mutually exclusive. One may not simultaneously operate under both sets of dynamics at the same time. One cannot possess full freedom and full knowledge. Nor can humans have the "best" elements of each set simultaneously. For example, according to the dynamics of the Tree of Knowledge, we cannot know ourselves fully or know God directly. Such universal truths are elements of the Tree of Life paradigm. Perhaps that is the meaning, at least in part, of two of the Bible's great maxims: "The secret things belong to the Lord our God; but the things that are revealed belong to us and to our children forever" (Deut. 29:29); "Now I know in part; then I shall understand fully" (1 Cor. 13:12).

According to this understanding of Genesis, it was actually humans who determined the expulsion from the Garden of Bliss, seeking the destiny of the Tree of Knowledge with all that the choice implies. Therefore, by choice and of necessity, humans no longer live in the Garden of Bliss, but rather East of Eden, where mortality and uncertainty but also faith and freedom dwell.

We have been taught that Adam and Eve sinned in partaking of the Tree of Knowledge, but I question that understanding. My interpretation is that while Adam and Eve acted contrary to divine caution, the category of classic "sin" here is not applicable. Rather Adam and Eve, the symbolic parents of humanity, exercised their divinely granted measure of freedom to decline the warning of the Divine, thereby choosing the path of dynamics known by the title "Tree of Knowledge." This high-risk approach to life, which humans embraced, may not have been favored by God, but it was definitely permitted. And the essential choice of that path, if one follows the story literally, was made by Eve, the mother of mankind. The one who bears the child and suffers the pain in childbirth chose to set her children along the more arduous, but hopefully more rewarding path of the Tree of Knowledge.

This approach raises the question of evil, suggesting that with the creation of potential for good—which is required for humans to reach their spiritual capacity—potential for evil indirectly came into existence as a consequence. Perhaps this is what Augustine meant when he noted that "Evil has its source in the good"; and what Thomas Aquinas had in mind when he stated "There is no possible source of evil except good"; and what the author of Isaiah had in mind when he quotes God as saying: "I form light and create darkness, I make weal [Heb. peace or harmony] and create woe [the Hebrew word here is the word for evil found in Genesis 2: 9 and is translated thus by the authors of the KJV], I the Lord do all these things" (45:7).

The reference to evil in Isaiah undoubtedly has in mind the Babylonian destruction of the temple in Jerusalem in the sixth century BC and the ensuing exile. However, in Jewish tradition, sovereign God is constrained from destroying evil for by doing so God could well destroy good. While omnipotent Deity could violate universal laws, to do so might unravel the cosmos.

One final principle needs to be mentioned, namely, that the two sets of dynamics represented by the trees in the Garden are in inverse proportion. The more one increases the influence and magnitude of elements inherent in one set, the more one decreases the influence and magnitude of the dynamics inherent in the other set. Those who embrace the security and certainty of the Tree of Life paradigm, including a full and aggressive Divine Providence, decrease the elements of the Tree of Knowledge paradigm—including the elements of challenge, freedom, and responsibility. Those who embrace the Tree of Knowledge way of life choose freedom and responsibility but also risk and uncertainty. The expansion of one set implies the contraction of the other.

According to J's interpretation of history, the source of sin is not to be traced to the world of nature, to the body, or to human finiteness. The first creation story (Genesis 1) contains the recurring refrain, "God saw that it was good." Judeo-Christian thought, when it has been true to its biblical heritage, has consistently emphasized the goodness of creation and has opposed religions or philosophies that regard the material world or the body as evil. Why then is history as it is? Which do humans repeatedly convert the world into a scene of struggle for power, the consequence of which is never ending suffering? The Bible drives to the heart of the matter: the source of our troubles lies in our freedom: "you will be like God, knowing good and evil" (Gen. 3:6). The words of the subtle serpent remind us that humans are incurably turned inward, making themselves the center of life. "The primeval revolt against God is an act of violence that disrupts all relationships—with God, with human beings, and with the earth itself. The consequence is that henceforth human beings must live in suffering and anxiety, with the prospect of death hanging over them like a Sword of Damocles."[11] Adam's freedom is our greatness; it can also be our downfall.

---

11. Anderson, *Understanding the Old Testament*, 149–50.

Part IV

Literary Topics

The Essential Message of the New Testament

Chapter 9

New Covenant

As we embark on the second journey through scripture, examining the documents that comprise the New Testament, we turn again to the three motifs that served us well during the first journey: covenant, community, and creation, this time through the lens of newness. To a greater extent than previously, in the New Testament these notions are so interwoven as to be inseparable.

Since the dawn of Christianity, "Old Testament" has been the standard label for the scriptures that the early Christian community inherited from ancient Israel. The term "testament," meaning "covenant," indicates that the Christian movement began in the heart of Judaism, that the Christian proclamation was based on the Jewish scriptures, and that the two communities of faith belonged to the Abrahamic tradition, sharing a common Bible and therefore a common story.

Hence, early Christians insisted that the Bible they read did not belong exclusively to the Jewish community; it belonged also to them. They could say, as did Paul: "For whatever was written in former days was written for our instruction, so that by steadfastness and by the encouragement of the scriptures we might have hope" (Rom. 15:4). Nevertheless, what was happening in their time seemed so radical and comprehensive as to constitute a "new covenant" (2 Cor. 3:6), a new beginning for Judaism and the world.

The New Covenant

The language "old covenant" recalls the famous prophecy in the book of Jeremiah (31:31–34) about two epochs: the time of the Mosaic covenant, which ended in human failure, and the time of the new covenant, when the divine *torah* (law, teaching) is written on the heart, resulting in such personal knowledge of God that religious teaching would no longer be necessary. In Jeremiah's prophecy the issue is the relation between the former age and the latter, not between two bodies of scripture.

During Jeremiah's life a wave of nationalism swept through the kingdom of Judah. For a while, under King Josiah's reign, it seemed that the nation stood on the verge of a golden age, like the glorious era of David's empire. Citizens were awakened from their patriotic dream by a succession of events that culminated in the fall of the nation and the exile of the population to Babylon. Competing prophets proclaimed a comfortable message of peace, promising that affairs would soon return to the good old days of national glory. Such prophets won a large audience, but in the long run the deepest impression was made by prophets such as Jeremiah, whose sharp words summoned people to face the realities of their history.

At the time of his call to become a prophet, Jeremiah realized that God's word had the double aspect of judgment and renewal, doom and promise. The first effect of the divine intention was judgment: "to pluck up and to pull down, to destroy and to overthrow" (Jer. 1:10). To be sure, judgment was not the final word, for God's intention was also "to build and to plant," but the rebuilding would come only after the destruction. Considering himself a second Moses, in fulfillment of God's promise to Moses in Deuteronomy 18:18 ("I will raise up for them a prophet like you from among their own people; I will put my words in the mouth of the prophet, who shall speak to them everything that I command"), Jeremiah announces a message of doom. This was not a message he had devised, nor one he wished to deliver. Questioning his vocation and viewed as a traitor, Jeremiah was thrown into a dungeon for announcing the fall of Jerusalem.

But the prophet never lost sight of the truth that God's purpose was not just to destroy and overthrow. Jeremiah understood that that the false had to be removed before the new could emerge (Jer. 24:6; 42:10). He would have been at odds with his deepest conviction and with the great prophets who preceded him had he not clung steadfastly to the vision of the New

People and the New Age that lay beyond catastrophe. This theme of hope is prominent in chapters 30–33 of Jeremiah, a section often called "The Little Book of Comfort."[1]

Even in his isolation from his nation and his people, Jeremiah knew that individuals experience God's "healing" or salvation within community. Thus, when Jeremiah looked to the horizon of God's future, he spoke of a New Community. The deepest rift in the people's history—the tragic separation of "the house of Israel" from "the house of Judah"—would be overcome, for God's love, working through the discipline of judgement, would make a new beginning for both Israel and Judah. Through their distress, not despite it, the people would be saved (Jer. 30:7).

This vision of the restored community of Israel is profoundly expressed in Jeremiah's prophecy of the new covenant (Jer. 31:31–34), a prophecy that eventually gave the name to the canon of Christian writings ("New Testament" means "New Covenant"). Several aspects of Jeremiah's prophecy seem to describe the Christian community's self-understanding as the new Israel of God (Gal. 6:16):

1. Unlike the covenant at Sinai, which marked the beginning of the divine intention for Israel, this covenant is new in that it pertains to the consummation of the divine purpose. The emphasis, however, is not on some abstract fulfillment in the afterlife, or on some place far removed from the concrete realities of time. Rather, this New Age will be realized on earth and in history.

2. Like the first covenant, this covenant is the result of God's initiative.

3. Unlike the covenant with Moses, which the people's history showed to have been broken, this covenant inaugurates a new history, a new relationship with God.

4. The covenant will be new in the sense that it will fulfill the original intention of the Sinai covenant. This covenant will be written upon the heart, not upon external tablets, and it will find expression not through obedience to religious ceremonies and written laws but through a personal response to the liberating voice of God.

5. The new covenant will create a new community—God's people—whose relationship with God will be based on trust and loyalty that cannot be broken.

1. Anderson, *Understanding the Old Testament*, 382.

6. The new covenant, like all covenants of promise, will rest upon divine forgiveness, not upon human effort. Such forgiveness, however, must be preceded by God's "discipline," which shatters human pride and self-sufficiency and results in gratitude and thanksgiving.

Early Christians, even those of Jewish descent, did not consider themselves either as an unbroken continuation of the old Israel or as a group attempting to return to an ancient pattern of faith. Instead they considered themselves to be living in the "last days": "Long ago God spoke to our ancestors in many and various ways by the prophets, but in these last days he has spoken to us by a Son, whom he appointed heir of all things, through whom he also created the worlds" (Heb. 1:2). While this passage says nothing about covenant,[2] it says a great deal about the conceptual framework within which the New Testament use of the term must be understood. Note the sharp separation of sacred history into two periods. This setting of new against old is defined by the mode of God's revelation: In the past it came through prophetic mediators, now it has come through a Son, the one through whom the plurality of previous modes of revelation is channeled, the antitype in whom is fulfilled a host of types. To say that Jesus Christ is "heir of all things," as elaborated by the author of Hebrews, means that multiple features of Old Testament religion must be seen as prefiguring this single individual, which comes to mean that he is the heir of the covenant idea as well. To show that Jesus bring a "better covenant, which has been enacted through better promises" (Heb. 8:6), the writer to the Hebrews quotes Jeremiah's prophecy of the new covenant and then asserts flatly that the new covenant made the first one obsolete" (Heb. 8:13). In a later passage he elaborates further, adding that Old Testament types such as high priest, tent, blood, sacrifice, and covenant, each has become a way of asserting what happened through Christ (Heb. 9:11–23).

When we hear Christ called "the mediator of a new covenant" (Heb. 9:15), we might think the author is implying that Jesus is another Moses, who was the mediator of the old covenant, but that would be incorrect. The writer's play with the biblical Greek word for covenant, *diatheke*, is significant in this connection. That word in ordinary Greek means "last will

---

2. The paucity of reference to the word "covenant" in the New Testament, while perhaps surprising, is understandable. For Judaism the term referred to the Mosaic law, whereas for the Roman Empire "covenant" meant an illegal secret society. This double-sided conflict made it nearly impossible for early Christianity to use the term meaningfully.

and testament." This word was chosen by the translators who prepared the Septuagint, the Greek version of the Old Testament, as an equivalent for the Hebrew *berith*, which never means "testament" or "last will." While the rationale for their choice is uncertain, their use of this term introduced an ambiguity which the writer to the Hebrews happily exploited. To show how Christ's death provides human being an "eternal inheritance," and to connect this with the Old Testament term, he uses the secular sense of *diatheke*, which permits him to introduce the idea that for a will to take effect "the death of the one who made it must be established . . . for . . . without the shedding of blood there is no forgiveness of sins" (see Heb. 9:15–22).

While elements of the Old Testament concept of the covenant are rare in the New Testament, primarily because the death of Christ so dominates the conception, traces of the old idea of the curse upon the faithless appear in Hebrews 10:28–29: Anyone who has violated the law of Moses dies without mercy 'on the testimony of two or three witnesses.' How much worse punishment do you think will be deserved by those who have spurned the Son of God, profaned the blood of the covenant by which they were sanctified, and outraged the Spirit of grace?" While this conception is relatively rare in the New Testament, it is possible to see in this passage an allusion to the old notion in which covenant partners brought a conditional curse upon themselves through the "blood of the covenant."

The Relation between the Testaments

For Christians, the relationship between the Old and New Testaments is one of continuity and discontinuity. Like two partners joined in marriage, neither is a substitute for the other, nor are they independent of one another. Rather there is relative independence, whereby they complement one another. For Christians, the gulf between the testaments is bridged by Jesus Christ, whose person and work "establishes a deep discontinuity with Israel's scripture and, at the same time, a deep continuity in the purpose of God."[3] The discontinuity is expressed in the Gospel of Matthew: "You have heard that it was said to those of ancient times, . . . but I say unto you" (Matt. 5:21–22, 27–28); the continuity is expressed in the same Gospel: "Do not think that I have come to abolish the Law or the Prophets. I have come not to abolish, but to fulfill" (Matt. 5:17). In short, both testaments

---

3. Anderson, *Contours of Old Testament Theology*, 12.

are theologically necessary if the church is to hear in the human words of the Bible the word of God.

The mystery of the relation between the testaments seems consonant with Paul's discussion in Romans 11 about the relation between the Jewish and Christian communities. In the face of Israel's rejection of Jesus as the Messiah, Paul grapples with the "mystery" of God's election that includes both Jews and Gentiles in "the Israel of God" (Gal. 6:16), declaring that "all Israel will be saved" (Rom. 11:26). God is thereby faithful to the promises made to the ancestors of Israel and extends the meaning and power of those promises to all who have faith.

The Jewish and Christian communities, bound together in God's creative purpose, have a common Bible and a shared history as the people of God while differing over the climax of the story, whether the pilgrimage of God's people leads to the Talmud and a continued life of messianic hope, or whether that pilgrimage leads through the Old Testament to Jesus the Christ, who came not to destroy but to fulfill the Law and the Prophets.[4]

One of the implications of this view of the relationship between the testaments is that it allows the Old Testament to speak with its own voice, even if that means interpreting passages differently than New Testament authors do. Of course, it is proper for Christians to regard the Hebrew scriptures as a whole in a Christological perspective, but this does not mean forcing particular texts to bear witness to Jesus Christ or to carry a Christian meaning if they do not. If the Old Testament can be understood as promise and the New Testament as fulfillment, as Christians maintain through their canonical approach to the Bible, this should not lead to the loss in the Old Testament of "its vertical, existential dimension which as scripture of the church continues to bear its own witness within the context of the Christian Bible."[5]

The New Testament: Responses to Jesus

The New Testament is best understood as the early Church's response to the historical Jesus (who he was, what he said and did), envisioned as five widening circles of response leading from "the Jesus of history" to "the Christ of faith," that is, from the experience of Jesus *by his disciples* to the

---

4. Anderson, *Understanding the Old Testament*, 597.
5. Childs, *Biblical Theology*, 77–78.

confession of him *by the church*. Most periods are said to have lasted approximately twenty years, with occasional overlap.

1. The period of *the earliest disciples* (AD 27–30): this includes their involvement with Jesus in ministry and their return to fishing and other occupations following his crucifixion.

2. *The oral period* (30–50): the years between the date of the crucifixion and the first letter written by Paul are years of silence, from which no writings have survived, a period characterized by preaching and proselytizing activity on behalf of the early followers of Christ, where the "Jesus material," including sayings of Jesus and stories about Jesus, circulated as single and detached units. Some scholars argue for the existence of proto-gospels and for the possibility the passion narrative reached a fixed form at an early period, but these assumptions cannot be corroborated with literary evidence.

3. The period of *the Pauline epistles* (49–64): this phase includes Paul's missionary travels and the authentic letters of Paul, Christianity's earliest written documents.

4. The period of *the Gospels* (65–95): this material, while going back to actual events in the life of Jesus, represents an expanding tradition of faith. To the Gospels should be added the book of Acts, written by the same author as the Gospel of Luke. Acts can be viewed as a sequel to the Gospels in that it describes the spread of early Christianity through the work of the apostles. While few details from this period can be verified historically, for believers they convey truth.

5. *The church* conscious of itself as society (80–100): this period overlaps significantly with that of the Gospels; literarily it features the writing of the latest books of the New Testament, including disputed letters of Paul such as the Pastorals, the General Epistles, and the book of Revelation.

To summarize, the message concerning Christ in the New Testament involves a process of development from the free period (the historical situation of Jesus) to the binding period (the historical situation of the Church), from faith *in* Jesus to *the* faith. The New Testament writings, therefore, represent a total response to the person of Christ, from experience to confession, from fact, through faith, to truth. When, at the close of the biblical period, the author of the Epistle of Jude speaks of "the faith that was once for all entrusted to the saints" (v. 3), this is biblically atypical. In the Bible faith is generally a relationship between human beings and God. Jude's view, referring to "the faith" with a definite article, reflects the situation of the church at the end of the apostolic age, when it became necessary to have a "rule of faith," a consistent system of teaching for the purpose of maintaining the identity of the community and defending its doctrines against novel teaching.

In examining the New Testament literature, we focus on three stages of that response: the Pauline epistles, the Gospels, and the period of the church. Though we title the Pauline response "new covenant," the Gospel response "new community," and the church period as "new creation," in actuality these headings are symbolic, for they represent dynamic concepts that flow seamlessly through the writings. Unlike the Exodus, which represented a new start for a Hebrew minority living under the oppression of the Pharaoh, the birth of Christianity represents a new beginning not only for a Jewish minority living under the oppression of a Pharaoh called Caesar, but also for all humanity.

Paul: Apostle of the New Covenant

Reversing the order of the New Testament, in which the Gospels stand first, our literary study of the New Testament begins with the letters of Paul, the earliest writings of the New Testament. Here we are in direct contact with living history. Paul's letters sparkle with life and grow out of specific situations, the exact nature not always clear because we have too little knowledge of the background. But from these letters we can see what early Christians believed, what they found difficult to believe, and where they were susceptible to aberration. What had been fluid in the period of oral tradition begins to crystalize into acceptable doctrine. But the Christians had as yet no Bible save the Hebrew scriptures. The last thing that Paul thought of in connection with his often hurriedly written letters was permanence. They were written for an immediate purpose, and once that purpose was fulfilled they might be expected to disappear. It was only accidental that some were preserved to become in due course sacred scripture.

The Impact of Paul

One of the heroic figures in the life of the early church, the apostle Paul emerged from being an arch-persecutor of Christians into an unrelenting missionary of the gospel. The impact of Paul upon the church was both widespread and permanent. His influence was fourfold:

- the first great theologian of the church;
- the first full-time missionary to the Gentiles;
- the founder of numerous congregations in Asia Minor, Greece, and Macedonia;
- the author (actual or alleged) of a group of letters that now comprise one-fourth of the bulk of the New Testament.

Paul is sometimes called the second founder of Christianity. As the first great theologian of the church, he was both a practical theologian—in that he addressed specific needs arising in the church—and a task theologian. To him belonged the unique task of developing or disclosing a theology for the Gentile church, indicating how Gentiles would be brought into full participation in the fellowship of Christ, what Paul would refer to as "the body of Christ" (Rom. 12:5; 1 Cor. 12:13, 27; Col. 1:18; cf. Eph. 4:4) and "the Israel of God" (Gal. 6:16; cf. Rom. 11:25–26).

The first full-time missionary to the Gentiles, Paul helped bridge the gap as the church became less Jewish and more Gentile in its makeup. Jesus had performed a revolution in religion, recognizing in Judaism a rich spiritual treasure, resulting in a distinct system of worship, a religious way of life, and a high ethical outlook. Yet that treasure was not available to everyone, for Judaism was an ethnic and deeply exclusive faith. Jesus believed himself to be not simply a teacher of truth but the Messiah, through whom God's eternal purpose for Israel and the nations would be fulfilled. This meant that Jesus undertook the task of liberating the spiritual treasure of Israel's faith for humanity. However, his ministry was almost exclusively to Jews, and his faithfulness to God led him to the cross. The work of Christ became entrusted to his followers, who would be empowered by the Holy Spirit to continue the mission Jesus had begun. It is in Paul and his work that we see the task being accomplished. Paul took the work of Christ and set it free from possession by any one ethnic group, sect, or clique. In so doing, Paul remains the classic exponent of the idea of freedom in Christ and of the universality of God's plan for all humanity (see Rom. 3:29–30; Gal. 3:14; 5:1; cf. Eph. 3:6).

Paul also founded new congregations during his missionary travels, providing exhortation, encouragement, and support through letters and personal visits. He helped heal doctrinal and moral difficulties in his churches, providing a form of moral instruction known as *paraenesis* (see, for example, 1 Thess. 4:1–12), such as one might expect to see in the philosophical letters of his day. His letters to the church of Corinth deal with numerous practical issues they were facing, helping later Christians more fully understand the nature of the Christian life.

In his letters Paul followed the common style of the day, beginning with introductory greetings, followed by the main body of the letter, and ending with concluding remarks, including a word of farewell, a feature that Paul regularly expanded with an expression of blessing and prayer for his readers. The middle section often consisted of two parts: doctrinal teaching (sometimes in response to questions raised by his audience), followed by practical teaching or advice concerning the Christian lifestyle.

While not all of his letters remain, by the end of the first century they became preserved through a collection that marks the church's initial Christian canon (see 2 Pet. 3:15–16). As part of scripture they became the most famous and influential set of letters ever written, impacting every major Christian thinker and practically every major revival. Central in the conversion of Augustine and Luther, they held a critical place in their life and teachings. During the Reformation, Calvin patterned his famous *Institutes of the Christian Religion* on Paul's letter to the Romans. While Paul had no idea he was writing scripture, there is no denying that he considered his writings to be invested with special authority, and furthermore, that he expected his readers generally to recognize this as factual (1 Cor. 2:16; 7:17; 14:37–38; cf. 2 Thess. 3:14).

Paul's Pedigree

Who, then, is Paul? What was his heritage, and how did he become both a Christian and an apostle of Christ? From his letters we know that his Jewish name was Saul and that he was born and reared at Tarsus, an important city in the Roman province of Cilicia, in southeastern Asia Minor (present day Turkey). Though Paul was brought up in the strict observance of the Hebrew faith and traditions, his father having been a Pharisee, he was born a Roman citizen. This privilege, possessed by only a few in the provinces of the empire, proved to be of great importance later in his Christian work and more than once saved his life. However, at an early age Paul went to Jerusalem, where he received religious instruction from the famous Jewish teacher Gamaliel. At Gamaliel's academy he became versed not only in the teachings of the Old Testament, but in the subtleties of rabbinical interpretation. In that setting Paul acquired a zeal for the traditions of Judaism, his training bringing him eventually into bitter conflict with the followers of Jesus Christ.

Paul first appears in Christian history in association with the persecutors of the Christian church (Acts 7:58). Later, looking back on the advantages in which at one time he had taken pride, he described his lineage thus: "circumcised on the eighth day, a member of the people of Israel, of the tribe of Benjamin, a Hebrew born of Hebrews, as to the law, a Pharisee, as to zeal, a persecutor of the church, as to righteousness under the law, blameless" (Phil. 3:6). That's quite a pedigree!

As a Pharisee, he belonged to one of the most prestigious sects in Judaism. Together with the Sadducees, an educated elite who exercised a widespread influence in politics, economics, and religion, they constituted the Sanhedrin, the great council of Jerusalem composed of seventy persons, presided over by the high priest. It was before such a body that Jesus was tried (Matt. 26:59; John 11:47), Peter and John were interrogated (Acts 4:5-7, 15; 5:27, 34), and, toward the end of his ministry, Paul made his defense (Acts 20:30).

Whereas the proportion of Pharisees to the total Jewish population was relatively small (the number of adult male Jews who belonged to the sect of the Pharisees at this time seems to have been around six thousand), they were quite popular with the Jewish masses. While the origin of the Pharisees is uncertain, it is commonly surmised that they came into existence in the second century BC, during the time of the Maccabean uprising. They seem to have come from a group called the Hasidim ("pious or strict ones"), the name possibly derived from the term *porash* or *perisha*, meaning "separated ones." In distinguishing the Pharisees from the Sadducees, the Jewish historian Josephus (AD 37–100) enumerated four doctrines held by the former and denied by the latter:

- Scripture: The Pharisees recognized as the supreme authority in religion the written Hebrew scriptures as well as the oral tradition (the accumulated body of pronouncements of Jewish teachers from the time of Ezra), whereas the Sadducees accepted the Torah alone as authoritative, discounting the authority of the prophetic literature, the Writings, and the oral tradition.

- Determinism: The Pharisees held a doctrine of divine foreordination or predestination, and considered it consistent with human free will, whereas the Sadducees denied that history was divinely controlled, insisting on individual freedom to direct one's life and thus history itself.

- Individual Eschatology: The Pharisees believed in the immortality of the soul as well as the resurrection of the body. They held that humans are rewarded or punished in the afterlife, whereas the Sadducees rejected these views, affirming that "souls die with the bodies" and that divine rewards and punishments are confined to the fortunes of this life.

- Spirit Beings: The Pharisees had highly developed views of angels and demons, whereas the Sadducees denied their existence (see Acts 23:6–8).

Though these doctrinal differences distinguished the Pharisees from the Sadducees, the essence of Pharisaism was its promotion of Jewish piety through prayer, fasting, tithing, giving alms, and otherwise living in conformity to the laws and ordinances of Judaism. Despite their depiction in the New Testament as legalistic, on the whole Pharisees viewed Judaism as a living and evolving religion. Combining conservative and progressive elements, this group alone, of the chief religious Jewish sects, survived the destruction of Jerusalem in AD 70, becoming the basis upon which rabbinic Judaism would be based.

In addition to their piety, the Pharisees prepared the way for Christianity by taking the Old Testament concept of the Messiah and working it into the common Jewish consciousness. Interestingly, it was through the Pharisaic wing, primarily as espoused by Paul, that many distinctive Christians doctrines emerged, including divine inspiration of scripture (2 Tim. 3:16), election and predestination of believers (Rom. 8:28–30; Eph. 1:4–5), bodily resurrection of the dead (1 Cor. 15), and belief in spirit beings. The two most controversial issues, however, which led to Paul's departure from Judaism and to the eventual schism between Judaism and Christianity, where Christological (the person of Jesus) and soteriological (the means of salvation). The Pharisees, stressing the primacy of Torah, limited God's grace to those who keep the commandments.

Paul's Conversion

By his own admission, Paul's first connection with the emerging Christian movement was as a persecutor (1 Cor. 15:9; Gal. 1:13). According to the testimony of Acts, Paul associated himself with the accusers of faithful Christian named Stephen, guarding the garments of the witnesses as, in conformity with the ancient law, they threw the first stones at his execution (Acts 7:58—8:1). Then he took part enthusiastically in the campaign of repression against the church of Jerusalem, arresting and imprisoning believers as far away as Damascus, intending to make them renounce their faith or face trial and punishment.

If Stephen saw the logic of the situation more clearly than the apostles, Paul saw it more clearly than the Pharisees. In the eyes of Stephen and Paul alike, the new order and the old were incompatible. Whereas Stephen might have argued, "The new has come; therefore the old must go," Paul for his part argued, "The old must stay; therefore the new must go." Only on one condition might Paul accept that the customs delivered by Moses might be changed. There was an ancient Jewish tradition, possibly predating Paul, that taught that when Messiah came, he would change the customs or even abrogate the law. But for Paul to believe that Jesus of Nazareth was that expected Messiah was out of the question. It is unlikely that Paul's conception of the status, career, and teaching of the Messiah conformed to that of Jesus. Furthermore, Jesus had been crucified; such a concept contradicted the meaning of the pronouncement in Deuteronomy 21:23 that "anyone that is hung on a tree is under God's curse." Since crucifixion was a Roman form of hanging, although a prolonged and more extreme version, it stood to reason that Jesus could not be the Messiah. The Messiah, by definition, was uniquely endowed with the divine blessing ("The Spirit of the Lord shall rest on him," Isa. 11:2), whereas the divine curse explicitly rested on one who was crucified. To the Jews, the very idea of a crucified Messiah was blasphemous (1 Cor. 1:23). Furthermore, it was believed by the Jews that the coming of the messianic age could be delayed by apostasy within the nation. Thus, as Moses took strong action in Numbers 25 when he hanged chiefs and slayed those who worshipped false gods, so Paul believed that in persecuting Christians he was following a righteous path

With astonishing suddenness the persecutor of the church became the apostle of Jesus Christ. He was in mid-course as a zealot for the law, bent on exterminating the plague which threatened the life of Israel, when, in his own words, "Christ Jesus made me his own" (Phil. 3:12). What cause this transformation? His own repeated explanation is that he saw the crucified Christ now exalted as the risen Lord: "Have I not seen Jesus our Lord?" he asks when his apostolic credentials are questioned (1 Cor. 9:1), referring to that same occasion later in the same letter where, after listing earlier appearances of Christ in resurrection, he adds, "Last of all, as to one untimely born, he appeared also to me" (1 Cor. 15:8). When, in 2 Corinthians 4:6, he says that "God . . . has shone in our hearts to give the light of the knowledge of the glory of God in the face of Jesus Christ," his language implies a reminiscence of his conversion on the way to Damascus, when about midday "a light from heaven flashed around him" and he fell to the ground, hearing a voice say: "Saul, Saul, why do you persecute me?" When Paul asked who was speaking he heard the reply: "I am Jesus, whom you are persecuting" (Acts 9:3–5).

No single event, apart from the Christ-event itself, has proved so determinant for the course of Christian history as the conversion and commissioning of Paul. It is so for the author of Acts, who provides three accounts of the conversion (Acts 9:1–22; 22:6–16; 26:12–18). "With no conscious preparation, Paul found himself instantaneously compelled to acknowledge that Jesus of Nazareth, the crucified one, was alive after his passion, vindicated and exalted by God, and was now conscripting him into his service."[6]

Paul's conversion represents a radical shift in his thinking about Jesus and the church. On the Damascus road Paul learned two things about Jesus: that he was not dead, but alive, and that Jesus was not cursed, but blessed by God. Hence the cross, rather than discrediting Jesus as an imposter, is truly God's provision for humanity and the fulfillment of the promise that through Abraham all nations and peoples would be blessed (Gal. 3:6–9). Jesus was indeed the expected Messiah, but also the "Son of God." This discovery became the subject of his first Christian preaching in Damascus (Acts 9:20). As a Christian, he still believed in only one God, but he became convinced that God could only be fully known through Jesus (2 Cor. 4:6). On the Damascus road he also learned that Christians are not heretics, but God's people. He discovered that in persecuting Christians he had been persecuting Christ (Acts 9:5). That correlation would lead him to one of his most profound insights, that the church was neither a building nor a sect but the "body of Christ" (1 Cor. 12:27). Theologically, the church was a microcosm of the transformation that God's new order would bring for

---

6. Bruce, *Apostle of the Heart Set Free*, 75.

the whole world. To be in the church was to have a foretaste of life in God's kingdom. Socially, the church in the Roman Empire was an alternative society, based on the new freedom and fellowship that Jesus had announced: freedom to love God and to love and serve others (Mark 12:29–31). It must have taken Paul some time to process his new understanding about Jesus and the church. His sojourn in the Nabatean wilderness after his conversion, followed by a three year stay in Damascus, certainly provided him time to reflect and rethink his theology, but as far as he was concerned, it was on the Damascus road that the essential core of his faith as a Christian was first revealed to him.

Paul and the Law

While Paul's Damascus-road experience may be said to have contained within itself the totality of his apostolic message, that totality was not grasped by him immediately. The revelation he received on that occasion coincided with his call to preach Christ among the Gentiles, but not until he was fully launched in his evangelistic career could he understand what this call entailed. Justification by faith was certainly implicit in his conversion, but it would take a decade or more of ministry to fully flesh it out, as he does in his letters to the Galatians and to the Romans. Speaking of his Christian standing by contrast with his earlier situation, he describes himself as "not having a righteousness of my own that comes from the law, but one that comes through faith in Christ, the righteousness from God based on faith" (Phil. 3:9).

Let us remember that he did not come to Christ through a process of failure, frustration, or disillusionment. Describing his former quest as a young Jewish male, he declares himself "as to righteousness under the law, blameless" (Phil. 3:6). The law he speaks of is not natural or social in nature but God's law, the revelation of God's will. Keeping God's law in its entirety was not an easy task, but it was not impossible. To be born under the law was an immense privilege. Unlike Gentiles, who lacked this privilege, a Jew who was instructed in the law could know God's will. He could qualify to be a "guide to the blind, a light to those who are in darkness, a corrector of the foolish, a teacher of children" (Rom. 2:17–20). In a context where Paul expresses sadness that his own people, the Jews, do not accept Jesus as God's Messiah, he lists seven historic privileges that belonged to Israel—eight if one counts the last statement that the Messiah sprang out of Israel: sonship; God's presence; the covenants; the giving of the law; the worship of God in the temple; the promises to Israel through Abraham, Moses, David, and the prophets; and the patriarchs.

At the time when Paul wrote these words he embraced another way. No longer did he rely upon the law and boast of his relation to God as one who had been born a Jew; no longer did he make his aim the attainment of that righteousness before God that was based on keeping the law. He had found a new way of righteousness, based on faith in Christ. Allegiance to a person had displaced devotion to a code and a way of life.

There were many early disciples of Jesus in the early church who though it quite possible—indeed desirable—to combine faith in Christ with the pursuit of righteousness through keeping the law, but Paul regarded this attitude as an impossible compromise. No one had kept the law with greater devotion than Paul, and the law, far from securing his righteousness before God, actually led him into sin. It was his devotion to the law that made him such a zealous persecutor of the church. But with the revelation on the Damascus road came the recognition that Jesus was the Messiah; the crucified Jesus was the risen Lord. The followers of Jesus had been right after all, and Paul had been terribly wrong. Instead of pursuing the path of righteousness, as he thought, he had been committing the sin of sins—attacking the witnesses of the Messiah and, through them, attacking the Messiah himself. His disillusionment with the law, when he understood where his devotion to it had led him, is reflected in his words: "For through the law I died to the law, so that I might live to God. I have been crucified with Christ, and it is no longer I who live, but it is Christ who lives in me. And the life I now live in the flesh I live by faith in the Son of God, who loved me and gave himself for me. I do not nullify the grace of God; for if justification comes through the law, then Christ died for nothing" (Gal. 2:19–21).

It is plain that Paul believed and taught that the law had been in a major sense revoked by Christ: "For Christ is the end of the law" (Rom. 10:4). The age of law, which was never designed to be other than a parenthesis in God's dealings with humanity (Gal. 3:19), had been superseded by the new age, which Christians call "the age of Christ" or "the age of the Spirit." In this age, it is not the Mosaic law that liberates us from "the law of sin and death," but rather "the law of the Spirit of life in Christ Jesus" (Rom. 8:2). For, Paul continues, God has done what the law could not do, because of the "flesh," that is, the powerlessness of the human nature. The law belongs to the old age, the age of spiritual weakness, whereas the Spirit belongs to the new age, the age of spiritual power. The transition from the old age to the new—from inability to ability—is brought about by the coming of Christ. Not only did Christ accomplish the will of God, but on behalf of others he endured the curse pronounced by the law on law-breakers, thereby redeeming from that curse those who were under law, so that they might through faith receive the promised Spirit and adoption as children in the family of God (Gal. 3:10–14; 4:4–6). Thus, by his life and death, Christ has "condemned sin in the flesh" (Rom. 8:3), thereby inaugurating the new age of spiritual freedom, the age, we may say, of the new covenant. The reference to the Spirit should remind us that Paul's teaching here points to the fulfillment not only of Jeremiah's "new covenant" oracle but also of the companion oracles in Ezekiel 11:19–20 and 36:25–28, where God promises to implant within the new community a new heart and a new spirit.

It is to this new heart that Paul refers when he says that the message of the new age is written "with the spirit of the living God, not on tablets of stone but on tablets of human hearts" (2 Cor. 3:3). A written law-code is an inadequate vehicle for communicating the will of God. The will of God was codified only for a temporary purpose—to reveal human sinfulness. Doing the will of God is not a matter of conformity to outward rules but a way to express inward love, such as the Spirit begets (Rom. 5:5). Hence, says Paul, "the letter kills, but the Spirit gives life" (2 Cor. 3:6). In 2 Corinthians 3:7–18 Paul demonstrates how the new covenant is the opposite of the old. In his writings, the two covenants are contrasted so sharply that there is little apparent continuity left between the Sinai covenant and the new covenant in Christ. For that reason he reaches back to the covenant with Abraham, using the narrative of Abraham's faith to demonstrate the priority of faith over law. Such faith, he argues, is reckoned as righteousness (Rom. 4:1–25). In Galatians 3 Paul extends his argument further, arguing that the law in its spiritual sense, as the embodiment of God's will, is upheld and fulfilled more adequately in the age of faith than was possible "before faith came," when law kept the people of God "imprisoned and guarded . . . until faith would be revealed" (Gal. 3:23). In these passages it becomes clear that for Paul the Sinai covenant is an interruption in the history of faith.

The affirmation that "Christ is the end of the law" (Rom. 10:4) has been variously understood. The word "end" (*telos*) can mean "goal" or "terminus," and in Romans Paul probably means both, for Christ was the goal of the law in the sense that the law had a tutorial role until Christ came (Gal. 3:19, 24). But Christ was, for that reason, the terminus of the law because his coming meant that the period of its validity was now at an end.

This possibility, easily misunderstandable, has left Paul open to the charge of antinomianism, a charge that Paul met and rebutted in his own day (Rom. 3:8; 6:1–23). As he makes clear, Paul does not condone lawless behavior: "Should we continue in sin in order that grace may abound? By no means!" (Rom 6:1–2). If Jewish Christians continued to observe various customs prescribed by the law as part of their way of life, Paul raised no objection; he himself conformed to those customs when he judged it appropriate. But what he is concerned with is the place of law in our approach to God: the righteousness attested by the law and the prophets comes solely through faith in Jesus Christ, for we are now justified by God's grace as a gift (Rom 3:21–26).

Because the law is the promulgation of God's will, it is "holy and just and good" (Rom. 7:12). But the spirit is holy both as being the Spirit of God and as creating holiness in human beings. It is the Spirit who renews the minds of the people of God so that they not only approve but do the will of God (Rom. 12:2). The holiness that the Spirit creates is nothing less than transformation into the likeness of Christ, who is the image of God. The purpose of the law, that humans should be holy as God is holy (Lev. 11:44–45), is thus realized in the gospel.

The traditional Lutheran doctrine of the threefold function of the law envisions it as:

- *spiegel* (mirror): as a summons to repentance, God's law provides moral guidance;
- *oregal* (curb or bridle): as a means of restraint, God's law provides civil guidance;
- *regal* (rule): as a means of instruction, God's law provides practical guidance.

The first use is recognized by Paul as a fact of experience: "through the law comes the knowledge of sin" (Rom. 3:20). Insofar as the second use involves the administration of law by magistrates for the restraint of evil and the maintenance of order, this is not an aspect of the gospel, though Paul speaks of this subject in Romans 13:17. As for the third use of the law, Paul's thoughts on the guidance of the church may sometimes be expressed by means of the term "law," but when he speaks of the "law of the Spirit" (Rom. 8:2) or the "law of Christ" (Gal. 6:2), he is referring to the "law of love," the law which Christ exemplified and which he laid down when he said that the whole law and prophets depended on the twin commandments of love to God and love to one's neighbor (Matt. 22:40). This reinterpretation of the law is echoed by Paul when he says that the whole law is summed up in a single commandment: "You shall love your neighbor as yourself" (Gal. 5:14) or that "Love does no wrong to a neighbor; therefore, love is the fulfilling of the law" (Rom 13:10).

But the law of love is a different kind of law from that which Paul describes as a yoke of slavery (Gal 5:1). Love is generated by inward qualities and cannot be enforced by legal sanctions. The law of love builds on the third use of the law in the Lutheran tradition—its use to provide guidance for the church. So far as Paul is concerned, guidance for the church is provided by the law of love, not the law of constraint. In his letters he lays down guidelines for his converts and others, often couched in the imperative mood, but these guidelines mostly concern personal relations. Food sacrificed to idols, for instance, is ethically and religious indifferent; what matters is the effect of our conduct and example on others. If we ignore their true interests, or cause weaker brethren to sin, then we are "no longer walking in love" (Rom. 14:15).

In his guidance, Paul walks a careful line between legalism and antinomianism, recognizing the importance of Christian freedom while remaining subject to the needs of others. The reformer Martin Luther best entered the mind of Paul when he declared that a Christian is "subject to none" in respect to personal liberty, yet "subject to all" in respect to charity. "This, for Paul, is the law of Christ because this was the way of Christ. And in this way, for Paul, the divine purpose underlying Moses's law is vindicated and accomplished."[7]

---

7. Ibid., 202.

Chapter 10

New Community

The central theme of the New Testament is a person, Jesus of Nazareth, a wandering preacher of the first century who has changed the course of history. Whether Christian or not, all who live in the Western world have been influenced by the teachings and life of this individual. Early disciples envisioned Jesus as the climactic historical figure, the Messiah who brought the long-awaited messianic kingdom of God, a rule that by ending evil and suffering would usher in an age of bliss. Later followers would view Jesus' role as pivotal, representing the midpoint of history. This view is maintained by Ernst Renan, famous nineteenth-century scholar, who wrote: "All history is incomprehensible without Christ"; by Napoleon, who confessed toward the end of his life: "This man, Jesus, vanished for eighteen hundred years, still holds the character of men as in a vise"; and by H. G. Wells, who once declared: "I am an historian. I am not a believer. But I must confess, as an historian, that this penniless preacher from Galilee is irresistibly the center of history."

The message of the New Testament is reducible to two claims: (1) that Jesus' appearance and career came at the climax of a series of historical events of which the Old Testament is witness, and (2) that God was in Christ, confronting humanity with reconciling power and transforming truth. The paradoxical emphasis upon both Jesus' humanity and deity is evident not just in his message but in his life, his actions, and his person.

Understanding Jesus through Jewish Eyes

The whole of the New Testament—every book, chapter, and verse—is theology: all is written from faith for faith (Rom. 1:17), by believers for the edification of other believers, or for those who are not yet believers that they might be brought to faith. All twenty-seven books are written to explain and promote faith in Jesus Christ. Biblical scholars famously distinguish between the "Jesus of history" and the "Christ of faith." While the New Testament writers had a great deal to say about the latter, what about the former? Who was Jesus of Nazareth?

Although we cannot be precise about the length of his life or even the duration of his ministry, it is believed that Jesus was born around 5 BC, shortly before the death of Herod in 4 BC, and that he died by crucifixion around AD 30. The New Testament is a response to Jesus of Nazareth, whom Christians call Christ, and to a cluster of events scholars call the "Christ event," centered around his birth, death, and resurrection.

Jesus of Nazareth, like other great religious teachers, left nothing in writing. While he may have familiar with some Greek words, throughout his ministry he seems to have spoken Aramaic, that form of Semitic speech akin to Hebrew and Syriac which became a lingua franca over a large part of the Middle East. This means that every saying attributed to him in the Greek New Testament has come to us through translation. Even his teachings and the traditions concerning Jesus were passed on orally, so little, if anything, was written down. During the oral period, the sayings of Jesus circulated mostly as isolated units, detached from their original context, and preserved in connection with the preaching and teaching activities of early Christians. The famous missionary doctor Albert Schweitzer, at the end of his survey of scholarly attempts to write the life of Jesus, concluded that such a task cannot be accomplished: "He comes to us as One unknown, without a name, as of old by the lake-side He came to those who knew Him not."[1] Jesus, he declared, could only be known by faith. Many current biblical scholars are less pessimistic, recognizing that in the Gospels, particularly in the Synoptic Gospels, there is a great deal of material that can be accepted as genuinely historical and therefore as going back to Jesus himself.

It is clear that the human Jesus must have been a figure of great power and originality. In him a force of immeasurable magnitude began

---

1. Schweitzer, *Quest of the Historical Jesus*, 403.

to operate in this world, unleashing a movement that has lasted through twenty centuries and is yet on the rise globally. When a person of such eminence appears, who can apprehend that person totally? One observer will see one aspect, another a different aspect; and even the collection of their observations cannot yield the whole person. Of course, no one can know another person completely. Even after years of marriage, husbands and wives often discover aspects of one another's being of which, up to that moment, they had been ignorant. This being so, it is not surprising that, when Jesus of Nazareth appeared, no single mind could encompass the whole of him, no single artist could paint the definitive portrait. What we have in the New Testament is a collection of fragments of memory and interpretation concerning Jesus, extruded through longstanding Jewish hermeneutical processes such as *testimonia*, *pesher*, typology, and midrash. Early Christians, believing that in Jesus all of God's promises were fulfilled (2 Cor. 1:20), added to this tradition, searching the Hebrew scriptures for passages that could be interpreted christologically.

At quite an early period in their corporate existence, before they called themselves Christians, the fellowship of disciples of Jesus in Jerusalem followed what they called the Way—the way of faith and life initiated by Jesus (see Acts 9:2; 19:9; also 18:25). This expression was not unprecedented in Judaism; it is found, for example, in the ancient Jewish writings known as the Dead Sea Scrolls as a designation for the Qumran community's faith and life, and may be understood as a shortened version of "the true way" or "the right way." As companions of the Way, the followers of Jesus found themselves assessing the place of Jesus in God's unfolding purpose for humanity. With increasing clarity they saw his identity and role foreshadowed in the Jewish scriptures, especially as he had taught them how to understand those scriptures.

In the apostolic speeches of the early chapters of Acts we find a number of christologies—explanations of the person and work of Jesus—in terms of biblical prophecy. Jesus is the anointed prince of the house of David (Acts 2:25-36); the humiliated and vindicated servant of the Lord (Acts 3:13-21); the promised prophet like Moses (Acts 3:22-23); and the one through whom the promises to Abraham were fulfilled (Acts 3:25-26). Jesus not only became identified with personal figures, but also with impersonal images, such as "the capstone" rejected by the builders of the temple.[2] At some point early Christians began collecting *testimonia*, biblical

---

2. The New Testament authors took themes such as the rejected stone and related

quotations about the Messiah, stringing them together as proof-texts. This technique, found in all strata of the New Testament, helps explain the chain of quotations found at the start of Mark's Gospel (Mark 1:2–3), where a quotation from Malachi is combined with passages from Isaiah. This literary genre is also evident in the Dead Sea Scrolls, in a short document called "Messianic Anthology" or 4QTestimonia. Antedating Christianity by about a century (dated to the middle of the first century BC), this document contains five biblical quotations dealing with messianic themes, connected by interpretation.

Pesher, a form of interpretation commonly used in the biblical commentaries found among the Dead Sea Scrolls, is based on the belief that readers are living in the final, climactic days of history, with the understanding that the ancient prophetic oracles were being fulfilled in the events of their time. Early Christians, viewing Jesus as the long-awaited Messiah, himself the fulfillment of God's promises to Israel, clearly used scripture in this way, understanding themselves to be living at the climactic end of history.

Typology is a special kind of symbolism in which a person, place, thing, or event in the Old Testament foreshadows a person, place, thing, or event in the New Testament, painting a picture of what Christ would be like and what he would accomplish in his ministry (see Luke 24:25–27). Paul refers to typology in Romans 5:14, where he identifies Adam as a type of Christ. Likewise, in Colossians 2:17 the Jewish festivals of the Mosaic period are said to be "a shadow of what is to come, but the substance belongs to Christ." In Hebrews 8–10, perhaps the greatest and clearest example of how typology is used in the New Testament, the author makes a lengthy argument that the tabernacle, sacrificial system, priesthood, and Mosaic Law were shadows of models that prefigured the person and work of Jesus Christ.

Midrash is a Jewish interpretive technique that recasts older stories into newer ones and thereby reads "deeper" meanings into old texts. It involves rereading and expanding a biblical text in the form of a new narrative to update the existential meaning in light of the ever-changing present situation. In this sense, midrash performs the function of recontextualizing an already existing text so as to enlarge and enhance its significance in and

---

them to other Old Testament "stone" oracles like the "rock one stumbles over" of Isaiah 8:13, the "foundation stone" of Isaiah 28:16, and the stone "cut out not by human hands" of Daniel 2:34. For their combination see Luke 20:17–18; Romans 9:32–33, and 1 Peter 2:6–8.

for the currently existing situational context. Such an approach is not concerned with objective accuracy but with meaning and understanding.

New Testament midrashic examples abound, so I limit myself to Matthew's use of prophecy, which by modern standards is quite skewed. Take the bizarre version of Zechariah 9:9 found in Matthew 21:7, where the Evangelist misunderstands the poetic parallelism in the original and has Jesus riding on two animals at the same time (while some modern translations attempt to clarify the confusion, it is clearly present in the original Greek of the passage). The parallel passages in Mark and Luke provide a more sensible explanation. Matthew's Gospel often interprets prophetically Old Testament passages not prophetic in their original context. This was done to demonstrate that events in the life of Jesus, particularly his birth, were part of a divinely pre-arranged pattern. The best-known example, the Emmanuel passage from Isaiah 7:14[3] (cited in Matthew 1:23), bore no reference in the original Hebrew text to the distant future. The context makes clear that it was given as a promise to King Ahaz, a contemporary of the prophet Isaiah who ruled from approximately 735 to 715 BC. The prophecy was a sign to the king that his wife was already, or soon would be pregnant. The birth of that child, born in the near future, was a promise to Ahaz that God would provide relief from impending political threat. Only later, through midrashic interpretation, were prophecies of this nature updated and applied to future events such as the coming of the Messiah (Matt. 1:22–23).

There are numerous additional midrashic examples in the New Testament writings. One such example appears in Matthew 2:23, where the relocation of the infant Jesus from Egypt to Nazareth is said to be a fulfillment of a saying found "in the prophets" to the effect that someone would be called a Nazarene. The vagueness of the reference (no particular biblical text seems to be in mind) makes clear that this is a piece of redaction made up by the author to prove his point and not the fulfillment of any specific prophetic message. A few verses earlier we read about the return from Egypt to Judea of Joseph, Mary, and Jesus. The author of Matthew cites this event as the fulfillment of a passage from Hosea 11:1, but that passage clearly referred to the original Exodus and not to the future at all. As many scholars note, Matthew's account contains numerous parallels to the story of Moses in Exodus. The exodus story was used by Matthew as the base

---

3. "Look, the young woman [Greek "the virgin"] is with child and shall bear a son, and shall name him Immanuel."

material for the story of the birth of Jesus, including the flight from Egypt and the slaughter of the male children by the Pharaoh and by Herod. While the midrashic approach might astound conservative readers of the Bible, the author of Matthew would not have considered this method questionable, since he was following a common Jewish exegetical approach.

The New Testament bears evidence that not only Jewish Christian churches but also early Gentile Christian churches had an almost excessive regard for the Old Testament, sharing with their Jewish Christian counterparts the interest in finding foreshadowing of the new revelation in the old. We have a clear picture of this phenomenon in Paul's Epistle to the Romans. Here, to an audience addressed as Gentiles, Paul bases his arguments on the Old Testament and assumes that his readers will have sufficient knowledge of the Jewish scriptures to enable them to understand his allusions and to follow his argument. We have no evidence anywhere of any early Christian congregation of which the same would not be true.

Jesus Christ as Prophet, Priest, and King

While it is true that the Old Testament can stand by itself, speaking with its own independent voices, the New Testament voices concerning Jesus Christ are "incomprehensible apart from the Old."[4] Early Christians affirmed that God's covenants with Israel had been "fulfilled," or better, "validated," by God's new covenant instituted through Jesus Christ. To speak of "fulfillment" is perhaps inadequate, because in one sense God's new revelation did not realize the promises of the covenants with Israel but rather introduced deep discontinuity with Israel's traditions. Yet in another sense these traditions were received and transformed, enriching the content of the Christian gospel. "The relationship between the old and the new is not a dichotomy--a division into two mutually exclusive parts—but a dialectic of continuity and discontinuity."[5]

Christian interpreters preferred the promissory covenants associated with Abraham and David to the Mosaic covenant of obligation, the latter suspect particularly by Paul and his followers, for it was feared that the emphasis on obedience to the law might put one's relationship with God on a basis of merit rather than on freely offered grace. Both traditions, however, are helpful in shaping our understanding of Christology. The

4. Childs, *Biblical Theology*, 77.
5. Anderson, *Contours of Old Testament Theology*, 337.

Mosaic covenant, with its traditions of exodus, torah-teaching, and wilderness sojourn, seem to have been influential in shaping the account of Jesus' Galilean ministry, while the Royal covenant, with its traditions of temple and kingship, have helped to shape narratives about Jesus in Jerusalem.[6]

The New Testament, from beginning to end, bears witness to the good news that God has come into this world supremely through Jesus Christ. It has always been a fundamental postulate of Christianity that human beings are made for fellowship with God. But that faith also recognizes a fatal power called sin, which disturbs this fellowship. Of all sin's consequences, by far the most serious is the loss of fellowship with God, evident in humanity by "alienation" and "hostility" (see Col. 1:21; Eph. 4:18). To overcome this estrangement, in "the fullness of time" the God of love came into this world through Jesus Christ.

To describe the meaning of the coming of Jesus, the New Testament portrays Jesus imaginatively through three major images, all derived from the Old Testament: Jesus is a prophet like Moses, though one greater than Moses; he is a priestly mediator of an everlasting covenant, though not standing in the succession of Israel's priests; and he is a king of the Davidic line, but his royalty is not like that of worldly rulers. The Old Testament speaks of a coming messianic age in which God would deliver Israel from its oppressors and establish it as the dominant kingdom on earth. The word Messiah ("anointed one") or "Christ" in Greek is used twice in the Old Testament to describe the coming deliverer (Ps. 2:2; Dan. 9:25). In ancient Israel kings, priests, and prophets who were chosen by God for special purposes were anointed with oil as a symbol of their divine appointment.

During the centuries immediately preceding Christ's birth most Jews believed that the coming Messiah would militarily defeat Israel's enemies and reestablish the nation as a strong earthly kingdom. While the Messiah was seen primarily as a political leader, he was also expected to exhibit strong religious leadership. Perhaps as a way to counter the first expectation, in the Gospels Jesus rarely refers to himself as "Messiah" (this may be why in Mark 8:29-30, Jesus instructs his disciples not to reveal his messianic identity to the Jewish people). Jesus' own understanding is stated in Mark 8:31, where he portrays his messianic role in terms of suffering. This view, probably influenced by the portrayal of the suffering servant in Isaiah 53, characterizes Mark's understanding of Jesus ("The Son of Man is to be betrayed into human hands, and they will kill him, and three days after

---

6. Ibid., 338.

being killed, he will rise again," Mark 9:31; see also 10:33–34). According to the Gospels, Jesus came to inaugurate a spiritual kingdom by dying on a cross (see John 18:36). At his trial Jesus was asked by Caiaphas whether he was the Messiah. His reply, interpreted as blasphemy, indicates that Jesus answered the question affirmatively, as Mark's version of the story confirms (Mark 14:61–65; see 15:32).

In the New Testament Jesus Christ is first, the eschatological prophet whom, according to Deuteronomy 18:15–19, God would raise up to speak God's words to the people. In the book of Acts, one of Peter's sermons portrays Jesus in this manner, citing the passage from Deuteronomy (Acts 3:12–26). The sermon portrays Jesus as standing in a succession of prophets, beginning with Moses, yet far greater (see Luke 24:27).

The priestly imagery of the temple and God's dwelling among the people greatly influenced the message of the New Testament. In the Old Epic tradition of the Hebrew scriptures, God's presence was visible in a "pillar of cloud" by day and a "pillar of fire" by night (Exod. 13:21–22). In the Priestly tradition, however, God's glory is manifest in the tabernacle, a prototype of the later temple (Exod. 40:34). In that perspective, God chooses to be present at the center of the community—in the tabernacle/temple, and in this sense to dwell in the midst of the people. As the Sabbath makes time holy, so the temple sanctifies space. The land around this center, that is, the land of Israel, becomes a holy land because it is the scene of a history that reaches its climax in the creation of a sanctuary where people have access to the holy God, who is Creator and Redeemer. This view is comparable to that in the prologue to the Gospel of John, which announces that the divine Logos was made flesh and "lived [tabernacle] among us", enabling people of faith to behold God's glory in Jesus Christ (John 1:14).

In connection with the announcement that God will dwell in the midst of the people, it is said that God designates Aaron and his sons to serve as priests (Exod. 29:43–46), representing the people to God. Exodus 29 sets forth the rite for the ordination of a person to the high priesthood. The individual was "anointed" with oil (29:7) and thus, like a king, could be considered "the Lord's anointed." In the Priestly theology, the role of the priest includes officiating at the altar. Priests occasionally taught, but primarily they served at the altar where sacrifices were performed that were believed to make atonement for the people and mediate God's forgiving grace. In the New Testament, Priestly theology comes to expression above all in the Epistle to the Hebrews (6:19—8:28), where Jesus is portrayed both as high priest (of the order of Melchizedek [Ps. 110:4], who performs his sacrifice not in an earthly temple but in its heavenly prototype) and as sacrifice (performed "once for all" and therefore not subject to repetition). Jesus is thereby see as the mediator of an "eternal covenant" (Heb. 13:20) that reconciles people to God and enables them to live in the presence of the holy God.

Finally, Jesus Christ is king, like the "son of God" of royal messianic tradition. In the Gospel of Luke, an angel tells Mary that the child to be born to her "will be called the Son of the Most High, and the Lord God will give to him the throne of his ancestor David" (Luke 1:32). Such titles belong firmly in Jewish tradition, echoing the Davidic covenant, which portrays the king in these terms: "I will be a father to him, and he shall be son to me" (2 Sam. 7:14). In royal psalms the anointed king of Israel is declared to be God's son "today," meaning on the day of coronation (Ps. 2:7). In Psalm 110:1 the king is portrayed as seated at the right hand of God, sharing the divine rule. In one instance, if we follow the unusual translation of the received text, the king is addressed as divine: "Your throne, O God, endures forever" (Ps. 45:6). This verse is without parallel in the Old Testament, though it is common in Near Eastern kingship ideology.

While most scholars understand this poetic imagery as symbolic, there is no question that the Old Testament writers view the king as God's agent, anointed for a specific task. While titles such as "messiah" or "son of God" are deeply rooted in Israel's covenant traditions and do not in themselves denote ontological relationship with God, such a shift is evident when one moves from the Synoptic Gospels to the quite different symbolic world of John's Gospel, which is introduced by identifying Christ with the Logos, the Word that in the beginning was "with God" and "was God" (John 1:1-2). This shift to ontology is also evident in post-Pauline writings such as the Epistle to the Colossians, which declares that God created the world in Christ (Col. 1:15-17) and that in him "all the fullness of God/deity dwells" (Col. 1:19; 2:9). Statements like these, rooted in Israel's wisdom literature (see Prov. 8:22-31; Wis. 7:22-30; 9:2, 10; 18:15; Sir. 24:1-12) but also in Greek philosophy, move in the direction of the Trinitarian discussions of the early Christian church.[7]

---

7. For an extended discussion of Logos in the writings of the first-century Jewish philosopher Philo of Alexandria, a contemporary of Jesus and of Paul, see Wilson, *Evolution of God*, 216-41. Using Jewish and Greek reasoning, Philo spoke of the Logos in ways that seemingly anticipated Christian conceptions of Christ and of the Holy Spirit.

No one image, motif or theme which has been reviewed is adequate in itself for the New Testament understanding of Jesus. "We have found him" (John 1:45), say the gospel and apostolic writers, echoing Philip. This note of fulfillment is struck throughout the New Testament, not so much one note as a harmony of notes:

> In Jesus the promise is confirmed, the covenant is renewed, the prophecies are fulfilled, the law is vindicated, salvation is brought near, sacred history has reached its climax, the perfect sacrifice has been offered and accepted, the great high priest over the household has taken his seat at God's right hand, the Prophet like Moses has been raised up, the Son of David reigns, the kingdom of God has been inaugurated, the Son of Man has received dominion from the Ancient of Days, the Servant of the Lord, having been smitten to death for his people's transgressions and borne the sin of many, has accomplished the divine purpose, has seen light after the travail of his soul and is now exalted and extolled and made very high.[8]

The Church as the New People of God

Every verse of the New Testament presupposes the new people of God, a new community called the church. From the beginning, Christians were characterized as "the body of Christ," followers of Jesus who showed by their lifestyle that they were a part of the new order that Jesus had announced and that they believed had now arrived. Theologically, the church was a microcosm of the transformation that God's new order would bring for the whole world. To be in the church was to have a foretaste of life as God's new people. Socially, the church in the Roman Empire was an alternative society, based not on selfishness and greed and exploitation, but on the new freedom and fellowship that Jesus had announced: freedom to love God and to love and serve others (Mark 12:29–31). As the church expanded across the Mediterranean world, it was indeed a new society—a context in which people of diverse social, racial, and religious backgrounds were united in a new and radical friendship. Because they had been reconciled to God, they found themselves reconciled to each other.[9]

---

8. Bruce, *New Testament Development*, 21.
9. Drane, *Introducing the New Testament*, 381–82.

Jesus himself conceived his mission to be that of calling the remnant of Israel—twelve disciples, corresponding to the twelve-tribe structure of Israel. And when the meaning of Jesus' life, death, and resurrection came upon these disciples with overwhelming power at the festival of Pentecost (Acts 2), a powerful movement emerged. This small community became a dynamic and militant church, with a message that "turned the world upside down" (Acts 17:6) and a gospel that was carried enthusiastically to the ends of the earth. The Acts of the Apostles gives the story of the emerging church. According to Acts, the church expanded because it fulfilled faithfully its two tasks in society: to evangelize, that is, to serve as Christ's witnesses "to the ends of the earth" (Acts 1:8; see also Matthew's Great Commission in Matthew 28:19–20), and to live by the ethics of love and mercy that Jesus had taught.

While stressing the newness of the church, we must also keep in mind the relation of this community to the entire Old Testament heritage. In a sense, the church may be called the "New Israel," for like ancient Israel, congregants had a special role in history. The Old Testament narrates how a people was formed to be the bearer of God's purpose in history and the instrument of God's saving work. Israel was not a race or a nation but a covenant community created by God's action. Having delivered Israel from slavery in Egypt, God made them a covenant people. Through many tumultuous years, God educated and disciplined them in order that they might understand more deeply the meaning of their special role.

It was Second Isaiah who understood most profoundly Israel's place in God's worldwide purpose. According to this prophet, Israel was called to be a "light to the nations" (Isa. 49:6) and a servant whose sufferings would benefit all humanity (Isa. 49:3; 53:4–6, 11–12). However, in the intervening years, this expansive vision was obscured. The last two centuries before Jesus witnessed a resurgence of Jewish nationalism that led in time to wars with Rome. In AD 70 the Romans destroyed the temple, leveled Jerusalem, and removed the last vestiges of Jewish statehood. So, in the fullness of time, God acted once again to reconstitute the community of Israel—no longer bound by ethnic or nationalistic limitations but open to all people, Jew and Gentile alike, on the basis of faith. The new community does not establish a clean break with the people of God whose life story is portrayed in the Old Testament. Rather, as Paul puts it in his important discussion in Romans 9–11, the community is a "remnant chosen by grace." It is, so to speak, a "wild olive shoot" grafted onto the olive tree (Israel); and the "branch" (Gentile Christians) is supported by the roots that reach down deeply into God's choice of Israel and God's faithful dealings with this people (Rom. 11:17–24).

Although some parallels can be drawn with the ancient Hebrew cultic observances, the church in the New Testament takes quite a different form. It is more similar to the Jewish synagogue (a learning center) than to the temple and its cultic activities. At first, homes of believers served as the places of worship; only later did Christians build church structures comparable to Israel's synagogues. The cross became the central cultic object, rather than the Ark of the Covenant or Torah scrolls. The cross served as a sign of Jesus' crucifixion and resurrection and symbolized the meaning of these events. The first day of the week (Sunday), which commemorated Jesus' resurrection, replaced the Jewish Sabbath as the primary cultic season. In addition to the regular activities of worship and education, which helped to unify the new Christian community, the basic cultic acts were baptism and the Lord's Supper (the Eucharist).[10]

Such worship and religious practices did not emerge without problems, however, and new leaders were required. Initially, the disciples of Jesus (the Twelve) became prominent leaders of the Jerusalem church, with a smaller number—consisting of Peter, John, and James "the Just"—exercising greater influence. A somewhat larger group, known as apostles, became the preeminent figures in the spread of Christianity. This group included the Twelve, but the total company of apostles was more numerous. The thing that made a person an apostle was a personal commission by Jesus. The Greek word *apostolos* means "one sent." Apostles were ambassadors of the risen Lord, understood to have extraordinary authority in the church.

In the world beyond Jerusalem, the church generally assumed the form of a synagogue, that is, a congregation. The Greek word for church (*ekklesia*) means a group of people called together. It is one of the words used in the Septuagint to designate the assembly of the people of Israel. Because the Jews chose another of the available synonymous words, *synagoge*, for their assemblies, it is quite likely that the first Christians deliberately, and to avoid confusion, rejected the term adopted by the Jews and chose the other. Almost from the start, church congregations were governed by elders (Greek, *presbuteros*), one of whom was chief. With the passage of time, the office of chief elder evolved into that of bishop. Ephesians 4:11 lists prophets, evangelists, pastors, and teachers after apostles among the

---

10. Bowne and Currid, "Biblical Society," 175.

spiritually gifted leaders of the early church. Apostles stand first in 1 Corinthians 12:28, followed by prophets, teachers, miracle workers, healers, helpers, administrators, speakers in tongues, and interpreters. In keeping with the order of both lists, Paul assigned particular honor to the office of prophet (see 1 Cor. 14:1–19). The authority of the apostle was derived from a connection with Jesus, while that of the church prophet was entirely charismatic. As the church developed, the authority of the apostles was passed from the apostles to the bishops through apostolic succession, an authority initially not concerned with the passing of power but of correct teaching. Over time the charismatic offices in the church waned, whereas apostolic authority was deemed irreplaceable.

As developed by Paul, the church presupposes a faith community that is the source of social unity. All life, whether politics, economics, education, or religion, stands under the covenant relation to God. Within that conception, every believer has a part to play. Whether Christians meet together for worship or fellowship, all members are indispensable for all have something to contribute (see 1 Cor. 14:26–33). As a result, Paul asserts that every Christian has a distinct *charism*, a ministry that is not restricted by either ordination or some other special experience, but which is given to all by the work of the Spirit in the lives of believers (1 Cor. 12:7).

In the church, all members are of equal importance, and that includes equality of women with men. Paul's letters contain conflicting statements about the place of women in the church's life, so in order to discern his own view, the recommended starting place is Galatians 3:28: "There is no longer Jew or Greek, there is no longer slave or free, there is no longer male and female; for all of you are one in Christ." Despite statements to the contrary, generally seen as interpolations (see 1 Cor. 14:33b–36) or post-Pauline (see 1 Tim. 2:11–15), the early Christian movement clearly affirmed sexual equality, prompting Thomas Cahill to call the primitive church "the world's first egalitarian society." Likewise, Cahill declares Paul's statement in 1 Corinthians 11:11 (that "in the Lord woman is not independent of man or man independent of woman") to be the clearest affirmation of sexual equality in the entire Bible—indeed, the first in world literature.[11] Paul himself was happy to work alongside women, some of whom were his close friends (Phil. 4:2–3). His most extensive list of greetings to Christian leaders includes many women (Rom. 16:1–15, and he refers to at least one of them as "apostle" (Junia, Rom. 16:7). Furthermore, when Paul advises the church

---

11. Cahill, *Desire of the Everlasting Hills*, 148.

at Corinth about the appropriate way to behave, he takes it for granted that both men and women should pray or prophecy in public worship (1 Cor. 11:4–5). In 1 Corinthians 11:1–16 Paul uses rabbinic arguments where it suits him, moving in two directions simultaneously: conserving tradition by upholding the custom of head-covering, yet breaking with tradition in allowing women to participate in worship. The whole frame of reference is determined by Paul's insistence that men and women have the same freedom and opportunity to play a full part in the life of the church.

The same point also comes out clearly when Paul discusses marriage in 1 Corinthians 7. Some of what he writes is obscure, no doubt because of its specific reference to details of the Corinthian situation. But the general principle is clear: Men and women relate to each other not through domination but by mutual love and service.

For Paul what determines a person's function in the church is the endowment of God's Spirit. In God's new society, social distinctions such as gender, race, and social class are irrelevant. The heart of the gospel is freedom: freedom from guilt, from the Law, from sin, and from all that would inhibit the development of one's God-given potential. To be set free by Christ is to be released into a new world in which people can find their own true identity, relating to each other in freedom and fellowship because they are related to Christ himself. That final transformation is yet in the future, when the "glorious freedom of the children of God" will be fully realized (Rom 8:21). In the meantime, the church stands as a testimony to that future hope, and as the context in which people can serve one another as they love and serve God.

The earliest church was undoubtedly charismatic. These early believers were dominated by their experience of the Holy Spirit at work among them, so they gave little thought to the problems of organizing the infant church. They believed the Holy Spirit was the only organizing force they needed. This understanding of Christian fellowship became central for Paul and quite likely for other apostles as well. The authentic picture of a church in the New Testament is of groups of Christians acting together in a spirit of mutual love and friendship. When Paul wrote to the church at Rome some twenty years after the events at Pentecost, there seems to have been no organized hierarchy. Yet within the space of about forty years, this changed rather dramatically.

During the second half of the first century, we see a distinction between itinerant and local ministries, which resulted in a two-tiered structure of authority consisting of:

- leaders with local authority (i.e., with oversight of individual congregations): these included presbyters (elders), "bishops" as Eucharistic celebrants, and "deacons" assisting in liturgy, with administrative and social duties;
- leaders with universal authority (i.e. with ministry to all churches): these included apostles, prophets, and teachers.

By the end of the first century (the close of the "apostolic" period), the church became more institutionalized. After the death of the apostles, leading cities such as Jerusalem, Antioch, Alexandria, Ephesus, and Rome became vested with greater status, their bishops with greater authority. Worship was now guided by trained clergy, and a fixed liturgy developed for the Lord's Supper. Baptism was no longer administered as a spontaneous expression of faith in Jesus, but as the culmination of catechetical instruction. The teaching often took place during Lent, followed by the baptism of converts on Easter.

We may trace four main reasons for these changes in the early church:[12]

1. *Church growth*: the early church grew at an amazing rate, due in part to evangelistic efforts like those of Peter and Paul but also to the fact that the church exhibited a remarkable ability to meet social and human needs. Leaders were needed, with specialized training, to meet these needs;

2. *Heresy and orthodoxy*: the charismatic approach was open to abuse as well as to false or abusive leaders. The need for a clearly delineated sense of tradition may have been the single most important factor that led to the development of a hierarchical church in the second century, which resulted in an ordained clergy and in the development of a canon of authoritative scripture;

3. *Social change*: like any organization, the church has no future unless it plans for the future. Growth requires planning, adaptation, and economic resources. The early church seems to have had elements of institutionalism from the start, including rites for initiates (baptism)

---

12. Drane, *Introducing the New Testament*, 398–406.

and for members (the Lord's Supper), and it was conscious of having traditions to hand on to future generations. Its leaders had great authority and were, at least on some occasions, paid by other church members. As long as the church saw itself as operating through the power of the Holy Spirit, change seemed unnecessary. But once it became suspicious of the exercise of charismatic gifts, due to their misuse, it was a short step from that to the institutionalized church;

4. *Frustrated hope*: the earliest Christians expected Christ's imminent return. The Christians at Thessalonica became so excited about the fact that Jesus was to return that they neglected work in order to prepare for this great event. Paul rebuked them for this, though he shared their sense of expectation (1 Thess. 4:13—5:11). Using the words of Jesus, he reminded them that "the day of the Lord will come like a thief in the night." In the meantime, they should be good citizens, working for their living and encouraging and helping other people. That is the best way to prepare for the coming of Christ. Paul, like Jesus, understood the kingdom of God as already present yet not fully so (see Matt. 12:28; Luke 17:21), and eternal life as a life in the future yet also as the life of God available in the present (John 6:47; 17:3). While early Christians expected the arrival of God's kingdom, this did not occur, and the prospect of a future return of Jesus diminished over time (2 Pet. 3:8). Eventually they came to terms with the fact that they needed to settle down for the long haul.

In the final analysis, the church became an institution not out of conviction but out of practical necessity. As a result of church growth, heresy, social change, and frustrated hope, the charismatic ideal no longer seemed a practical way forward.

The Foundation of the New Community

Of the many passages in the New Testament that deal with the calling and mission of the new community, 1 Peter 2:4-10 is one of the most instructive. It establishes the biblical truth that the church has been built upon Jesus Christ, the "living stone," upon which foundation a "spiritual house" is built. The church is not essentially a social organization or a human institution that can be analyzed sociologically, but is rather a creation of God, who has chosen the rejected stone (Jesus Christ) as the foundation.

In 1 Peter three "stone" oracles appear as *testimonia* about the ministry of Jesus: Isaiah 28:16; Psalm 118:22; and Isaiah 8:14–15. In the first passage, delivered by Isaiah in the course of a warning about the impending Assyrian invasion of Judah, the stone is the righteous remnant of the people of God, the hope of the future, which in other oracles of Isaiah is embodied in the promised prince of the house of David. Isaiah 28:16 views the stone not only as a reliable foundation stone but as a cornerstone, a tested stone that keeps the entire structure intact. The figure is used also in Ephesians 2:20–22, where Christ Jesus is "the cornerstone" in whom "the whole structure is joined together and grows into a holy temple in the Lord."

The second *testimonium*, taken from Psalm 118, bears the jubilant cry that the stone which the builders would have rejected as poor material has become the cornerstone of the foundation. The stone referred to in this royal psalm is also the righteous remnant of Israel, but according to 1 Peter, the remnant is reduced to one—to Jesus Christ, the church's one foundation. In the parable of the vineyard (Mark 12:10–11), Jesus addresses this *testimonium* to hearers who "realized that he had told this parable against them" and sought to arrest him. Its application is made even more explicit in Acts 4:11 where Peter, standing with John to reply to the Sanhedrin's inquisition into the healing of the lame man in the temple court, assures the court that the healing was effected by Jesus, "whom you crucified." The third rock *testimonium* in 1 Peter 2 is an oracle from Isaiah 8:14–15, which also relates to unbelievers. To those who believe, the cornerstone is "precious," but for unbelievers, Jesus is "a rock that makes them fall" (1 Peter 2:8). It is used by Paul in Romans 9:32–33, where it is thoroughly conflated with the oracle from Isaiah 28:16 to provide a *testimonium* of Israel's refusal of the gospel.

The expression in 1 Peter 2:9, previously applied to the chosen people at the time of the making of the covenant (see Exod. 19:4–6), is here applied to the New Israel, which was once "not a people" (1 Peter 2:10; compare Hos. 2:23), but in the grace of God has become "God's people."

The place of the church in the movement of God's purpose for the world, from creation to consummation, is developed with majestic splendor in the Epistle to the Ephesians. In addition to describing the church in terms of the image of the temple, of which Jesus Christ is the chief cornerstone (Eph. 2:19–22), a second image is used, the distinctively Pauline image of the body, of which Christ is the head (2:16; see 1:22–23; 4:15–16). The theme of peace is sounded in 2:17, the words "to you who were far off" and "to those who were near" echoing God's great promise to Abraham in Genesis 12:4: "in you all the families of the earth shall be blessed." While we usually think of peace as the absence of war, in the Bible "peace" has a more positive meaning, pointing to a state of harmony, wholeness, and welfare within the community. And it is a basic biblical premise that there cannot be right relations within the community unless human beings are in right relation with God, for when separated from God, people are at odds with one another as well as with themselves. Thus the command about loving God comes first and supplies the basis for loving the neighbor.

As Old Testament prophets looked away from the fractured society of Israel, they anticipated the coming of the age of the Messiah, when the barriers of separation would be overcome and human beings would be brought into a new relation with God, with one another, and with the natural environment. In Ephesians love is not a commandment but a new reality in human relationships that has been initiated by God's prior love through Jesus Christ. The church is a fellowship of love, the highest endowment of God's Spirit (see 1 Cor. 13:13; 1 John 4:7–21).

Jesus' Prayer for the Church

The theme of the unity and faithfulness of the church in the world is elaborated in John 17, Jesus' so-called "high-priestly prayer." In his final prayer, two prepositions are important: "out of" and "into." God has summoned a people for Christ "out of" the world (John 17: 6). Indeed, the New Testament word for church (*ekklesia*) literally means "called out" and suggests the idea of God calling people out of the world into a new and unique fellowship. However, the church is not taken out of the world into a detached life, but rather is sent "into" the world (John 17:15, 18).

The church is God's new community in the world. As God's mission for the world, the church has inherited the vocation to be a light to the nations and the instrument of God's healing of the brokenness of society. This cannot be done without unity, and so above all, Jesus' prayer is for the unity of the church: "that they may be one, even as we are one" (John 17:11, 22). "And this unity is to be the most convincing demonstration to the world that Jesus has been sent by God as the Way, the Truth, and the Life" (John 14:6).[13]

---

13. Anderson, *Unfolding Drama of the Bible*, 79.

Chapter 11

New Creation

We have said that the Bible views history as a purposive drama, and that the drama sweeps forward from beginning to end, from the initiation of God's plan in the book of Genesis to the realization of God's design in the book of Revelation. All things—history and nature, heaven and earth—are caught up in the purpose of the God who is the First and the Last, the Alpha and the Omega. Unlike the ancient Greek historians who believed that history moves in circles, and unlike some modern historians who believe that the historical process is a phase of the growth and decay of nature, the Bible affirms that our lives are part of a great drama that moves in the direction of a goal. It is not accidental that the Christian Bible moves from the creation of "the heavens and the earth" (Gen. 1:1) to the creation of "the new heaven and the new earth" (Rev. 21:1). Creation and consummation, first things and last things, are inseparably joined together, like Siamese twins. The Bible, therefore has an eschatology, that is, a doctrine of the end (*eschaton*) or "last things" (*eschata*) of history, and because the first words of the Bible, "in the beginning," have as their counterparts the expectation "in the end," creation is an eschatological belief.[1]

It should be obvious that we cannot speak of either the first things or the last things except in the language of religious symbolism, that is, the language of myth. In both cases we are dealing with ultimates that lie beyond the range of our finite knowledge, beyond our immediate historical experience. Therefore, we must speak in the language of faith—faith that

---

1. Anderson, *Creation versus Chaos*, 110.

rests upon the meaning that has been disclosed in the unique historical tradition beginning with the Exodus and culminating in the Christ event.

From Prophecy to Apocalyptic

To consider properly the eschatological element in the New Testament, we must turn again to the prophets, for eschatology was basic to their message. They consistently looked beyond the present, in which God's purpose seemed to be temporarily opposed by Israel's rebellion, to a time when God would triumph over the forces of evil. Prophetic predictions of the triumph of God's purpose were expressed in phrases like "the Day of the Lord," "the Age to Come," and "the kingdom of God." In their vision the consummation of history was to be a time of reckoning, when all rebellious powers would be judged and destroyed. It was also to be the beginning of a New Creation in which nature and human nature would be transformed. No longer would there be war, and even wild animals would be tame (Isa. 65:17–25). The pictures of the messianic age remind us of the idyllic peace and harmony of the Garden of Eden prior to the expulsion. The prophets proclaimed that the Day was imminent, as the very next moment of history.

The prophetic message was further elaborated in a type of literature called "apocalyptic," which flourished in the postexilic period. The theme of apocalyptic, as in the case of prophecy, is the nearness of the time when God will assert sovereignty over history and nature. It is characteristic of apocalyptic, however, that specific historical events recede into the background, and the contest between God and rebellious forces assumes a cosmic scale. Apocalyptic writers are dualistic in their view of history. They perceive two dominions (kingdoms) struggling for dominance. The kingdom of God stands opposed to the well-organized kingdom of Evil that is under the leadership of Satan. This is not a metaphysical dualism, rooted in ultimate reality or in the depths of divinity, for God's original creation was good. Rather, this is a postcreation dualism rooted in creaturely rebellion against God—rebellion that is evident not only in human sin but also in cosmic revolt by celestial beings. The conflict between the forces of God and the forces of evil was eventually expressed in terms of the myth of Satan, a heavenly being who revolted against God and set up a rival kingdom into which human beings are enticed. These two dominions may also be described as two "ages" or "worlds," that is, times of history. The present "age," in the apocalyptic view, is under the dominion of evil, and it will be succeeded by the "new age," when evil is overcome and all things are made new.

The End will be heralded by unusual "signs" and cataclysms in nature. On the Day of Judgment God (or God's messianic agent) will destroy all powers of evil and will create a new heaven and a new earth. As we see in the book of Daniel, the purpose of apocalyptic writers was to encourage the faithful to remain steadfast in a perilous hour when allegiance to God was temporarily eclipsed by foreign tyranny or the victory of evil (in this light see the account of Daniel's friends cast into the "fiery furnace" [Dan. 3] or of Daniel cast into the "den of lions" [Dan. 6], symbols of the Maccabean faithful under the forced Hellenization by the tyrant Antiochus Epiphanes around 165 BC). The use of fantastic imagery in books like Ezekiel and Daniel clearly indicates that the language was intended to be imaginative. The heart of the apocalyptic message was the certainty that God's purpose could not be frustrated—a certainty that found expression in the nearness of the End. This is the only way that a new age of peace and justice can come: God must destroy the whole evil system.

The movement from classical prophecy to apocalyptic can be traced within the book of Isaiah, from its inception in the message of the eighth-century prophet Isaiah of Jerusalem (chapters 1–39), to the message of the so-called Second Isaiah during the exile (chapters 40–55), to the message of the so-called Third Isaiah, dated to the postexilic period and found at the conclusion of the book (chapters 56–66). To appreciate the theological significance of this shift, we turn to the message of Second Isaiah, which represents the transition from prophecy (First Isaiah) to apocalyptic (Third Isaiah).

Like a pastoral theologian, Second Isaiah offers comfort to a dislocated, suffering people whose faith in God has been strained to the breaking point: "Comfort my people, says your God. Speak tenderly to Jerusalem, and cry to her that she has served her term, that her penalty is paid, that she has received from the Lord's hand double for all her sins" (Isa. 40:1–2). The substance of the "good news" that is to be carried from heaven to earth is that the time of the coming of God's dominion is near. While Second Isaiah does not refer directly to the Mosaic covenant, the people are told that though they have suffered the penalty for their sins, and they are assured that God's covenant promises made of old are still valid: "the word of our God will stand forever" (Isa. 40:8). Like the former exodus from Egyptian bondage, God is about to do a "new thing," which will be so wonderful that the former things pale in significance: "I am about to do a new thing, now it springs forth, do you not perceive it?" (Isa. 43:16–19). The heart of Second Isaiah's message is the proclamation that the new creation is happening in the present as God conquers the chaos of the Babylonian exile and makes a path through the sea for his redeemed to pass over and return with singing to Jerusalem (Isa. 51:10). The prophet has taken creation completely out of the realm of mythology. For him creation is a historical event in the now. Here is a faith that turns not to the archaic past, longing for the good old days, "but stands on tiptoe, facing the new age that God is about to introduce."[2]

Second Isaiah turns to the Davidic covenant, announcing the rebuilding of the temple through the agency of a foreign ruler, Cyrus of Persia, here called God's anointed (Messiah) because he will accomplish God's purpose (Isa. 44:28—45:7). The Davidic covenant is reaffirmed by shifting the promises of this "everlasting covenant" from the Davidic dynasty to the new community (Isa. 55:3). The poet continues by stating that this community will be instrumental in including other nations in the saving purpose of God, as promised in the Abrahamic covenant (Isa. 55:5; see Gen. 12:3; 22:18).

The final section of the book of Isaiah, so-called Third Isaiah (56–66), is sometimes designated proto-apocalyptic or the "dawn of apocalyptic," since it is not apocalyptic in the full-blown sense. In the final edition of the book of Isaiah, materials of more definite apocalyptic character were added, including "the little apocalypse" of Isaiah 24–27 and chapters 34 and 35. In these passages we notice a shift in emphasis from the history of the people Israel to the cosmic dimension, which includes heaven and earth and the whole course of human history from creation to consummation. Nations like Assyria and Babylon are no longer agents of God chastening the people Israel but are symbols of sinister powers at work in history, threatening God's divine plan for Israel and the nations. God's victory over these forces of evil represents a new creation in which God vindicates Zion, the city of God, and ends the suffering of the poor and helpless of the earth (see Isa. 65:17–19).

Whereas classic prophecy explained suffering as retribution for the people's failure or sin, apocalyptic writers found this explanation of evil to be inadequate. It was not enough to call for repentance or to blame the people for their irresponsibility. They perceived that Israel and all peoples were caught in the grip of monstrous forces that challenged the sovereignty of God. Evil, in their view, is located not in the human heart but in oppressive

---

2. Anderson, *Contours of Old Testament Theology*, 294.

empires and other structures of power. Accordingly, apocalyptic writers revived the ancient myth of the battle of the Divine Warrior against the powers of chaos and the decisive victory that demonstrated God's power as King. This ancient myth influenced the pattern of the Song of the Sea (Exod. 15:1–18), a poetic response to the Exodus. At one point Second Isaiah invoked the myth to portray Yahweh's power to create a people and give them a future. In this poetic view, the victory over the army of the Pharaoh is symbolized by the monster of chaos, Rahab (Isa. 51:9–10), and the author addresses Yahweh to achieve a similar victory in the future.

In apocalyptic imagination the Divine Warrior's victory is not restricted to Israel's history but belongs to a universal drama, in which the kingdom of God opposes the powers of evil that afflict people. These visionaries portray a New Jerusalem, a new age, indeed, a new creation. In this perspective, the coming of God's kingdom on earth will be the time of God's triumph—not only over human sin but also over all the powers of evil that have corrupted human history. In the Isaiah Apocalypse (Isa. 24–27), the writer portrays the final triumph of the Divine Warrior over the monster of evil known as Tiamat in Babylonian tradition and as the sea serpent Leviathan (Rahab) in Canaanite mythology (Isa. 27:1).

Thus in apocalyptic literature the whole historical drama, from creation to consummation, is viewed as a cosmic conflict between the divine and the demonic, creation and chaos, the kingdom of God and the kingdom of Satan. According to this view, the outcome of the conflict will be God's victorious annihilation of the powers that threaten creation, including death, which apocalyptic writers regarded as an enemy hostile to God. Seen in this perspective, the role of the Messiah would be not just to liberate humanity from the bondage of sin but to battle triumphantly against the powers of evil.

A line can easily be drawn from this apocalyptic passage to the portrayal of the consummation found in the book of Revelation. In this Christian apocalypse, at the time of the final triumph of God, the powers of evil—symbolized by "the great dragon . . . that ancient serpent, who is called the Devil and Satan" (Rev. 12:9)—will be overcome. Moreover, "the sea"—the locus of the powers of chaos—will be no more (Rev. 21:1).

The First Coming of Christ as Eschatological Event[3]

The New Testament is saturated with the belief that something new has happened in the history of humanity, in and through the life and death of Jesus Christ, and above all through his resurrection from the dead. In order to make sense of the New Testament, we need to begin with Easter, for Easter is central to Christianity. Whatever occurred on that first Easter, it had incredible power. Before the Easter experience Jesus' followers forsook him and fled. After the Easter experience they were willing to die for their conviction that whatever their understanding of God, it had to include Jesus of Nazareth. This shift in God consciousness revolutionized the theology of a group of Jewish people so dramatically that the world has never been the same. In addition, the Easter event led Jewish Christians to create Sunday, a new holy day, different from yet fulfilling the notion of the Jewish Sabbath.

The continued experience of God's presence in this community of faith was so real that in time even this experience was redefined. Through this definition the concept of the Holy Spirit and later the doctrine of the Trinity became the very cornerstone of the Christian faith. No matter how one understands the meaning of Jesus' resurrection and the message of Easter, there must be about it something real enough to account for these measurable effects.[4] But what really happened, and what does it mean?

When we examine the Gospel accounts, which describe in some detail the event we call the resurrection, we find that they do not give a clear-cut and harmonious picture as to what happened. The Easter narratives, taken literally, raise more questions than they answer. And so we dare to ask whether Paul and the authors who write about the resurrection, writers we call Mark, Matthew, Luke, and John, assumed the literal objective quality of the Easter stories as they described them. Is it possible, we must ask, to affirm the reality of the Easter experience without taking literally the details of the resurrection moment? This is a crucial and necessary distinction. Were the Gospel stories of Easter written to capture a literal description of something that actually happened? Can Easter be real without this kind of objectivity?

When we look at the story of Jesus' life as the Gospel writers portray it, particularly when they deal with the birth and death of Jesus, can we think

---

3. The material in this segment is adapted from the discussion on the resurrection in my book, *Beyond Belief*, 136–39.

4. Spong, *Liberating the Gospels*, 278.

that they intended their words to be understood literally? They were not writing history or biography. They were trying to interpret a life-changing experience that had been very real to them, but all they could use were limited human words. The Gospel writers signaled this weakness of vocabulary to their readers by exaggerating their language to the point at which their words became literally absurd. The entire Gospel narrative is illustrative of this, but it reaches a climax in the stories of Jesus' birth and death.

Symbolic language is obviously present in the story of Jesus' birth. Do virgins conceive? Do angels sing to shepherds? Do stars wander through the sky so slowly that magi can follow them? Would wise men travel with symbolic interpretive gifts for a newborn child, including myrrh as a sign of what that baby's eventual death would accomplish? Even in the first century these things would be recognized as the stuff of fairy tales, not unlike narratives of those who seek a pot of gold at the end of the rainbow.

The Gospel narratives go on to relate accounts of Jesus walking on water, transforming five loaves of bread into enough food to feed multitudes, and even raise people from the dead. The narratives then culminate in tales describing the final events in Jesus' life. Were the graves of the "saints in Jerusalem" really opened by Jesus' death so that the bodies of those long deceased ones could rise up, be resuscitated, and walk the streets of that city in the sight of many (Matt. 27:52)? Were these ever meant to be literal stories, even in the first century, or is there something else going on in these narratives that we miss because we have for so long been taught to read them as historical?

Did the risen Jesus miraculously appear out of thin air to the two people on the road from Jerusalem to Emmaus and then just as miraculously disappear into thin air after they had recognized him in the sacrament of the broken bread (Luke 24:13–35)? Did the risen Jesus walk through locked doors and barred windows to get into that upper room to join his disciples at the time of the evening meal on the first day of the week following the crucifixion (John 20: 19–23)? If people really believed that Jesus could do that, why would the stone in front of the tomb have been a problem and thus why was angelic help needed to remove it?[5]

Once we get beyond the simple inadequacy of human language to describe the realm of the divine, we must then face the incongruities present in the biblical texts of Easter. How many angels were at the tomb? Was it one, as Mark and Matthew state, or were there two angels, as Luke and John

---

5. These questions are taken from the discussion in Spong, *Eternal Life*, 174–77.

assert? Where were the disciples when the reality of Easter first dawned on the disciples? Mark and Matthew indicate that they were in Galilee. Luke directly contradicted this understanding, insisting that every appearance of the risen Christ occurred in Jerusalem or in its environs. Did the women see the risen Lord at the tomb at the dawn of Easter? No, said Mark; yes, said Matthew; no, said Luke; yes, said John, but it was not "the women" but only one woman, and her name was Mary.[6]

Was the resurrected body of Jesus physical? Matthew seemed to think so when he portrayed the women taking hold of the feet of Jesus (Matt. 28:9). Luke portrays Jesus as eating fish in the presence of the disciples and as inviting the disciples to handle him, claiming that a spirit does not have flesh and bones (Luke 24:39–43). Such descriptions sound quite physical. But in the Emmaus road account this body could appear out of thin air and disappear into thin air. John had the same internal conflict in his text. John's Jesus could walk into a locked room, but once inside he also offered his physical wounds for inspection (John 20:19–25). "Everywhere one turns in the biblical texts of Easter there is confusion, for assertions made in one gospel are contradicted in another."[7]

Next, we examine the order of resurrection appearances as given in 1 Corinthians 15:1–6. The first witness was Cephas (Peter), then the twelve, then five hundred witnesses, and last of all, Paul. In Mark, the first Gospel to be written, there is no mention of an actual appearance of the risen Jesus. This Gospel announces an anticipated reunion in an unspecified future (Mark 16:1–8). Matthew, writing more than twenty years after Paul, states that the first appearance was not to Cephas, but to the women in the garden. Later he describes an appearance to the eleven, not to the twelve, but he never relates an account of a moment when an appearance to Peter might have occurred (Matthew 28). Luke does affirm that Peter was the first (Luke 24:34); second in his listing, however, was not the appearance to the twelve, as Paul had asserted, but to an unknown man named Cleopas (Luke 24:13), who was traveling with a friend on the road to Emmaus. Only after this episode, according to Luke, did Jesus appear to the disciples (Luke 24:36). John, the last gospel to be written, mentions that the risen Christ appeared first to Mary Magdalene, and only second to the disciples, but not to all twelve, since both Thomas and Judas clearly were absent. No source in

---

6. Spong, *Liberating the Gospels*, 280–82.
7. Ibid., 283.

the biblical tradition corroborates Paul's mention of an appearance to five hundred brethren or to James.[8]

Ask yourself, if you are still confined to the literal sense of the story, why it was that though the Christian community attached great weight to the resurrection, no two accounts of it were alike? Also note why the described events are seen as taking place at the dawn of the day, and why the resurrection takes place privately and not publicly. Are we dealing, in these ancient biblical narratives, with a different level of reality and a different kind of language? How does one explore and seek to make rational sense out of experiences that occur at the edges of life? Do these questions not give us a clue that these writers were trying to say something that stretched ordinary human language beyond its normal limits? Surely these writers were aware that they were describing an internal, profoundly real and reorienting psychic and mystical experience that had altered human consciousness and, therefore, human history. Should we expend time and energy looking for proofs of the literalness of these details so that we can, first, convince ourselves that they are true, and then pass on that understanding to the next generation? Can our fear of death ever be transcended by these literalistic approaches? In each of the above-cited examples I would argue that the words were not, and were never intended to be, literal descriptions of real happenings, and that to treat them as if they were is to distort them.

Regardless of one's stance on these matters, one point is clear: Jesus appeared only to his followers; unbelievers did not see him. This should warn us against supposing that the resurrection was an objective event capable of being seen by all persons. Only in faith could one behold the risen Christ. To the church, the resurrection was the sign and assurance that God had won a decisive victory over "the law of sin and of death" (Rom. 8:2) and had made available "newness of life." Already believers could participate in the life of God's kingdom. As God raised Christ from the dead, so God had raised them from "death" in order that they might share, both now and hereafter, in the "new creation."

Up to this point we have attempted to project ourselves into the mindset of early Christians, who thought Hebraically about the resurrection. Since the Bible is written in an idiom more or less strange to us, we must learn the new language, lest we completely misunderstand the faith early Christians attempted to communicate. E. P. Sanders, in his classic text *Jesus and Judaism*, maintains that before the outbreak of the War of the Jews

---

8. Ibid., 280–81.

against Rome in AD 66, Judaism held the following hopes for the future: the restoration of the tribes of Israel; the conversion, destruction, or subjugation of the Gentiles; the renewal of Jerusalem, including a new or rebuilt temple; and the purification of God's people and their worship.[9] Christians inherited the Hebraic view that history is the interval between the beginning and the end. This eschatology, however, was radically transformed by the Christian gospel, which affirmed that already the powers of God's kingdom had broken into history in the person of Jesus of Nazareth, above all in his death and resurrection. As Peter proclaimed on the day of Pentecost, quoting an eschatological passage from the prophecy of Joel, already men and women were living "in the last days" (Acts 2:16–21).

Like their Old Testament counterparts, the followers of Jesus were shaped by an event so profound that it continues to be celebrated as decisive for Christians around the world. The early Christians found in Easter a correlation with the Exodus—a path from darkness to light, despair to hope, inability to possibility, bondage to freedom—and with creation, for the resurrection constituted a new beginning for humanity.

While the line between the eschatology of Jesus and that of the church cannot be clearly drawn, it seems likely that Jesus thought in the framework of Jewish apocalyptic, though purging it of features such as nationalism, revenge on enemies, and desire for a sensuous paradise. While he seemed to have conceived his messianic role to be that of Isaiah's Suffering Servant, quite likely he also related himself to the figure of the coming Son of Man, Daniel's heavenly figure who would appear on the clouds at the consummation of history (Mark 14:62; see Dan. 7:13–14). In any case, early Christians clearly believed that the appearance of the Messiah in the role of the Suffering Servant was an eschatological even. It was their conviction that already the *eschaton* had entered history, giving assurance of the near approach of the Day of Judgment and "the time of universal restoration" (Acts 3:20–21). The cross was God's sentence of judgment upon human sin and all the powers of darkness, but God's victory in the resurrection had already made possible a "new creation" for those who were in Christ (2 Cor. 5:17).

While later Christians focused on the vision of a second coming of Christ, it is important to recognize that in the early Christian message the center of gravity lay not in the anticipation of Christ's return but in the proclamation that Christ's "first coming" was itself an eschatological event. The New Testament places the emphasis on the victory that has already

---

9. Sanders, *Jesus and Judaism*, 279–303.

been won in the cross and resurrection and shuns any attempt to pry into the mystery of the future which lies in the sole authority of God (Acts 1:7; Matt. 24:26). Oscar Cullmann expressed this matter aptly using an analogy from World War Two. Speaking of the invasion at Normandy, known as the Decisive Day (D-day), he noted that the decisive battle in a war may occur at a relatively early stage of the war, and yet the war continues. While the war continues until Victory Day (V-day), the tide turns on D-day, guaranteeing the final outcome.[10] As a result of Christ's resurrection, early Christians were assured that the goal of history had been achieved proleptically by Christ's victory over death. The End would merely vindicate the faith of the present.

At the cross, one of the seven last sayings of Jesus is "It is finished" (John 19:30), a statement not of resignation but of accomplishment. At a certain point the earthly career of Jesus of Nazareth came to an end; what he accomplished would not be done again or anew. Nevertheless, with God every end is a new beginning. The end of Jesus known in the flesh is the beginning of Christ known in the Spirit. It is faith in this living Christ, encountered through the living Spirit, that keeps New Testament hope alive.

The Present Nature of the Kingdom of God

The dominant theme in the preaching of Jesus—indeed the center of his mission and message—is the coming of the kingdom of God. While the phrase "kingdom of God" is rare in contemporary Jewish writings, it is widely regarded as one of the most distinctive aspects of the preaching of Jesus. Because almost everywhere in the Old Testament the idea of the kingdom is related to the people of Israel and the rule of the house of David in Jerusalem, Jesus is at pains to divest his teaching of this former understanding of the nature of the kingdom. What Jesus proclaims is the immediate sovereignty of God, who will take control of the destinies of all humans, restore humanity to what God had intended it to be, and overthrow the evil powers that had led astray human beings from their proper destiny.

In Mark's Gospel, Jesus' first act upon returning from his sojourn in the wilderness is to proclaim the coming of the kingdom (Mark 1:15). Here Jesus is picking up where Second Isaiah left off half a millennium earlier. Isaiah had envisioned a day when God would finally bring justice to the world, when the long-suffering faithful could rejoice at the end of

10. Cullmann, *Christ and Time*, 84.

oppression. Jesus shared Isaiah's anticipation but was more specific about when this time would come: "Truly I tell you, there are some standing here who will not taste death until they see that the kingdom of God has come with power" (Mark 9:1). His audience was to repent and "believe in the good news."

Whatever Jesus envisioned in his proclamation about the kingdom, it was going to be on earth. Despite Matthew's preference for the expression, "kingdom of heaven," it is clear that the concept, as Jesus used it, refers to the destiny of good people on a new, improved earth. It has nothing to do with the souls of dead people ascending to heaven.

In New Testament teaching the coming of the kingdom is always dependent on divine initiative, never on human achievement. Humans may enter the kingdom; they may proclaim it and inherit it (Matt. 25:34; 7:21), but they can neither earn it nor bring it forth. Because the word "kingdom" in the Gospels suggests a geographical region or realm, which is misleading in this context, scholars prefer the term "kingship" or "kingly rule of God."

The term "kingdom" is complex and paradoxical at its core. In the Synoptic Gospels, the paradoxical nature of the kingdom is manifested in several ways: (a) it is present (Matt. 12:28; Luke 17:21), yet not fully present (Matt. 8:29; 13:30); (b) it is a gift (Matt. 25:34; Luke 12:32), yet it also involves human effort (Matt. 6:33; Luke 12:31); (c) it is an internal reality (Luke 17:20–21), yet it has external implications for the world (Matt. 6:10). Scholars are particularly interested in the first of these, for it addresses the tension between the present time and the future, the "already" and the "not yet." In that regard, they have introduced the term "inaugurated eschatology" to refer to the relation of the present inauguration and the future fulfillment of the kingdom.

There is a present element in the New Testament concept of the kingdom, particularly in the teaching of Jesus, which is colored by a sense of intense urgency. God has already taken the initiative; humans are challenged to recognize the reality of the present situation and to make such decisions as will qualify them to become citizens of the kingdom. The signs of the presence of the kingdom are already present in the ministry of Jesus. When John the Baptists questions the mission of Jesus and asks for signs, he is given clear evidence: "the blind receive their sight, the lame walk, the lepers are cleansed, the deaf hear, the dead are raised, and the poor have good news brought to them" (Matt. 11:5). All these are signs that the power of the kingdom is presently at work. Those who refuse to recognize that the power evident in Jesus is a power from God are told: "if it is by the finger of God that I cast out the demons, then the kingdom of God has come to you" (Luke 11:20). When one person, for a period of some thirty-five years, lives in total dependence upon God, with a unique understanding of God's will and in unconditional surrender to it, the kingdom is already present. As Jesus tells the Pharisees in answer to their question about when the kingdom was coming: "the kingdom of God is among you" (Luke 17:21).

According to the New Testament, Christians are kind of hybrid creatures who live in two dimensions. They are citizens of the present age while at the same time living under the dominion of Christ's kingdom. As Paul put it somewhat paradoxically, they live "in the flesh" (human nature) and also "in the Spirit" (the new dimension introduced by Christ). Awareness of this dual citizenship led early Christians to say that they were "strangers" in the historical era on earth (Heb. 11:13). Ever since the New Testament period Christianity has had to steer between two dangers. On the one hand, Christians have been tempted to withdraw from society on the assumption that Christ's kingdom is not of this world (John 18:36). On the other hand, they have been tempted to make a too easy identification of the kingdom with something in this world, such as the institutional church or the ideal human society. However, the essential message of the New Testament is this: The kingdom is not of this world, yet it has been manifest in this world through the life, death, and resurrection of Christ. Although God's kingdom is a higher order than any political reality or human ideal of the present age, it has influenced and penetrated the kingdoms of this world—not as a tangent touches a circle but as a vertical line intersects a horizontal plane. The task of the church is to bear witness to this "vertical dimension" of history and, in so doing, to seek to leaven and redeem society in the name of Christ. This attitude toward society is not one of "detachment" but one of "transfiguration," involving a rhythm of withdrawal and return through worship and action, faith and good works.

For those interested in understanding how Jesus' teachings on the kingdom affect faith and practice, a good place to begin is the Sermon on the Mount, found in Matthew 5–7 (an abbreviated and revised version appears in Luke's Sermon on the Plain; 6:17–49). This so-called "sermon" should not be considered as having been delivered by Jesus on one occasion, but was most likely formed by the author of Matthew's Gospel for his community, gathered from collections of memorized sayings of Jesus. Some find here a new moral code, to be followed literally, while others, noting the severity of the standards, call them "interim ethics," supposing that Jesus' envisioned them as rules applicable only in a time of crisis.[11] Biblical theologian N. T. Wright finds in these words "the challenge of the kingdom: the summons to Israel to be Israel indeed at the critical junction of her history, the moment when, in the kingdom announcement of Jesus, the living God is at work to reconstitute his people and so fulfill his long-cherished intentions for them and for the whole world."[12]

Those who wish to follow literally the words of Jesus' Sermon will not only fail to understand the character of Jesus' teachings, but unknowingly transform Christianity into the very legalism it once opposed. One of Jesus' reasons for making such pronouncements as are found in Matthew 5–7 was to shatter the notion that one could be "righteous" before God through effort. To be sure, Jesus came not to destroy the Law but to fulfill it, something only he could do. The Sermon on the Mount stands witness to the fact that no one can merit God's approval by human effort.

At the heart of the Sermon on the Mount we find these words: "But strive first for the kingdom of God and his righteousness" (Matt. 6:33). According to this teaching, the kingdom is to be the believer's first and main concern. It was certainly so for Jesus, who gave up everything for the sake of the kingdom. The theology of Jesus does not admit compromise; there must be a complete break with conventional morality or piety. For example, a rich young man is told by Jesus that he must sell all that he has and give to the poor (Mark 10:17–22). To understand the meaning of such severity, this story must be read contextually. Jesus is on his way to Jerusalem, and the final conflict in which he is to be engaged looms before him. At such a time there can be no hesitation; it must be all or nothing. This is a moment of crisis for those who would follow Jesus. In Matthew's Sermon, when Jesus says, "You cannot serve God or wealth" (Matt. 6:24), he is not giving a new commandment. He is simply stating a fact about the choices his followers must make. Before them lie two mutually exclusive worlds. Those who choose to live in one are automatically excluded from the other. When money has priority, God's lordship is compromised: "No one who puts a hand to the plow and looks back is fit for the kingdom of God" (Luke 9:62).

---

11. Albert Schweitzer coined the phrase "interim ethics" to express his belief that Jesus understood himself to be living at the end of human history. The interim period was to be short; hence the stern ethic. A valuable study of this problem is McArthur, *Understanding the Sermon on the Mount*.

12. Borg and Wright, *The Meaning of Jesus*, 39.

These are radical sayings. It is quite plain that if everyone gave away all their possessions to the poor, the only result would be that the rich of today would become the poor of tomorrow and vice versa; the social situation would be neither changed nor improved. Not every command is of equal application to every situation; there must be a measure of adaptation and flexibility. But before we become too easily dismissive of Jesus' radicalism, let us remember that Christian ethics is derived from Christian theology. The central point of that theology is the example of Jesus Christ and his demand that citizens of the kingdom recognize unconditionally the sovereignty of God (the six antithetical sayings found in Matthew 5:21–48 indicate how God's sovereignty might be realized in daily life).

We must always remember that the context of Jesus' sayings was the message that God's kingdom was near at hand. Jesus' claims placed persons on the very borderline between the old age and the new. The new law of the kingdom, presented by Jesus in this Sermon, has several important characteristics. First, it internalizes the demands of God, showing that we should look beyond legal codes ("You have heard that it was said") for God's original intention ("but I say to you"). Humans are condemned for anger even though they refrain from the outward act of murder (Matt. 5:21–26), for lust even though adultery is not committed (Matt. 5:27–30), for the insincerity that makes oaths necessary (Matt. 5:33–37). God looks upon the heart, that is, to the motives behind our actions. Second, the new law intensifies the requirements of the original law, not to frustrate us or to increase our guilt, but to produce sincerity and gratitude. Finally, Jesus made love central. This love is no natural sentiment or calculated act but is patterned after the love of God. As God's love is bestowed unconditionally upon those least deserving to be loved, so likewise Christians must love even those who seem to be most loveless, including social outcasts or despised enemies. The Sermon on the Mount discloses the truth that our relationship with God is not on the basis of ethical or religious attainment. The Sermon on the Mount fulfills God's Law by destroying legalism: Christ is the "end of the law" (Rom. 10:4). Rather than setting a standard of perfection that drives us to despair, Christ's Sermon provides a compass that gives direction to our efforts to improve and transform society. Christian ethics, then, are essentially "resurrection ethics," since they derive their motive and patterns from the love of God manifested in Christ: "Beloved, since God loved us so much, we also ought to love one another" (1 John 4:11).

Despite the emphasis on the present nature of the kingdom, the New Testament also looks forward to the End, to the time when the last enemy has been overthrown and God's absolute sovereignty is established with finality. Thus the expression in the Lord's Prayer: "Your kingdom come" has both a present and a future element, for while it has to do with daily realities, it looks forward to the end of evil on earth, when God's sovereignty is unopposed.

The tension between the "already" and the "not yet" is evident also in Paul's eschatology. At several points Paul emphasizes that the coming of Jesus inaugurates a new era or "age," which he designates a "new creation" (2 Cor. 5:17). While the presence of this new age can already be experienced, for Paul the ultimate transformation of the world is yet to come. Viewing the resurrection of Jesus as eschatological event, for it confirms that the "new age" is truly present, Paul also looks ahead to the future coming of Jesus Christ in judgment at the end of time. Another theme of Paul's eschatology is the coming of the Holy Spirit. This theme, which builds on a long-standing aspect of Jewish expectation, sees the gift of the Spirit as a confirmation that the new age has dawned in Christ. One of the most significant aspects of Paul's thought is his interpretation of the gift of the Spirit to believers as a "guarantee" or "first installment" of ultimate salvation (2 Cor. 1:22; 5:5).

Emphasis on the kingdom is found in all genres and strands of the New Testament literature. It is introduced in a number of different contexts quite naturally and as though it formed part of the ordinary vocabulary of Christian thought. As one might expect, the book of Revelation also speaks of the kingdom. There the fulfillment is said to be close at hand, leading the expectant church to affirm: "The kingdom of the world has become the kingdom of our Lord and of his Messiah, and he will reign for forever and ever" (Rev. 11:15).

The church is aware of living in an interim, "between the ages." It cannot bring in the kingdom; it can only testify to its reality, living by the spiritual and ethical principles established by Jesus. Because the citizens of the kingdom belong to a community of believers and are not isolated individuals, they are responsible to maintain the four "notes" or marks of the church, that is, its four defining characteristics as noted in the creeds of Christendom:

- *one*: the unity of the church;

- *holy*: the purity of the church (to be "holy" is to be set apart for and dedicated to service);
- *catholic*: the universality of the church (every Christian is part of an inclusive and welcoming whole);
- *apostolic*: the faithfulness of the church to its founding principles.

Through discipleship, the church models God's "new creation," exhibiting the presence of the kingdom of God to the world, thereby fulfilling individually and communally the cultural mandates associated with the covenant of creation (see Gen. 1:26—2:3). These ordinances, instituted for human wellbeing, include family, labor, and worship. The covenant of creation binds all humans to God and to one another. It entails that, as image-bearers, humans are to reflect God's concern for all of life.

Christian Transformation of Apocalyptic

As we have seen, the New Testament writings are heavily influenced by apocalyptic thinking. This perspective is evident from the earliest Gospel, the Gospel of Mark, which shares with apocalyptic writings a set of beliefs. In his book on Mark, *Community of the New Age*, Howard Kee mentions several convictions held in common:

1. Revelation of the Divine Secret: Knowledge of God's purpose for the world, and especially for God's people, has been revealed through God's chosen agent;
2. Martyrdom in the Face of Opposing Evil Powers: The faithful must be willing to accept suffering or even death in the face of opposition from the religious and political powers that are presently in control;
3. The Apocalyptic Dawn of a New Age: Beyond the present time of testing lies a new age, in which God's purpose in and for the creation will be achieved, and God's people will be fully and eternally vindicated.[13]

Also the letters of Paul are heavily influenced by apocalyptic thinking. To underscore the future vindication of the faithful, early Christians employed the apocalyptic theme of resurrection from the dead (1 Cor. 15). Apocalyptic prophecies viewed resurrection to be an end-time event, which

---

13. Kee, *Community of the New Age*, 12.

makes it possible for faithful martyrs, who have predeceased the arrival of God's kingdom, to take part in the final consummation.

While the early Christians shared basic convictions with Jewish apocalyptic, one finds not only similarities but striking differences. For example, the New Testament has transformed the apocalyptic view by announcing that God has done something totally and radically new through the life, death, and resurrection of Jesus Christ. A "new creation" has begun to appear (2 Cor. 5:17). The New Testament portrays Jesus not merely as an apocalyptic visionary who announces the mystery of God's kingdom to a select few; rather, he himself is the sign of God's kingdom in the present historical age. Jesus' crucifixion, crowned with resurrection, signifies that Jesus is the victor in the long struggle with evil. The New Testament announces that the period of waiting is over, for the king has come and the dominion of God has already been inaugurated. In other words, the Christian gospel has altered the time scheme of apocalyptic, with its sharp separation of "the present evil age" from "the age to come," so that the old must pass away before the new can come. Rather the two ages are like overlapping circles, for already God has introduced the new age through Jesus Christ even while the old age persists. In the Christian reinterpretation of apocalyptic, the supreme sign of the new age is the resurrection of Christ from the dead. As Paul argues in 1 Corinthians 15, this end-time event has already occurred in the midst of the present age. So near and certain is God's triumph that Paul can go so far as to say that not everyone will die (1 Cor. 15:51; Matthew's Gospel refers to a strange apocalyptic event occurring at the moment when Jesus was crucified, when many who were dead are said to have come forth from their graves; 27:51–54).

To be sure, the Christian community lives in the tension of the "already" and the "not yet." Using the symbolic language of apocalyptic, the trumpet signaling God's final triumph has not yet sounded. There is still a period of waiting for the final consummation, the coming of God's kingdom fully on earth and the appearance of Jesus Christ in glory. But this waiting is not the expectation of counting the days or speculating on an apocalyptic timetable. For already God's triumph has been manifest in the resurrection of Christ.

Finally, "apocalyptic has given to the early Christian community a profound grasp of the meaning of God's triumph in Jesus Christ. God's victory is liberation from the power of sin through divine forgiveness, displayed in the vicarious and atoning death of Jesus. The apocalyptic perspective, however, pushes Christian interpreters to go beyond the prophetic message of sin and forgiveness and to proclaim God's triumph over all the powers of darkness, chaos, evil, and death."[14] Paul lists some of those powers in his great victory proclamation at the end of Romans 8, where he declares that through Christ we are "more than conquerors" (Rom. 8:37).

The call to conquer is fundamental to the structure and theme of the book of Revelation, the apocalypse that brings the Christian canon to a close. Everything that is said in the seven messages to the churches has this aim, expressed in the promise to the conquerors that concludes each (Rev. 2:7; 11, 17, 28; 3:5, 12, 21). Like Jesus, the real victors are the martyr-witnesses, those who are faithful to God even to the point of death. Conquering is not represented as something to which only some are called, but as the only way for Christians to reach their eschatological destiny. According to Revelation 21:7–8, there are only two options: to conquer and inherit the promises or to suffer the second death in the lake of fire. John's message in Revelation is a call for resistance against evil, not however, through violence but through kingdom living and witnessing.

The book of Revelation brings to a magnificent climax the biblical drama that opens in Genesis with creation and the Garden. The whole historical drama is embraced within the redemptive timespan of the one who is "the Alpha and the Omega, the beginning and the end" (Rev. 21:6). True to the Christian faith, the author of Revelation affirms that the kingdom of Christ has already broken into history. The divine victory, which in the present evil age can be discerned only by faith, ultimately will be openly manifest, for every creature will attest the triumph of God's redemptive love (Rev. 5:13). Thus the Lamb (Christ) that was slain is pictured imaginatively as the final conqueror who at the end will overthrow all forces of evil that had corrupted history. Christ's victory ushers in the "new heaven and the new earth" (Rev. 21:1).

In Revelation, the outcome of history is assured: Jesus has already won the victory through his death and resurrection. Because God reigns, hope is always near. This letter was not written to terrify people but to awaken and encourage them, to sustain their hope when things seemed bleakest. Hope is the most important message of Revelation. Readers must always take into consideration the goal in Revelation 21:5, which acts as a compass pointing to the book's "true north": "I am making all things new." Notice that the emphasis is on the present progressive tense: Because of Christ's victory,

---

14. Anderson, *Contours of Old Testament Theology*, 335.

God's work is always "new." In Revelation, these are the *only* words spoken directly by the one sitting on the throne. This is where the Bible's storyline is headed, and it is incumbent upon people of faith to discern that the arc of history is bent toward hope.

Think of all that's wearing out, that's running down, of all that science teaches about entropy, of all the oldness about our routines and our lives. Yet history, we are told, is headed toward newness. The word "new" doesn't mean simply another, however, but a new kind of heaven and earth. Heaven and earth are part of God's creation; God is not about to destroy it all just to start over, but rather will bring about radical alteration. As in Isaiah's earlier vision (65:17), "new heaven" suggests "new spirituality" and "new earth" suggests "new physicality." In this case newness need not be equated with discontinuity or dissimilarity, for embedded in the biblical concept of newness is the notion of continuity as well as discontinuity with what precedes. When Paul states that the whole creation is longing for redemption (Rom. 8:19–22), he has in mind the double connotation of *kainos*, the Greek word for "new," which means either "renewed" or "new." Newness—like resurrection—is an image of renewal, similar to Paul's description of "new creation" in Galatians 6:15 and 2 Corinthians 5:17. T. S. Eliot's classic statement about life's journey, "and the end of all our exploring will be to arrive where we started and know the place for the first time," can be read in this way, as a statement about renewal. This is the sense in which there will be a new creation in Revelation. There will be continuity in that the earth is renewed but also discontinuity in the distinction between God's vision of what the world can be and the imperial visions that came before (Rev. 21:1–2).

In *The Chronicles of Narnia* C. S. Lewis describes the place he calls "New Narnia" in terms of both continuity and transformation. In *The Last Battle*, the New Narnia where the children find themselves at the end of their journey is not an escape from old Narnia but rather an entry more deeply into the very same place. New Narnia has the same hills and the same houses as their hometown, but everything is more radiant. New Narnia is a "deeper country; every rock and flower and blade of grass looked like it meant more." New Narnia is "world within world," where "no good thing is destroyed." This kind of vision provides a wonderful picture of how all of creation will be renewed.[15] The fact that John refers twice (21:2 and 10; cf. 3:12) to the holy city "coming down" does not mean that he saw the city come down from heaven on two separate occasions. John is identifying

---

15. Rossing, "Journeys Through Revelation," 72.

a permanent characteristic of the city; its nature is defined by its having come down.

Belief in a heavenly city of Jerusalem, often personified as a feminine figure or "mother," was widespread in biblical times (see Gal. 4:26). According to Isaiah 54, the renewed Jerusalem would be made of precious stones and would be "married" to God in covenantal love. Following the destruction of Jerusalem in AD 70, people's longings for a renewed Jerusalem intensified. John would have been well aware of such a longing and likely experienced it himself. What is unique to Revelation is that the heavenly city does not stay in heaven. It comes down from heaven to earth, offering a welcoming home to all humanity. A fundamental example of apocalyptic hope is the message we find at the end of Revelation: God is coming to make a home among us. "See, the home of God is among mortals," this vision declares (Rev. 21:2–3). Contrary to ideas about the "rapture" of the church from earth, there is no "rapture" in Revelation. Instead it is God who is "raptured" to earth to live with us. As Christians come forth out of "Babylon" (John's code word for Roman imperial domination but for us a reference to worldly power and values), God comes to us. At the end of Revelation, humans are not in heaven; there is no longer need for dualistic thinking, because God dwells on earth. And where God is, there is heaven.

This vision fulfills the people's deepest longings for residing with God. The promise of God's dwelling on earth recalls God's "tabernacling" with Israel in the wilderness, after the Exodus. The theme also echoes Ezekiel 37:27, "My dwelling place shall be with them; and I will be their God, and they shall be my people." This idea is also found in John 1:14, where the verbal form of the word translated "dwell" (Greek *skene*) refers to the residence of God in Jesus and Jesus with us, and then again in Revelation 21:3, where God's presence with mortals is made permanent. Matthew's usage of Isaiah's promise of the birth of a child named Emmanuel (Matt. 1:23), which means "God is with us" (Isa. 7:14), reminds us that God's intention has always been to dwell with humanity. In Revelation that promise is fully consummated. There will be no temple in God's new city, for the presence of God and the Lamb will be the temple.

It is characteristic of biblical eschatology that the myths of the End draw elements from the myths of the beginning. So, for example, the symbol of the "tree of life" reappears in Revelation (22:2), and the idyllic peace of the Garden of Eden is matched by the New Creation, in which there will no longer be suffering, anxiety, or death. It would be wrong, however, to view this as a return to a utopia, as though the biblical drama moves in a vast circle that returns to the starting point. The book of Revelation does not envision a return to the innocence of nature; rather, it visualizes human beings, like returning prodigals, receiving the forgiving and redemptive love that conquers sin and brings humanity to true maturity. It is significant, then, that the mythological End is described not under the figure of the Garden of Eden but in the symbolism of the New Jerusalem.

Two strands of language and symbolism run through John's account of the New Jerusalem, a combination of particularism and universalism. In the first place, the history of both Israel and the church comes to fulfillment in this vision, the fulfillment of God's promises to the covenant people, whose destiny is portrayed as being "a kingdom and priests" serving God (Rev. 5:10; cf. 1:6 and 22:3b–5). It is, after all, the New *Jerusalem*. On the other hand, references to the nations as sharing in the promised blessings are equally prominent. The nations will walk by the city's light, the glory and honor of the nations are brought into it (21:26), and the kings of the earth bring their glory into it" (21:24). The significance of Revelation 21:3, which states the overall meaning of 21:1—22:5 at the outset, is to reiterate evidence found throughout Revelation to the effect that the witness of the church is intended to bring about the conversion of the nations. The implication of Revelation 21:3—that all nations are to become covenant peoples—is stunning. John's intention in this passage seems clear: the history of God's covenant people (both Israel and the church) will culminate in "the full inclusion of all the nations in its own covenant privileges and promises."[16]

To the earth God makes a commitment in Revelation, earth being the location of salvation. Such is the meaning of "a new heaven and a new earth," a phrase coterminous with God's bridal city. But the "new heaven" will be on earth, and God will dwell in the midst of that renewed city. There can be no more sea in that city, neither the heavenly sea before the throne nor the earthly sea, symbolic of the chaos monster and all the Leviathans of violence, injustice, and despair in the old order of things. And there can be no more tears, sorrow, and mourning in this new world of joy and life eternal. Positioned at the end of the Bible, the vision of the New Jerusalem brings to fulfillment all biblical promises of restoration and renewal. It fulfills Isaiah's promise of newness (Isa. 43:19; 65:17) as well as the promises made to the seven churches in the opening letters of Revelation, when

---

16. Bauckham, *Theology of Revelation*, 139.

those who "conquer" receive their inheritance (Rev. 21:7). As we might expect, John dismisses seven elements of the old order in the holy city: sea, death, grief, crying, pain, all that is under God's curse, and night (Rev. 21:1, 4; 22:3, 5).

The Bible invites us to drink deeply from its metaphors of promise and warning, vision and blessing. God is with us through every beginning and every ending, our Alpha and Omega. If the Bible is a journey, then the final scene of the New Jerusalem is the homecoming. Listening to scripture being read aloud in the worship service, early Christians traveled on a life-changing apocalyptic journey. They traveled to heaven to see the throne of God and the Lamb, to taste and see the gifts of God. They witnessed conflict and victory, and they endured. As believers gather around the Eucharistic table, they see their own world more clearly, their own lives glimpsed in a new and deeper way.

That kind of transformational experience is Revelation's goal for each of us. Like Dorothy in *The Wizard of Oz* waking up in Kansas, everything is different for us now because of our apocalyptic journey. The message is clear: stay on course, keep the faith—follow the yellow-brick road. Faithful companions and a vision of the New Jerusalem can help us resist the temptations of "Babylon" and lead us to celebrate boldly: "Ding dong! The witch is dead; the wicked witch is dead!" With new eyes, ears, voices, limbs, and hearts we can see the Lamb standing in the middle of the street, reminding us that love never fails (1 Cor. 13:8). Together we find ourselves transported beyond our invisible mountains into thin places, glimpses of New Jerusalem beyond belief. We see rivers of life flowing from the heart of God; we catch a glimpse of God's tree of life and taste its medicinal healing leaves.

Visions of the new creation are essential; we cannot live without them, for they bring healing to our lives and to our troubled world. The message of Revelation is clear: The One who dwells in our midst is making all things new. That is the promise of Revelation: God's people gather around the throne of the Lamb, beside the river, beneath the healing tree of life, singing "Amen. Come, Lord Jesus!" Faith indicates that if Christ is our companion and the Spirit is within, then God's dwelling is with us. If that perspective holds true, then heaven is here, evil is defeated, the world is renewed, and all creatures are beloved, for reality is undergoing cosmic transformation. This vision of promise and faith keeps "making all things new."

In the Bible, when all is said and done, we are left not with a new heaven only but with a new heaven and a new earth—joined together completely and forever (cf. Eph. 1:10). The new city is not just a dream, a comforting fantasy. Those who follow the Lamb already belong in that city and already have the right to walk its streets, for that city is the Bride. The new creation is God's kingdom; its citizens are dressed in white—the garment of the bride—and all have childlike faith, for it is "to such as these that the kingdom of heaven belongs" (Matt. 19:14). Life has been secured, promise is fulfilled, and that is cause for rejoicing.

Epilogue

Reading the Bible

The Bible is a controversial book. And that can be a good thing. For controversy helps us learn and grow. But the Bible is also one of the most misunderstood and misinterpreted books, and that's not good. In the past, Biblical literalists have used the Bible to perpetuate slavery, exterminate the Indians, subjugate women, marginalize minorities, and exploit the environment, among other atrocities. For this and other reasons, many educated people today simply ignore the Bible or view it as a museum piece from antiquity. Of course, the Bible has also been instrumental in liberating slaves, women, and other minorities, and it contains a most powerful motivation for ecological responsibility.

Perhaps you have heard it said that the modern age has problems with authority in general, and with the authority of scripture in particular. However, according to an important and oft-quoted passage found in 2 Timothy 3:16, the Bible should not be considered as an authority in the modern sense of the word; in other words, the Bible does not exist for its own sake. Note that 2 Timothy 3:16 does not say, "All scripture is inspired by God and is *authoritative*." It says that all scripture is inspired and *useful*—useful to teach, rebuke, correct, instruct, and equip us for our mission as the people of God. For too long we have read the Bible as if it were God's encyclopedia, God's rule book, God's answer book, God's scientific text, God's easy-steps instruction book, God's little book of morals for all occasions. In Jesus' day, the only people who would have had anything close to these expectations of the Bible would have been the scribes and Pharisees. And Jesus certainly disapproved of their attitudes and methodology regarding scripture.

When you let go of the Bible as God's answer book, you get it back as something so much better. It becomes the family story—the story of the people who have been called by the one true God to be his agents in the world, to be his servants to the rest of the world. So I suggest we stop reading the Bible as a "modern" answer book. But that doesn't mean we should discard it. Just the opposite! When we let it go as a modern answer book, we get to rediscover it for what it really is: an ancient book of incredible spiritual value for us, a kind of universal and cosmic history, a book that tells us who we are and what story we find ourselves in so that we know what to do and how to live. Of course, the Bible is even more than a book of wisdom and wisdom development. It's a book that calls together and helps create a community, a community that is a catalyst for God's work in our world.

In his intriguing fable, *A New Kind of Christian*, Brian McLaren captures the spirit of the Emerging Church Movement, where personal interaction with God is more important than institutional church structures, faith more a way of life than a system of belief, being authentically good more important than being doctrinally correct, and where one's direction in life is more important than one's present location. In one of the conversations between the protagonist named Neo (an ordained minister now teaching high school science) and pastor Dan, whose daughter is in Neo's class, the former criticizes modern liberals and conservatives alike for reading the Bible in very modern ways:

> Modern conservatives treat the Bible as if it were a modern book. They're used to reading modern history texts and modern encyclopedias and modern science articles and modern legal codes, and so they assume that the Bible will yield its resources if they approach it like one of those texts. But none of those categories even existed when the Bible was written. Sure, there was history, but not with all of the modern trimmings like a concern for factual accuracy, corroborating evidence, or absolute objectivity. Sure there was law, but I'm not sure there is a one-to-one correspondence between an ancient Near Eastern concept of law and our modern concept. The conservatives seem somewhat blind to these kinds of differences, I think. . . . The modern liberals seem to make a corresponding mistake. They acknowledge that the Bible is a different kind of text from our modern texts, but then they in a sense judge it by modern standards. If something doesn't fit in with a modern Western mindset that reveres objectivity, science, democracy, individualism, that sort of thing, it is dismissed as primitive and irrelevant.[1]

---

1. McLaren, *A New Kind of Christian*, 55–56.

Neo suggests a third option: instead of reading the Bible, what if you let the Bible read you? If that sounds a bit ethereal, perhaps even mystical, think of it this way. Think of a scientist preparing to dissect a northern leopard frog, *Rana pipiens*, or think of a detective at a crime scene. How would you describe their attitude or approach? Now think of a teenage girl meeting a boy at the mall. Surely her attitude differs from the scientist's or the detective's. Her approach wouldn't be so analytical or objective. And there would be some fun in it, a sense of personal investment, a feeling of adventure. In one sense there's less caution, less holding back. Yet in another way there is holding back, because she wants to make her move and then leave room for him to respond. It's less aggressive, less controlling, and more . . . relational. We need to approach the Bible more that way; we need to flirt with it, romance it—or possibly let its message romance us.[2]

Our modern age has predisposed us to only a limited range of postures with the Bible, like the objective analysis of a scientist or like forensic science, always trying to prove something. It's all about a kind of aggressive conquest of the text—reducing it to something explainable by our preconceptions, turning it into moralisms or principles or outlines or conclusions or proofs or whatever. What would happen if we approached the text less aggressively but even more energetically and passionately? What would happen if we honestly listened to the story and put ourselves under its spell, so to speak, not using it to get all of our questions about God answered but instead trusting it to pose questions about us. What would happen if we simply trusted ourselves to it—the way a boy opens his heart to a girl, the way a patient trusts herself to an oncologist?

There are two ways to "kill" the Bible:

1. You can dissect it, analyze it, and abstract it. You can read its stories and poetry and from them derive neat abstractions, sterile propositions, and sharp-edged principles. You can sanitize the text of all evocative language, paradox, multiple perspectives, and interesting, three-dimensional people to end up with cute morals, simple two-dimensional systems, and flat, boring prose. As a result, the Bible itself begins to vaporize, leaving the desired residue of systematic theology, which is all people in this approach ever wanted anyway.

2. You can also kill the Bible by demythologizing it. You can read it like an engineer and dismiss anything that doesn't fit your modern, Western, rationalistic, reductionist mind-set. You're left with a pickled specimen, a

---

2. The following discussion is adapted from McLaren, ibid., 56–57.

hollow shell, a stuffed tiger this way also, through a kind of expert theological taxidermy.

What a relief to have a third alternative—to read the Bible as a premodern text, emerging from a people who believed that truth is best embodied in story and art and human flesh rather than abstraction or outline or moralism. This option relieves the biblical writers of having to conform to modern expectations. Instead, it enables us to join them in our common human predicament as humans whose three-pound brains can't hope to contain the wonder of one grain of wheat or sand, much less the Creator of the universe!

The Bible deals with the question of the ultimate meaning of human life. To be sure, the biblical drama is staged in an ancient setting and describes events that happened long ago. But these pages bear witness to the victory that God accomplished in history once for all, to the revelation that casts its light across the centuries. According to the Bible, humans shall not live by systems and abstractions and principles alone but also by stories and poetry and proverbs and mystery. And best of all, instead of handing us morals that we must try to impose on followers of different stories, it calls us to live as part of its own story, the story of a loving Creator who started something wonderful and beautiful that in spite of our many failures God will bring to completion. As we live by that story, we find followers of other stories interested in ours because our story, rightly understood, has plenty of room for them and for their stories as well.

If in the decision of faith the Christ of the Bible reveals the true meaning of history, then one unhesitantly will join the generations of Christians in affirming that this scripture is the Word of God.[3]

---

3. Anderson, *Rediscovering the Bible*, 267.

Bibliography

Achtemeier, Paul J. *The Inspiration of Scripture: Problems and Proposals.* Philadelphia: Westminster, 1980.
Anders, Max. *30 Days to Understanding the Bible.* Expanded edition. Nashville, TN: Thomas Nelson, 2011.
Anderson, Bernhard W. *Contours of Old Testament Theology.* Minneapolis: Fortress, 1999.
———. *Creation versus Chaos.* New York: Association Press, 1967.
———. *Rediscovering the Bible.* New York: Association Press, 1951.
———. *Understanding the Old Testament.* 5th ed. Upper Saddle River, NJ: Pearson Prentice Hall, 2007.
———. *The Unfolding Drama of the Bible.* 4th ed. Minneapolis: Fortress, 2006.
Archer, Gleason. *A Survey of Old Testament Introduction.* Rev. ed. Chicago: Moody, 1979.
Armstrong, Karen, *The Bible: A Biography.* New York: Grove, 2007.
———. *A History of God.* New York: Ballantine, 1993
———. *A Short History of Myth.* New York: Canongate, 2005.
Bauckham, Richard. *The Theology of the Book of Revelation.* Cambridge: Cambridge University Press, 1993.
Beker, J. Christiaan. *Paul the Apostle: The Triumph of God in Life and Thought.* Minneapolis: Fortress, 1980.
———. *The Triumph of God: The Essence of Paul's Thought.* Minneapolis: Fortress, 1990.
Borg, Marcus J. *The God We Never Knew.* New York: HarperSanFrancisco, 1998.
———. *Meeting Jesus Again for the First Time.* New York: HarperSanFrancisco, 1994.
———. *Reading the Bible Again for the First Time.* New York: HarperSanFrancisco, 2001.
Borg, Marcus J. and N. T. Wright. *The Meaning of Jesus: Two Visions.* New York: HarperSanFrancisco, 1999.
Bowne, Dale R. and John D. Currid. "Biblical Society: A Covenantal Society." In *Building a Christian World View*, edited by W. Andrew Hoffecker, 2:156–85. Phillipsburg, NJ: Presbyterian and Reformed, 1988.
Brown, Raymond E. *An Introduction to the New Testament.* New York: Doubleday, 1997.
Bruce, F. F. *The New Testament Development of Old Testament Themes.* Grand Rapids, Eerdmans, 1968.
———. *Paul, Apostle of the Heart Set Free.* Grand Rapids: Eerdmans, 1991.
Brueggemann, Walter. *Genesis.* Interpretation: A Bible Commentary for Teaching and Preaching. Atlanta: John Knox, 1982.
———. *Theology of the Old Testament.* Minneapolis: Fortress, 1997.

BIBLIOGRAPHY

Caird, G. B. and L. D. Hurst. *New Testament Theology*. Oxford: Clarendon, 1994.
Childs, Brevard, *Biblical Theology in Crisis*. Philadelphia: Westminster, 1970.
———. *Biblical Theology of the Old and New Testaments*. Minneapolis: Fortress, 1977.
———. *Introduction to the Old Testament as Scripture*. Philadelphia: Fortress, 1979.
Cory, Catherine, *A Voyage through the New Testament*. Upper Saddle River, NJ: Pearson Prentice Hall, 2008.
Countryman, L. William, *Biblical Authority or Biblical Tyranny? Scripture and the Christian Pilgrimage*. Valley Forge: PA: Trinity International, 1994.
Cross, Frank Moore. *Canaanite Myth and Hebrew Epic: Essays in the History of the Religion of Israel*. Cambridge, MA: Harvard University Press, 1973.
Cullmann, Oscar. *Christ and Time*. Philadelphia: Westminster, 1950.
Drane, John. *Introducing the New Testament*. Revised and Updated. Minneapolis: Fortress, 2001.
Duvall, J. Scott and J. Daniel Hays. *Grasping God's Word*. 3rd ed. Grand Rapids, MI: Zondervan, 2012.
Fox, Matthew. *Creation Spirituality*. New York: HarperSanFrancisco, 1991.
———. *Original Blessing*. Santa Fe, NM: Bear & Co., 1983.
Eichrodt, Walther. *Theology of the Old Testament*. Vol. 1. Philadelphia: Westminster, 1961.
Friedman, Richard Elliott. *Who Wrote the Bible?* New York: HarperSanFrancisco, 1997.
Gnuse, Robert Karl. *No Other Gods: Emergent Monotheism in Israel*. Sheffield: Sheffield Academic Press, 1997.
Guthrie, Donald. *New Testament Theology*. Downers Grove, IL: Inter-Varsity, 1981.
Harrison, R. K. *Introduction to the Old Testament*. Grand Rapids, MI: Eerdmans, 1969.
Hendricks, Howard G. and William D. *Living by the Book: The Art and Science of Reading the Bible*. Chicago: Moody, 2007.
Hillers, Delbert R. *Covenant: The History of a Biblical Idea*. Baltimore: Johns Hopkins Press, 1969.
Kee, Howard C. *Community of the New Age: Studies in Mark's Gospel*. Philadelphia: Westminster, 1977.
Klein, William W. et al. *Introduction to Biblical Interpretation*. Rev. ed. Nashville, TN: Thomas Nelson, 2004.
Ladd, George Eldon. *A Theology of the New Testament*. Grand Rapids, MI: Eerdmans, 1974.
McArthur, Harvey E. *Understanding the Sermon on the Mount*. New York: Harper & Row, 1960.
McGrath, Alister E. *Christian Theology: An Introduction*. 5th. ed. Malden, MA: Wiley-Blackwell 2011.
McLaren, Brian D. *A New Kind of Christian: A Tale of Two Friends on a Spiritual Journey*. San Francisco: Jossey-Bass, 2001.
———. *A New Kind of Christianity: Ten Questions That Are Transforming the Faith*. New York: HarperCollins, 2010.
Miles, Jack. *God: A Biography*. London: Simon & Schuster, 1995.
Neill, Stephen. *Jesus Through Many Eyes: Introduction to the Theology of the New Testament*. Philadelphia: Fortress, 1976.
Newberg, Andrew. *The Spiritual Brain: Science and Religious Experience*. Course Guidebook. Chantilly, VA: The Great Courses, 2012.
Plotkin, Bill. *Nature and the Human Soul: Cultivating Wholeness and Community in a Fragmented World*. Novato, CA: New World Library, 2008.

BIBLIOGRAPHY

Richardson, Alan. *Genesis I–XI*. Torch Commentary. London: SCM, 1953.

———. *An Introduction to the Theology of the New Testament*. New York: Harper, 1958.

Rohr, Richard. *Falling Upward: A Spirituality for the Two Halves of Life*. San Francisco: Jossey-Bass, 2011.

Rossing, Barbara R. "Journeys Through Revelation." *Horizons* 23:3 (2010) 1–76.

Schulweis, Harold M. *For Those Who Can't Believe*. New York: HarperPerennial, 1995.

Schweitzer, Albert. *The Quest of the Historical Jesus*. New York: Macmillan, 1968.

Spong, John Shelby. *Eternal Life: A New Vision*. New York: HarperOne, 2009.

———. *Liberating the Gospels: Reading the Bible with Jewish Eyes*. San Francisco: HarperSanFrancisco, 1996.

———. *Rescuing the Bible from Fundamentalism*. New York: HarperSanFrancisco, 1991.

———. *Why Christianity Must Change or Die*. New York: HarperOne, 1999.

Smith, Mark S. *The Early History of God: Yahweh and the Other Deities in Ancient Israel*. 2nd ed. Grand Rapids: Eerdmans, 2002.

Vande Kappelle. Robert P. *Beyond Belief: Faith, Science, and the Value of Unknowing*. Eugene: OR: Wipf & Stock, 2012.

———. *Dark Splendor: Spiritual Fitness for the Second Half of Life*. Eugene: OR: Wipf & Stock, 2015.

Vande Kappelle, Robert P. and John D. Currid. "The Old Testament: The Covenant Between God and Man." In *Building a Christian World View*, edited by W. Andrew Hoffecker, 1:11–30. Phillipsburg, NJ: Presbyterian and Reformed, 1986.

Virkler, Henry A. and Karelynne Gerber Ayayo. *Hermeneutics: Principles and Processes of Biblical Interpretation*. 2nd ed. Grand Rapids, MI: Baker, 2007.

Wright, N. T. *The Climax of the Covenant: Christ and the Law in Pauline Theology*. Minneapolis: Fortress, 1993.

———. *Jesus and the Victory of God*. Minneapolis: Fortress, 1996.

———. *The New Testament and the People of God*. Minneapolis: Fortress, 1992.

———. *The Resurrection of the Son of God*. Minneapolis: Fortress, 1993.

Wright, Robert. *The Evolution of God*. New York: Little, Brown, 2009.

Subject/Name Index

Abraham (patriarch), 16, 31, 40, 69, 70, 72, 76, 95, 98, 110, 131, 132, 176, 191
   call of, 111–12, 141
   sacrifice of Isaac, 114–18
   See also covenant, with Abraham
Achan, 123
Acts, book of, 28, 29, 49, 161, 167, 168, 176, 181, 184
Adam, 73, 131, 140, 143, 144, 147, 149, 151
Agassiz, Louis, 58
Albright, William, 73, 75
Amos (prophet), 78, 79, 107–8
Ancestral History, 132
Anderson, Bernhard, x, 146
angels, 166
animism, 69
anthropology
   biblical, 17, 80–81
   Hebrew, 144
Apocalypse of Peter, 50
apocalyptic, 193–96, 201, 208–15
   Christian, 208–15
   Jewish, 201, 209
Apocrypha, 25, 27–28, 47
apostolic authority, 186
apostolic period, 188
Apostles Creed, 87
apostolos (apostle), 185, 186
Aquinas, Thomas, 149–50
Aramaic, 175
Aristotle, 87, 133

ark (of the covenant), 120–21, 124, 126, 127, 139, 185
Armstrong, Karen, x, 68, 137
Asherah (Canaanite deity), 74
Astruc, Jean, 40
Athanasius (bishop), 50
Augustine (bishop), 145, 149, 164

Baal (Canaanite deity), 77–78
Babylonian exile, 38, 195
baptism, 185, 188
Barnabas, letter of, 49
believe, belief, 113–14
berith (covenant), 159
Bethke, Jefferson, 13–14
Bible, ix, 22–23, 31–32, 136, 155
   as drama, 31–32, 136–37, 192, 219
   as literature, 23
   as premodern text, 219
   as sacred, ix, 22
   as scripture, 21–23, 57
   as Word of God, 22, 33n1, 57, 160, 219
   authority of, 35, 51, 216
   authorship of, 37, 51–52
   See also canonical process
   books of, 21, 25–30
   canonization of, ix, 45–50
   inspiration of, 33–36
   interpretation of, 1, 5, 53–64
   literal (verbal), 8, 22, 34, 35, 198, 200
   myth in, 137–38
   poetry in, 138
   reading the, 216–19

SUBJECT/NAME INDEX

Bible *(cont.)*
   social views in, 121–22, 130–31, 141–42
   See also scripture
biblical anthropology, 84–91
biblical theology, 59, 67–79, 80–84
bishop, 185, 188
Boff, Leonardo, 91
Book of the Covenant, 26, 104, 123
Borg, Marcus, x, 80–81, 87
Brueggemann, Walter, x, 144–45

Cahill, Thomas, 186
Calvin, John, 54, 164
canon, 45–46
   Christian, 32, 164
canonical process, 36
   New Testament, 61–64
   Old Testament, 59–61
charism (charismatic gift), 186, 187
Christianity
   as "the Way," 176
   Jewish heritage, 184, 200–201
Christology, 166, 176, 179
Chronicles, books of, 25, 47
church, 185
   and charismatic ministry, 186, 187
   and synagogue, 185
   as new community, 183–91
   four notes or marks of, 207–8
   growth of, 188–89
   unity of, 191, 207
Clement, first letter of, 49
Colossians, letter to, 28, 29, 30, 44, 177, 182
Columbus, Christopher, ix
community, 110–31
   new, 32, 157, 183–91
concordance, 59n3
conscience, role of, 117
conservatives. *See* theological conservatives
Corinthians, first letter to, 28, 29, 30, 44, 62, 164, 166, 167, 168, 186–87, 199, 209
Corinthians, second letter to, 28, 29, 30, 31, 44, 155, 168, 171
corporate personality, 131–31

Countryman, William, 35
covenant, 7, 26, 40, 95–109, 155, 158n2, 179
   eternal, 182
   law, 98–99, 102, 103–5, 110, 129, 179–80
   lawsuit, 107–9
   new, 31, 155–73
   of creation, 141, 208
   promise, 98–99, 110, 129, 179–80, 194
   with Abraham, 112–18
   with David, 125–30, 195
   See also Book of the Covenant
creation, doctrine of, 82–83, 96–97, 132–44
   and consummation, 192
   and evolution, 139–40
   and worship, 138–41
   new, 134, 192–215
   theology of, 88–89
creation mandates, 141–42
creation spirituality, 87, 89–91
Cullmann, Oscar, 202

Daniel, book of, 27, 28, 30, 31, 46, 96, 194, 201
Darwin, Charles, 69
David (king), 16, 26, 79, 98, 124, 125–30, 131, 156, 190
   covenant with, 125–30
   See also royal theology
Day of Judgment, 194, 201
Day of the Lord, 193
deacon, 188
Dead Sea Scrolls, 176, 177
death, origin of, 145
deuterocanonical, 24, 25
   See also Apocrypha
Deuteronomic Reform, 38, 71, 79
Deuteronomist (D), 38, 40–41
Deuteronomistic History (historians), 26, 118–27, 130
Deuteronomy, book of, 26, 40, 41, 72, 101–2, 104, 118, 122–23, 156, 181
DeWette, Wilhelm, 40–41
diatheke (covenant), 158
Didache, the, 49

SUBJECT/NAME INDEX

discipleship, 208
Documentary Hypothesis, 37–43
dualistic thought, 13, 87, 89, 134, 193–94

Easter, 188, 197, 198–99
  and creation, 201
  and Exodus, 201
Ecclesiastes, book of, 25, 27, 47, 140
Eichhorn, Johann, 40
Eichrodt, Walther, 97
ekklesia (church), 185, 191
El, Elohim, 75–77
election, 111–12
Elijah (prophet), x, 71, 77–78, 145
Eliot, T. S., 10, 211
Elohist (E), 16, 38, 40, 41, 42
El Shaddai, 75, 76, 113
Emmanuel passage, 178
Enlightenment, 8, 54, 97
Enuma Elish, 133, 141
Ephesians, letter to, 28, 29, 30, 44, 166, 185, 190, 191
Epistles. *See* Paul, epistles of
eschatology, 166, 181, 192, 193, 201
  inaugurated, 203
eschaton, 201
Esther, book of, 25, 27, 47
etiology, etiological, 144
Eucharist (Lord's Supper), 185, 188
Eve, 143, 144, 149
evil, 145, 149–50, 193–94, 195, 210, 214
exegesis, 1, 58–59
Exodus, book of, 26, 72, 76, 99, 101, 102–4, 123, 181
Exodus, the, 71, 85, 95, 96, 97, 99, 110, 162, 178, 193, 196, 201
exodus theology, 99–101
Ezekiel (prophet), 38
Ezekiel, book of, 145, 171, 194, 212
Ezra (reformer), 38, 46, 134, 165
Ezra, book of, 25, 26, 37, 46

faith, 7, 8, 9, 110, 111, 112, 148, 162, 175, 210
  language of, 192, 200
  testing of, 113–18
Fall, the. *See* temptation narrative, the

first half of life (first journey), 1–3, 5, 6, 34, 36, 64, 81
formation, 15
Fox, Matthew, 87, 89–90
freedom, 187
Friedman, Richard, 38
Friedrich, Georg Wilhelm, 69
fundamentalism, 55

Galatians, letter to, 6–7, 28, 29, 30, 44, 48, 157, 169, 170, 171, 172, 173
Garden of Eden, 193, 212, 213
  See also temptation narrative
General (Catholic) Epistles, 28, 30, 45, 161
Genesis, book of, 16, 17, 26, 31, 40, 69, 70, 72, 75, 76, 96, 98, 99, 110, 111–15, 134–51
genre, 23
Gilgamesh Epic, 133
gnostic, gnosticism, 48–49
God, 5, 12–13, 14, 31, 34, 68–69, 91, 99, 109, 110, 111, 137, 146, 184, 192
  as Creator, 31, 132–44, 181, 219
  as Redeemer, 181
  fear of, 5
  love of, 191, 206
  meaning of, 9
  monarchical model, 80–84, 87
  nature of, 100–101
  providence of, 117–18
  Spirit model, 80–84
  testing of Abraham, 113–18
  will of, 171
  See also biblical theology
gospel, 43, 111, 179
Gospels, 23, 28, 43, 44, 45, 48–49, 161
  reliability of, 175
Graf, Karl, 41, 42
Great Commandment, the, 12, 172–73, 191
Great Commission, 184

heaven, 4, 9, 214
Hebrew Bible. *See* Old Testament
Hebrews, letter to, 30, 48, 49, 158–59, 177, 181–82
hell, 4, 9, 85

227

SUBJECT/NAME INDEX

Hendricks, Howard, 59
henotheism, 70, 73, 145
Herder, Johann von, 55
hermeneutical principles, 61–63
hermeneutics, 56–57
    goal of, 64
hesed (steadfast love), 106, 109, 127
higher criticism, 55
Hobbes, Thomas, 39
Holiness Code, 26
Holy Spirit, 6, 34, 54, 64, 81–83, 163, 170, 171, 172, 186, 187, 197, 207, 214
    and love, 95, 96, 191
Hosea (prophet), 79, 95, 108, 145, 178
human task, 146

illumination, 63–64
imago dei (image of God), 90, 140, 142–44
interim ethics, 205
Irwin, James, ix
Isaiah (prophet), 38, 150, 190, 213
Isaiah, book of, 72, 109, 177, 178, 190, 194, 195
    Second, 72, 78, 150, 184, 194, 195, 202, 211
    Third, 194, 195
Israel, 130, 146
    New, 184–85, 190
    social system, 121–22, 130–31
    See also corporate personality

Jacob (patriarch), 16, 40, 69, 72, 76, 131
James (the Just), 44, 185
James, letter of, 30, 49, 141
Jeremiah (prophet), 31, 38, 72, 86, 108, 145, 156, 157
    prophecy of new covenant, 31, 156, 157–58
Jeremiah, book of, 108, 145, 156–57
Jerusalem (Zion), 125–26
    destruction of, 156, 184
    New, renewed, 212, 213, 214
    vindication of, 195
Jesus Christ, 31–32, 158, 159, 160, 163, 174, 176, 177, 180
    as eschatological event, 197–202
    as foundation stone, 189–90
    as prophet, priest, and king, 179–83
    birth of, 179, 198
    crucifixion of, 167, 168
    law of, 7
    meaning of, 184
    miracles of, 198
    priestly prayer of, 191
    resurrection of, 185, 197, 198–200, 202
    second coming of, 189, 201
    teaching of, 14, 87
    words of, 6, 48
Jesus of history and Christ of faith, 175, 202
Jesus of Nazareth, 175–76, 197, 202
Jewish Bible. *See* Old Testament
Jews and Christians, 160
Job, book of, 25, 27, 72, 76, 106, 138
Joel, book of, 25, 201
John (apostle), 185
John, Gospel of, 14, 29, 45, 109, 181, 182, 191, 198, 199, 202, 212
John, letters of, 30, 49
Josephus (Jewish historian), 165
Joshua, 26, 73, 120, 121, 123
Joshua, book of, 26, 73, 102, 104, 118, 120, 123
Josiah (king), 38, 40, 79, 156
Jude, letter of, 30, 49, 161–62
judge(s), 26
    definition of, 122
Judges, book of, 26, 118–19, 123, 124
judges, period of, 69, 118–24

kainos (new, renewed), 211
Kee, Howard, 208
Kierkegaard, Søren, 115–16
kingdom of God, 130, 174, 189, 193, 200, 201, 202–8, 215
    future nature, 207, 208, 210
    paradoxical nature of, 203
    present nature of, 202–8, 209, 210
kingship ideology, 182
Kings, books of, 25, 26, 74, 118, 124–25
Kings, first book of, 71, 74, 76, 124
Kings, second book of, 40, 74

SUBJECT/NAME INDEX

Lamentations, book of, 25, 27, 46
law of love, 172–73
legalism, 6, 169–73, 205, 206
Lent, 188
Leviathan (chaos monster), 196
Leviticus, book of, 26, 101, 171
Lewis, C. S., 211
Lex Talionis, 105
liberalism, 55
liberals. *See* theological liberals
Lindbergh, Charles, ix
Luke, Gospel of, 29, 45, 48, 60–61, 62, 90, 161, 177, 178, 181, 182, 198, 199, 204, 205
Luther, Martin, 53, 164

Maccabean period, 27, 165, 194
Maccabees, books of, 25, 27
Malachi, book of, 177
Marcion, 49
Mark, Gospel of, 45, 48, 62, 169, 177, 180–81, 198, 199, 202–3, 208
marriage, 141, 142, 187
Mary Magdalene, 199
Matthew, Gospel of, 6, 24, 45, 62, 90, 136n2, 159, 173, 178–79, 178–79, 184, 204–6, 209
McGrath, Alistair, 86
McLaren, Brian, 87, 217, 218n2
Megilloth, 27
Messiah, messianic hope, 130, 136n2, 163, 166, 169, 170, 174, 177, 178, 180–81, 182, 193, 195, 196, 201
   Jesus as, 167
Metzger, Bruce, x
Micah, book of, 108–9
Michener, James, 95
midrash, 177–78
mishpat (justice), 105, 109
monolatry. *See* henotheism
monotheism, 70, 72, 77–78, 79
Moses, x, 26, 31, 37, 39–40, 41, 46, 52, 71, 72, 73, 75, 98, 99–102, 121, 131, 156, 158, 167, 176, 181
Mount Sinai (Horeb), x, 26, 52, 69, 71, 76, 98, 101–5
Muratorian Canon, 49–50
myth, language of, 137–38, 192

Napoleon Bonaparte, 174
nature
   as sacrament, 88–89
Neoplatonism, 87
nephesh (breath, spirit), 81–82, 144
Nero (emperor), 44, 45
New Testament, 28–30, 31–32, 50, 155, 159, 180, 183
   centrality of Jesus Christ in, 175, 197–202
   composition of, 43–45
   message of, 174
   relation to Old Testament, 159–60, 179
   responses to Jesus, 160–62
Noah, 98, 131
Numbers, book of, 37, 101, 121, 167

Old Testament, 24–25, 31, 49, 72, 95, 96, 155, 159, 160, 174, 176, 179, 184
   doctrine of God in, 67–79
oral period, 161

Paradise Lost, 144
paradox, 13
Passover, 22, 46, 101
Pastoral Epistles, 44–45, 48, 161
patriarchal period, 110
Paul (apostle), 44, 48, 145, 155, 162–73
   and apocalyptic, 208
   and charismatic offices, 186, 187
   and covenant, 171
   and Holy Spirit, 187, 207
   and Israel, 184–85
   and justification by faith, 169
   and law (Torah), 169–73, 179
   and new creation, 207
   and women, 186–87
   conversion of, 167–69
   doctrine of the church, 168–69
   epistles of, 28, 29–30, 43, 44–45, 48, 49, 161, 164
   impact of, 162–64
   moral instruction (*paraenesis*), 164
   relation between Jews and Gentiles in, 160
peace, 191

SUBJECT/NAME INDEX

Pentateuch, 24, 25, 26, 37, 70, 95, 96, 98, 103, 110, 118
 composition of, 37–43
 See also Documentary Hypothesis
Pentecost, 184, 187, 201
People's History, 132, 157
pesher, 176, 177
Peter (apostle), 45, 185
Peter, first letter of, 30, 45, 49, 130, 189–90
Peter, Gospel of, 48
Peter, second letter of, 30, 34, 44, 45, 48, 49
Pharisees, 47, 164, 165–66, 216
Philemon, letter to, 28, 29, 30, 44, 48
Philip, Gospel of, 48
Philippians, letter to, 2, 28, 29, 30, 44, 165, 167, 169, 186
Philistines, 124, 125, 126
Phoenicia, 126
pietism, 55
Plato (philosopher), 87, 133
Plotinus (philosopher), 87
Plotkin, Bill, 3
polytheism, 70
Postcritical Paradigm, 8–9
practical theology, 60
Precritical Paradigm, 8, 9, 81
predestination and free will, 166
presbuteros (elder), 185
Priestly writer (P), 38, 41, 42, 99, 113, 134–36, 137, 139, 140, 181
priests, 124, 181
prophetic task, 106–9
Prophets (Nebiim), 24, 25, 46, 47, 165
prophets, prophecy, 27, 124, 145, 156, 193
Proverbs, book of, 25, 27, 182
providence, divine, 148, 150
Psalms, 25, 27, 47, 127, 139, 175, 182

Rabia (Sufi saint), 4–5
Rahab (chaos monster), 196
rapture, 212
religion
 false, 13–14
 role of, 9
Renan, Ernst, 174

resurrection, doctrine of, 166, 197–200, 202, 208–9
 and creation, 201
retribution, doctrine of, 145, 195
Revelation, book of, 4, 16, 23, 30, 32, 45, 49, 161, 196, 207, 210–15
Richardson, Alan, 140
Romans, letter to, 28, 29, 30, 44, 101, 155, 160, 164, 166, 169, 171, 172, 173, 177, 179, 184–85, 186, 187, 190, 210
royal theology, 125–30, 182
ruach (wind, Spirit), 81
Ruth, book of, 25, 27, 46

Sabbath, 52, 141, 181, 185, 197
Sadducees, 47, 165–66
salvation, doctrine of, 14, 84–88, 111, 213
Samuel (judge), 124, 125
Samuel, books of, 25, 26, 118, 124–27
Samuel, first book of, 124, 125
Samuel, second book of, 126, 127, 128, 129
Sanders, E. P., 200
Sanhedrin, 165, 190
Satan, 193, 196
Saul (king), 124–25, 128
Schulweis, Harold, 117
Schweitzer, Albert, 175, 205n11
scripture(s), 48, 164, 165, 219
 inspiration of, 33–36
 interpretation of, 9, 219
 role of, 4
second half of life (second journey), 1–2, 3–4, 5, 6, 9–14, 36, 81
 spirituality, 9–14
Second Isaiah. *See* Isaiah, Second
securing life, 14
Sermon on the Mount, 22, 90, 204–6
Septuagint, 24, 47, 185
shalom, 111
Shechem, 104, 120
Shema, 71–72
Shepherd of Hermas, 49
Shiloh, 104, 120, 124
sin, doctrine of, 83, 84, 88, 89, 201
 original, 84–85, 87, 89, 149, 150

230

SUBJECT/NAME INDEX

Sinai. *See* Mount Sinai
Smith, Morton, 78–79
Solomon (king), 37, 128, 129–30, 145
Son (son) of God, 159, 168, 170, 182
Son of Man, 31, 180, 183, 201
Song of Songs (Song of Solomon), 25, 27, 46
soteriology, 166
Spinoza, Baruch, 39
spirituality, 9–14, 91
Spong, John Shelby, x
Spurgeon, Charles, 62
stewardship, 141–42
Suffering Servant, 31, 201
Sunday, 185, 197
Suzerainty Treaty, 98, 103–5, 107, 108, 128
synagoge (synagogue), 185
systematic theology, 59–60, 218

Tanakh. *See* Old Testament
temple, 126, 127, 128, 139, 170, 181
    destruction of, 150, 184
temptation narrative, the, 144–51
Ten Commandments, 52, 72, 101, 103, 104, 131, 146
testimonia, 176–77, 190
theocracy, theocratic, 110, 119, 124
theological conservatives, 1, 7, 217
theological liberals, 1, 7, 217
Thessalonians, first letter to, 28, 29, 30, 44
Thessalonians, second letter to, 28, 29, 44, 30, 48
Thomas, Gospel of, 48

Tiamat (chaos monster), 196
Timothy, first letter to, 44, 48
Timothy, second letter to, 33–34, 44
Titus, letter to, 28, 29, 30, 45
totemism, 69–70
Torah (Law), x, 6, 24, 25, 31, 46, 71, 156, 165, 166
transformation, x, 9–12, 15, 83, 87, 168–69, 172, 187, 207, 214
treaty pattern (Hittite), 103, 104
    See also Suzerainty Treaty
Tree of Knowledge, 147, 148–51
Tree of Life, 148–51, 212
Trinity, Trinitarian, 182, 197
truth, 15, 140, 219
Twelve, the, 185
Tylor, Edward, 69
typology, 177

Vatke, Wilhelm, 41, 42, 70–71

Wellhausen, Julius, 42–43, 69, 71
Wells, H. G., 174
wisdom literature, 25, 27, 182
Wisdom of Solomon, 25, 50, 96, 182
Wright, N. T., 205
Wright, Robert, 73n4, 75n5, 88
Writings (Kethubim), 24, 25, 27, 46, 47, 165

Yahwist (Jahwist, J), 16–17, 40, 41, 42, 113, 132, 134, 139, 143–47, 150

Zechariah, book of, 25, 178
zedek (righteousness), 105–6

www.ingramcontent.com/pod-product-compliance
Lightning Source LLC
Chambersburg PA
CBHW062018220426
43662CB00010B/1386